CW00501415

Hotpot Crockpot *One Pot*

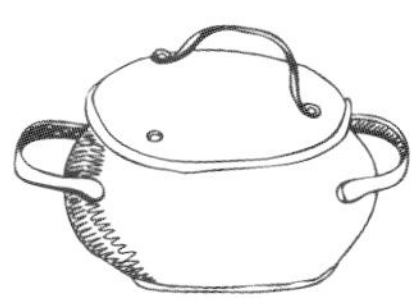

Hotpot
Crockpot
One Pot

140 easy time-saving, flavour-packed recipes

Contents

Food for family and friends – without the fuss

Casserole dishes, slow-cooker appliances and pressure cookers are the busy cook's saviour. They take the hard work out of cooking, help to **save time** in the kitchen and produce wonderful, flavoursome results.

Often, too, they help **save money** because the cooking methods used to make many one-pot dishes make the very best of the cheaper cuts of meat and other low-cost ingredients.

All the recipes in this book are **easy to prepare.** You won't find any tricky techniques here, or recipes asking you to juggle five pots and pans at once. Just honest-to-goodness dishes that are full of flavour, made from everyday ingredients. And the experience won't be spoiled by having a big pile of pots and pans to wash up afterwards.

Most of our recipes are complete **one-pot** meals, meaning all the ingredients are cooked in the one pot and simmered together; others just need a simple side dish to complete them, or some bread or salad.

One-pot meals also include **hotpots,** a term originally used to refer to dishes from China and South-East Asia, where fresh ingredients are simmered in a flavoursome broth in a communal pot at the table. On page 307, you'll find simple hotpot recipes to use as a base for creating all manner of aromatic Asian-style hotpots.

Nowadays 'hotpot' is also a general name for robust stews, such as Lancashire hotpot, in which simple ingredients are cooked together.

Crockpot meals are slowly simmered in a slow-cooker appliance to melt-in-the-mouth perfection. And so you'll find recipes such as crab chowder, beef bourguignon, pulled pork, and even octopus in tomato and red wine. If you don't have a slow cooker, don't worry: these recipes can also be cooked in the oven or on the stovetop, or sometimes even in a pressure cooker when speed is of the essence. Simply check the instructions given at the end of the recipes.

This confidence-inspiring book features more than 140 fail-safe recipes for **soups, mains** and **desserts,** and will quickly become your go-to book for super-easy, fabulous meals.

THE EDITORS

Hotpot, crockpot, one pot

The appeal of 'one pot' cooking lies in its sheer simplicity — easy on effort, full of flavour, and with the added bonus of minimal washing up! You might be surprised just how many satisfying dishes you can cook in just one pot. Soups and stews are the obvious candidates, supported by a wide variety of healthy grain and pasta dishes, and wonderful desserts, too — opening the door to a whole world of flavours.

What pot?

'HOTPOT' is often used as a general term for a stew or casserole, but it is also known as an Asian dish, with different countries having their own versions. An Asian-style hotpot usually involves a communal pot of broth, which is kept at a gentle simmer on the table over a gas flame. Each diner then briefly dips different very thinly sliced ingredients — such as vegetables and raw meat or seafood — into the broth to cook. Various accompanying condiments are also offered at the table. You'll find more information about Asian hotpots as well as great recipes on pages 306–307. Another style of hotpot is exemplified by the famous dish Lancashire hotpot. It is a traditional English recipe comprising lamb and potatoes and other ingredients, slowly cooked together in the oven.

'CROCK-POT' was the original brand name for a slow cooker, and this has become a generic term over time. Many other companies make slow cookers now, so the proprietary term 'Crock-Pot' is used less and less.

'ONE POT' cooking is, in essence, no-fuss cooking, with all the ingredients being simmered together in the one vessel. To make an all-in-one one-pot meal, the dish will typically contain a protein, vegetables, and usually a carbohydrate, such as rice, pasta or potatoes, all cooked in a sauce or liquid, such as stock or water, in the one pot.

Which pot?

Many different types of vessels can be used for one-pot cooking. The type you use will depend on the recipe you are making, the amount of food you are cooking — and, of course, the ingredients in your cupboard.

The most important criteria, particularly for dishes that need to cook for a long time, is that your pot or pan has a good-quality heavy base. This will distribute the heat evenly, without creating hot spots that may result in uneven cooking or scorched food.

Versatile stews such as lamb with apricots (see page 111) can be cooked in a slow cooker, or a large casserole dish.

Beef pot roast (see page 51) can be gently cooked in a large saucepan, or left to simmer in a slow cooker.

SAUCEPAN If you are cooking on top of the stove, you will need a saucepan of some sort. The size will depend on the number of people you are cooking for.

The largest saucepan is sometimes referred to as a stockpot, as this is the type of pan chefs use to make a large batch of stock. Larger pots usually have two small handles, one at either side, which makes them easier to move when they are full, compared to a regular saucepan with one long handle.

Stainless steel saucepans are best because they are durable and easy to clean. However, they need to have a heavy reinforced base (often with a layer of copper), as stainless steel itself is not a good conductor of heat.

CASSEROLE DISH A casserole refers both to a cooking vessel, and the meal cooked in it. Casserole dishes are most commonly used in the oven, and can be made from metal, glass, ceramic or earthenware.

Most cultures have their own version of this type of cooking. The northern African tagine is a good example. The distinctive shallow dish with its tall, conical lid is called a tagine, and so usually is the recipe cooked in it.

Another type of casserole is the Dutch oven, which is a heavy, round cast-iron lidded pot, usually with a small handle on each side. These are brilliant for campfire cooking, but can also be used in the kitchen. They need to be lightly greased after being washed or they will rust.

Even more durable are the very heavy enamelled cast-iron casseroles favoured by the French. These are very versatile and perfect for one-pot cooking. They are flameproof and ovenproof, meaning you can brown meat and other ingredients on the stove, then add the remaining ingredients, put the lid on and finish cooking the meal in the oven. These pots come in various sizes and colours, and while expensive, will last a lifetime.

SLOW COOKER AND PRESSURE COOKER These two appliances are designed to save time in the kitchen, though in very different ways.

The slow cooker simmers food at a very low temperature over a long period of time. You put all the ingredients in, turn it on and then go about your day, coming home to a ready-cooked meal in the evening.

A pressure cooker, on the other hand, steams food under high pressure, cooking it at a much faster rate, thereby greatly reducing cooking time. See pages 12–13 for information on slow cookers and pressure cookers.

IN THE POT

Many of the recipes in this book are what could be called a stew, casserole or braise. These terms are quite often interchanged when talking of these types of dishes.

A stew is usually a dish of meat, vegetables and a liquid (such as a broth or sauce), cooked slowly in a pot on the stovetop. A braise is really the same thing.

A casserole is almost the same as a stew, but is more often cooked in the oven. The vessel itself is also called a casserole, or casserole dish. Another style of casserole is a mixture of ingredients such as meat or seafood, vegetables and or/pasta, with an often creamy sauce, and a browned cheesy topping.

A pot roast usually consists of a large whole piece of meat, rather than meat that has been cut into smaller cubes; it is sometimes tied with kitchen string to help retain its shape. Vegetables are cooked with the meat, in a flavoursome broth. The cooked meat is then sliced to serve, with the vegetables served alongside. The resulting sauce can be served as it is, or thickened to make it more gravy-like.

Slow cookers

The advent of the slow cooker in the 1970s revolutionised meal preparation. It offered the liberating convenience of being able to put a simple bunch of ingredients into the cooker in the morning, then venture out all day, knowing that a meal awaited in the evening.

Anatomy of a slow cooker

Traditional slow cookers have a heavy ceramic insert that sits in a housing. This housing, or body, contains the heating elements. The ceramic insert conducts heat gently and evenly. A lid sits on top and seals in all the moisture for cooking.

Some modern slow cookers have an insert made from a heavy non-stick material, similar to a non-stick frying pan, allowing you to brown meat and vegetables on the stovetop, before placing the insert back into the body of the slow cooker to finish cooking. This feature allows for true one-pot cooking as preliminary browning or sautéing does not need to be done in a separate pan.

The real advantage of the slow cooker is that it is plugged into an electrical outlet, and, because it cooks at a controlled low temperature, it can be left safely to cook a meal unattended.

Settings

Slow cookers vary between brands in terms of the settings they offer. They all have a high and low setting, and sometimes one marked 'auto' and/or 'keep warm'.

LOW If you are out for a whole day, or you want to cook a dish overnight, use the low setting. This setting is so low that it is virtually impossible to overcook your food, so there is no need to panic if you run a little late getting back to it.

HIGH As a rule of thumb, if a shorter amount of time suits you, cook the dish on high for half the time that you would cook it on low.

AUTO This setting has the food starting on a higher setting, then switching to low. The cooking time will fall halfway between times given for low and high settings.

KEEP WARM This switches from the cooking setting to just keeping your food warm. It is not advisable to leave food on this setting for more than a few hours.

Size matters

If you are purchasing a new slow cooker, the main guideline is how many people you will be cooking for.

SLOW COOKER SIZE RECOMMENDATION	
1 person or for a side dish	1 to 1½ litres (quarts)
2 people	2 to 3½ litres (quarts)
3 or 4 people	3½ to 4½ litres (quarts)
4 or 5 people	4½ to 5 litres (quarts)
6 or more people	5 to 6 litres (quarts)
Fill the dish at least half-full, but no more than two-thirds full.	

To brown or not to brown?

Early slow cooker recipes didn't bother with browning meats when cooking stews and casseroles, preferring to accentuate the simplicity of slow cooker use by just combining all the ingredients and turning the cooker on and leaving it to do its work.

This certainly is possible, and the result is acceptable, but for real depth of flavour it is preferable to sear meat in batches to caramelise and brown the surface. This adds to the flavour and colour of the final dish.

If you have one of the more modern slow cookers with a stovetop-proof insert, you will be able to fully follow the 'one-pot' ethos. However, if you have the time and inclination, it can be worth getting out a frying pan for the initial stages of some recipes. See page 308 for more information on browning and searing meat.

Desserts

Desserts cooked in the slow cooker are a revelation to those who think these appliances are just for stews. Self-saucing puddings work particularly well, as does fruit, which poaches beautifully at low temperatures. The real benefit is that the dessert cooks itself in the slow cooker, leaving the oven and stovetop available for other cooking, which is handy if you are having a crowd for dinner. See our desserts chapter for slow-cooker dessert recipes.

How to adapt a recipe for the slow cooker

Adapting a conventional recipe for a slow cooker may take some trial and error, but any errors are unlikely to be disastrous. If in doubt, find a similar slow cooker recipe to the one you wish to adapt, and use that as your guide.

- One general tip is to reduce the quantity of liquid: the slow-cooker lid is designed to prevent evaporation, so you won't lose any liquid. For a standard stew-type recipe, you can generally halve the amount of liquid required. To start with it might not seem like you have enough liquid, but many ingredients exude liquid during cooking, which produces a flavoursome sauce.
- A general rule for converting the cooking time is this: 1 hour stovetop simmering or moderate oven cooking is equivalent to 8 hours on low, or 4 hours on high.

Slow cooker hints and tips

- If using frozen vegetables, always thaw them completely before adding them to the slow cooker.
- Don't peek! Lifting the lid allows precious heat to escape, which can add 15–30 minutes to your cooking time every time you open it. Resist the temptation to stir, unless instructed otherwise.
- Don't overfill the cooker. Ideally, it should be at least half full, to distribute the heat evenly, but no more than about two-thirds to three-quarters full.
- If using firm vegetables such as carrots or turnips, arrange them in the bottom of the cooker, then place the meat and other ingredients on top of them. This is because hard vegetables will take longer to cook.
- Use dried herbs and spices sparingly: they have such a long time to impart their flavour in a slow cooker that the result can overpower the dish. Fresh herbs, however, are best stirred in just before serving.
- Cut your meat and vegetables into uniform sizes so they cook through at the same rate.
- For handy tips on cooking dried beans in a slow cooker, see page 309.

Make this crustless lime cheesecake (see page 290) in a slow cooker, or a pressure cooker. It's your choice.

SAFE AND SOUND

While slow cookers are very safe appliances, some care must still be taken — particularly as the cooker will be left unattended for lengthy periods.

- Read the instruction manual thoroughly before you first use your slow cooker, and keep it accessible for future consultation.
- Stand the cooker on a stable surface, well away from the edge.
- Don't place the cooker near the sink or any other wet area.
- Make sure the electrical cord is away from heat or water, and is in good condition.
- Use oven mitts to lift the insert from the housing.
- When lifting the lid, tilt it away from you to avoid the surge of steam.
- Don't forget to turn the switch off the cooker when removing the insert.

Pressure cookers

Like the slow cooker, the pressure cooker has been around for decades and is enjoying a fresh wave of popularity. These fabulous appliances are a boon for busy households, cooking meals in a fraction of the time taken by conventional cooking methods.

Why use a pressure cooker?

Pressure cookers allow you to produce stews, casseroles and other dishes with the same long-simmered flavour, but minus the long cooking time.

Cheaper 'secondary' cuts of meat, which normally need to be cooked for hours at a low temperature, can be turned into delicious and economical meals in about one-third of the conventional time.

The greatest advantage is that no advance planning or preparation is required: you can decide what you want for dinner when you get home, then enjoy a healthy, hearty meal in the same time that it would take to have pizza delivered.

How does it work?

The pressure cooker looks like a bulky saucepan or stockpot, with thick walls and a very tightly sealed lid, designed to withstand all the pressure that will build up during cooking.

Pressure cookers work by heating liquid to very high temperatures, which creates steam that cannot escape. This steam reaches temperatures higher than the boiling point of water, cooking the food quickly and efficiently. As well as saving time, you save on power costs, and also retain nutrients in food which may otherwise be lost during long cooking times.

Pressure cookers have gone through several changes over the years to make them safer and more efficient. The modern pressure cooker is a much less intimidating device than those of old, with safe, reliable valves to release pressure when the food has finished cooking. Reassuringly, they often have several valves as back-up should the main valve block up or fail to operate for some reason.

The first pressure cookers were designed to sit on a regular stovetop, over either gas or electricity as the heat source. A gas flame is particularly good as it allows you to regulate the heat instantly. If cooking on an electric hotplate which does not adjust as quickly, you can simply move the cooker to a different hotplate set to the desired temperature.

You can now buy electric pressure cookers that stand alone and cook on the benchtop, rather than on a hotplate. These are convenient as their automation looks after the timing for you. However, they don't reach the pressure levels of stovetop pressure cookers, so food will take a little longer to cook. Also, they don't have as long a life span as good-quality, stainless steel stovetop pressure cookers.

If you are thinking of buying a pressure cooker, it's best to buy a brand new one made by a reputable company. It will have up-to-date safety features, and will last a lifetime if looked after properly. If you buy from a well-established company, you will also be able to purchase any spare parts your pressure cooker may require over the years.

Do plenty of research before buying a pressure cooker, as they are a relatively expensive appliance. The internet is a useful source of information.

How to adapt a recipe for the pressure cooker

If you are already familiar with using a pressure cooker, you may want to convert favourite recipes to use in your appliance. As a starting point, it is best to compare your recipe with similar recipes that have been developed and tested in a pressure cooker. See opposite for some general guidelines.

Some companies make an electrical appliance which you can use as a slow cooker, or as a pressure cooker. These usually also have the function where you can brown ingredients such as meat and onions first, which add flavour to the finished dish, and mean you don't have to use a different pot, thereby minimising washing up.

Pulled pork (see page 131) takes about 45 minutes in a pressure cooker, compared to 8 hours in a slow cooker.

- Reduce the quantity of liquid. Because the food cooks quickly and is sealed in tight, you won't lose liquid to evaporation. You do, however, need some liquid to create the steam required for cooking.
- Reduce the cooking time to about one-third of the time specified in a standard recipe. For instance, if your recipe requires 1 hour of simmering on the stove, it will take 20 minutes in a pressure cooker.
- Make sure food is cut into uniformly sized pieces, so they cook evenly in the same time.
- Don't overfill the pressure cooker. Two-thirds is the maximum you should fill it, to allow space for it to operate correctly. However, if you are cooking foods that may froth during cooking, and any that expand, such as pasta or rice and other grains, only fill the pressure cooker to halfway. You need plenty of room for the steam to gather, and froth can block valves.
- Season the dish at the end of the cooking time, rather than before, as the flavours can become quite concentrated.
- For the best flavour, brown your meat first. In a stovetop pressure cooker, simply brown the meat and deglaze the pot as you would in a saucepan or frying pan. Electric pressure cookers often have a browning option. See page 308 for more information on browning ingredients.
- Always release the pressure as recommended in the manual.

LOW PRESSURE OPTION

While it may seem that pressure cookers are all about high pressure working on tough meat or robust beans, some cookers have an option for low pressure cooking. Food will still cook more quickly than with conventional methods, but using the low pressure option suits more delicate dishes such as fish, custards, and other egg dishes. Check your manual for more information.

Safety first

Although pressure cookers aren't the scary, potentially dangerous contraptions they used to be, care must still be taken to operate them safely.

They vary in their style and methods of releasing the pressure, so before you use the appliance, make sure you read thoroughly the accompanying instruction manual.

It is a good idea to try out a few of the recipes in the manual to start with, as this will help give you a feel for how your pressure cooker works.

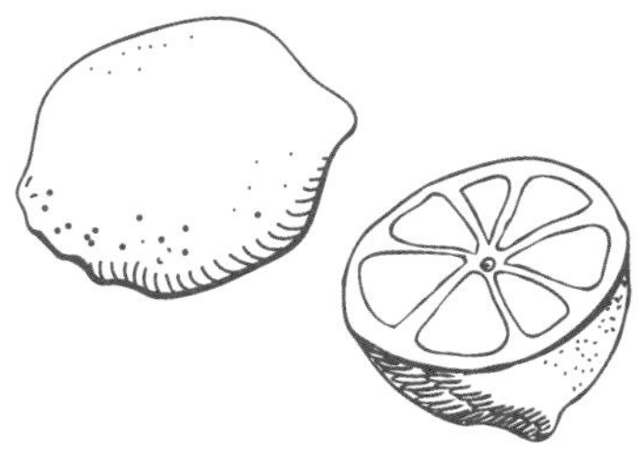

Hearty soups

Potato and vegetable soup

A dollop of pesto enriches the flavour and texture of this healthy soup and also adds extra nutrition. If you don't have time to make your own pesto, just use a good-quality ready-made one instead.

1 tablespoon olive oil
4 potatoes (600 g/1¼ lb), peeled and chopped
1 onion, chopped
2 cloves garlic, crushed
6 cups (1.5 litres) vegetable stock
1½ cups (185 g) small cauliflower florets
2 small carrots, sliced
1 cup (125 g) sliced green beans
1 cup (45 g) baby English spinach leaves
pesto (see page 39), to serve

- The soup goes well with cheesy toasts: cut a baguette into thick diagonal slices and place a slice of brie on each. Place under a hot grill (broiler) and cook until the cheese melts.
- This soup doesn't freeze very well, but leftovers can be refrigerated for several days.
- Frozen green beans are convenient and nutritious and can be used instead of fresh beans in this soup. There is no need to thaw them first if cooking the soup on the stove. If using frozen green beans in the slow-cooker version, make sure they are first fully thawed, and add them to the slow cooker with the spinach.

PREPARATION 15 minutes **COOKING** 25 minutes **SERVES** 4

1 Heat the oil in a large saucepan over medium heat. Add the potatoes and onion and sauté for 5 minutes, or until the potatoes start to soften. Add the garlic in the last minute.

2 Pour in the stock and add the cauliflower. Bring to a boil, reduce the heat and simmer for 10 minutes.

3 Add the carrots and beans and simmer for a further 5 minutes, or until the vegetables are cooked. Remove from the heat and stir in the spinach. Serve topped with a spoonful of pesto.

PER SERVING 923 kJ, 221 kcal, 8 g protein, 6 g fat (1 g saturated fat), 32 g carbohydrate (12 g sugars), 6 g fibre, 1578 mg sodium

Slow cooker

If you have a slow cooker you can sauté in, or you don't mind using another pot, follow step 1 as above. (Alternatively, omit the oil and the sautéing step.) Transfer all the ingredients to the slow cooker, except the spinach and pesto. Gently combine, then cover and cook on low for 7 hours.

Stir in the spinach, cover and cook for a further 10 minutes. Serve topped with pesto.

- When tomatoes are not in season, use 200 g (7 oz) canned peeled tomatoes or 2 tablespoons ready-made tomato pesto instead. You can use any white beans instead of the borlotti beans.
- This soup keeps well for up to 2 days after cooking. Reheat thoroughly and add some fresh stock if the liquid needs replenishing.

Garden soup with herbs

Beans and pasta noodles add extra substance to this vegetable-packed soup. The pasta can be cooked right in the soup, or just add leftover cooked pasta near the end to warm through.

4 tablespoons olive oil
1 onion, finely diced
2 small zucchini (courgettes), sliced
2 celery stalks, finely diced
4 savoy cabbage leaves, thick central vein removed, leaves cut into strips
1 small leek, white part only, thinly sliced
2 carrots, thinly sliced
6 cups (1.5 litres) vegetable stock
1 bay leaf
1 sprig fresh rosemary
1 teaspoon dried oregano
2 tomatoes
420 g (15 oz) can borlotti (cranberry) beans, drained and rinsed
125 g (4 oz) short pasta noodles, such as macaroni or rotelle
3 tablespoons shredded fresh basil
grated parmesan, to serve

Slow cooker

If you have a slow cooker you can sauté in, or you don't mind using another pot, follow step 1 as above. (Alternatively, omit half the oil and the sautéing step.) Increase the stock to 8 cups (2 litres) and add to the slow cooker with all the ingredients except the pasta, basil and parmesan. Gently combine, then cover and cook on low for 7 hours.

Stir in the pasta, then cover and cook for a further 45 minutes. Serve as directed in step 5.

PREPARATION 25 minutes **COOKING** 30 minutes **SERVES** 4

1 Heat half the oil in a large saucepan over medium heat. Add the onion, zucchini, celery, cabbage, leek and carrots and sauté for 5 minutes, or until softened.

2 Pour in the stock and bring to a boil. Add the bay leaf, rosemary and oregano, then cover and simmer for 10 minutes.

3 Meanwhile, cut a shallow cross in the base of each tomato. Place the tomatoes in a heatproof bowl and cover with boiling water. Leave for about 30 seconds, then drain and rinse under cold water. Leave until cool enough to handle, then peel the skin away from the cross. Dice the tomatoes and set aside.

4 Add the beans and pasta to the soup. Cook the pasta for 10 minutes, or for the time given on the packet directions, until al dente. Stir in the diced tomatoes.

5 Season to taste with salt and freshly ground black pepper. Stir in the basil and divide the soup among bowls. Drizzle with the remaining 2 tablespoons oil, sprinkle with parmesan and serve.

PER SERVING 1832 kJ, 438 kcal, 14 g protein, 23 g fat (4 g saturated fat), 45 g carbohydrate (14 g sugars), 9 g fibre, 2028 mg sodium

Scotch broth

Instead of mutton, as traditionally used, this soup features richly flavoured and convenient lamb leg chops. Alternatively, use lamb shanks instead of lamb chops in this satisfying soup.

1 tablespoon olive oil
750 g (1½ lb) lamb leg chops
4 cups (1 litre) salt-reduced beef stock
½ cup (110 g) pearl barley
2 carrots, cut in half lengthwise, then thickly sliced
2 swedes (rutabagas), peeled and cut into 2.5 cm (1 inch) cubes
½ cup (15 g) chopped fresh parsley

- When buying lamb, check that it has creamy white fat — a yellowish tinge may indicate the lamb is old.
- You can replace some or all of the carrots and swedes with chopped cabbage and leek.

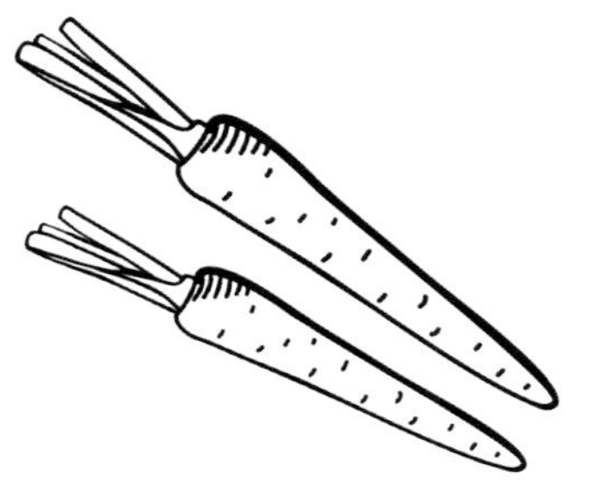

PREPARATION 10 minutes **COOKING** 1 hour 45 minutes **SERVES** 4–6

1 Heat the oil in a large heavy-based saucepan over medium heat. Add the lamb chops and cook for 3 minutes on each side, or until browned. Pour the stock and 8 cups (2 litres) water over the chops and bring to a boil. Reduce the heat to low and gently simmer for 45 minutes, skimming the froth regularly.

2 Add the barley, carrots and swedes and partially cover. Simmer gently for 45 minutes, or until the barley is tender.

3 Remove the chops from the soup. Strip off the meat, chop it roughly and return to the soup, discarding the bones.

4 Season with salt and freshly ground black pepper, ladle into bowls and serve sprinkled with the parsley.

PER SERVING 1763 kJ, 421 kcal, 41 g protein, 14 g fat (5 g saturated fat), 34 g carbohydrate (14 g sugars), 8 g fibre, 1141 mg sodium

Slow cooker

If you have a slow cooker you can sauté in, or you don't mind using another pot, brown the lamb as directed in step 1. (Alternatively, omit the oil and the browning step.) Transfer all the ingredients except the parsley to the slow cooker. Gently combine, then cover and cook on low for 8 hours. Continue from step 3 above.

Easy minestrone

Here's a tip from Italian cooks: there are really no hard-and-fast rules or secret ingredients when it comes to making minestrone, so long as it contains beans, pasta and an abundance of vegetables.

1 tablespoon olive oil
3 slices rindless bacon (bacon strips), chopped
1 onion, finely diced
2 celery stalks, thinly sliced
2 cloves garlic, crushed
4 cups (1 litre) beef stock
1/4 cup (60 ml) red wine
2 roma (plum) tomatoes, chopped
2 carrots, quite thinly chopped or diced
1/2 cup (120 g) risoni pasta
420 g (15 oz) can red kidney beans, drained and rinsed
1/3 cup (50 g) frozen peas
3 tablespoons chopped fresh parsley
finely grated parmesan, to serve
pesto (see page 39), to serve (optional)

- If you have any leftover cooked pasta, omit the risoni and add the pasta to the soup in the last few minutes to warm through.
- Vary the vegetables depending on the season and what your garden or fridge has to offer. Savoy or white cabbage, fennel, zucchini (courgettes) or green beans — virtually any vegetable belongs in minestrone.

PREPARATION 20 minutes **COOKING** 25 minutes **SERVES** 4

1 Heat the oil in a large saucepan and sauté the bacon, onion, celery and garlic over medium heat for 5 minutes, or until the vegetables have softened and the bacon is golden.

2 Add the stock, wine, tomatoes and carrots, then bring to a boil and simmer for 5 minutes. Stir in the risoni and simmer for a further 6 minutes, stirring occasionally.

3 Add the beans and peas and simmer for 4 minutes. Remove from the heat and stir in the parsley. Serve with a sprinkling of parmesan, and a dollop of pesto if desired.

PER SERVING 1372 kJ, 328 kcal, 20 g protein, 12 g fat (3 g saturated fat), 32 g carbohydrate (5 g sugars), 6 g fibre, 1618 mg sodium

Slow cooker

If you have a slow cooker you can sauté in, or you don't mind using another pot, follow step 1 as above. (Alternatively, omit the oil and the sautéing step.) Increase the stock to 5 cups (1.25 litres) and add to the slow cooker with all the ingredients except the risoni, peas, parsley, parmesan and pesto. Gently combine, then cover and cook on low for 7 hours.

Stir in the risoni, then cover and cook for 15 minutes. Add the fully thawed peas, replace the lid and cook for a further 15 minutes. Stir in the parsley and serve as directed.

Chicken noodle soup with vegetables

If you have made your own chicken stock, use the cooked chicken meat in this soup. Leftover cooked chicken, turkey or pork are also perfectly suited to this nourishing favourite.

1 tablespoon olive oil
1 onion, cut in half, then into thin strips
1 leek, white part only, thinly sliced
6 cups (1.5 litres) chicken stock
500 g (1 lb) carrots, thinly sliced
400 g (14 oz) boneless, skinless chicken breasts, cut into bite-sized chunks
1 bay leaf
1/2 teaspoon dried thyme
150 g (5 oz) thin soup noodles (short vermicelli)
2/3 cup (100 g) frozen peas
1/4 teaspoon sweet paprika
pinch of freshly grated nutmeg
2 tablespoons finely chopped fresh parsley

PREPARATION 25 minutes **COOKING** 20 minutes **SERVES** 4

1 Heat the oil in a large saucepan and sauté the onion and leek over medium heat for 5 minutes, or until softened but not browned.

2 Pour in the stock and bring to a boil. Add the carrots, chicken, bay leaf and thyme and simmer for 3 minutes.

3 Add the noodles and cook for 2 minutes, then add the peas and simmer for a further 3 minutes.

4 Stir in the paprika and nutmeg and season to taste with salt and freshly ground black pepper. Serve sprinkled with the parsley.

PER SERVING 1732 kJ, 414 kcal, 32 g protein, 11 g fat (2 g saturated fat), 46 g carbohydrate (13 g sugars), 6 g fibre, 1368 mg sodium

---

The leek and carrots can be chopped ahead of time and sealed in a freezer bag or storage container and refrigerated until required.

Slow cooker

If you have a slow cooker you can sauté in, or you don't mind using another pot, follow step 1 as above. (Alternatively, omit the oil and the sautéing step.) Transfer all the ingredients to the slow cooker, except the noodles, peas and parsley. Gently combine, then cover and cook on low for 7 hours.

Stir in the noodles, then cover and cook for 15 minutes. Add the fully thawed peas, replace the lid and cook for a further 15 minutes. Serve sprinkled with the parsley.

Smoked fish and cannellini bean soup

Smoked fish adds a lovely depth of flavour to this simple, snappy dish, in which pantry items are paired with fresh vegetables and accented by the aniseed flavour of dill.

1 tablespoon olive oil
1 onion, chopped
1 celery stalk, chopped
2 small zucchini (courgettes), chopped
2 cups (500 ml) salt-reduced fish or chicken stock
175 g (6 oz) smoked fish fillet, skin removed, flesh diced
2 x 420 g (15 oz) cans cannellini beans, drained and rinsed
1 tablespoon chopped fresh dill
2 tablespoons thick (heavy/double) cream (optional)
crusty bread, to serve

PREPARATION 10 minutes **COOKING** 15 minutes **SERVES** 4

1 Heat the oil in a large saucepan and sauté the onion, celery and zucchini over medium heat for 5 minutes, or until softened but not browned.

2 Add the stock and bring to a boil. Add the fish and season lightly with salt and freshly ground black pepper. Cover and simmer gently for 5 minutes, or until the fish flakes easily.

3 Stir in the beans, dill and cream, if using. Heat until almost boiling, then ladle into bowls and serve with crusty bread.

PER SERVING 792 kJ, 189 kcal, 19 g protein, 6 g fat (<1 g saturated fat), 15 g carbohydrate (4 g sugars), 9 g fibre, 999 mg sodium

- If you can, buy pale golden, undyed smoked fish. Bright yellow smoked fish is artificially coloured, and usually not smoked at all, but treated with a smoke-flavoured liquid.
- A delicious alternative is to substitute 150 g (5 oz) cooked, peeled prawns (shrimp) for the fish. Instead of the beans, you could also use 250 g (8 oz) frozen or drained canned corn kernels.

Slow cooker

If you have a slow cooker you can sauté in, or you don't mind using another pot, follow step 1 as above. (Alternatively, omit the oil and the sautéing step.) Transfer all the ingredients to the slow cooker, except the dill and cream. Gently combine, then cover and cook on low for 3 hours. Just before serving, stir in the dill and cream.

Classic seafood soup

Unlike the famed French seafood stew bouillabaisse on which it is based, this elegantly simple but equally flavoursome version doesn't take hours to prepare. Use any combination of seafood you like, or to make it even simpler, use a good-quality seafood or 'marinara' mix.

- 2 tablespoons olive oil
- 1 onion, finely chopped
- 1 celery stalk, finely chopped
- 3 cloves garlic, crushed
- 1/4 teaspoon saffron threads (optional)
- 1/2 cup (125 ml) white wine
- 700 ml (24 fl oz) tomato passata (puréed tomatoes)
- 2 cups (500 ml) salt-reduced fish or chicken stock
- 2 bay leaves
- 1.5 kg (3 lb) prepared seafood, such as firm white fish fillets cut into chunks, shelled and deveined raw prawns (shrimp), scallops, chopped calamari, scrubbed mussels
- 2 tablespoons chopped fresh parsley
- lemon wedges, to serve

PREPARATION 20 minutes **COOKING** 30 minutes **SERVES** 6

1 Heat the oil in a large saucepan and sauté the onion, celery and garlic over medium heat for 5 minutes, or until softened. Stir the saffron through, if using, then add the wine and bring to a boil.

2 Stir in the passata, stock and bay leaves, then reduce the heat and simmer for 10 minutes.

3 Add the prepared seafood and simmer until it is all cooked. Depending on their size, the fish pieces will take 8–10 minutes to cook through, and the prawns, calamari, scallops and mussels 4–5 minutes.

4 Season with salt and freshly ground black pepper. Serve sprinkled with the parsley, with lemon wedges on the side.

PER SERVING 1649 kJ, 394 kcal, 50 g protein, 10 g fat (2 g saturated fat), 21 g carbohydrate (11 g sugars), 3 g fibre, 2165 mg sodium

- A finely shredded fennel bulb can be added with the onion.
- For some extra warmth, add a pinch of dried red chilli flakes or chilli powder with the saffron.

Slow cooker

IF YOU HAVE A SLOW COOKER you can sauté in, or you don't mind using another pot, follow step 1 as above. (Alternatively, omit the oil and the sautéing step.) Transfer all the ingredients to the slow cooker, except the parsley and lemon wedges, and mussels if using. Gently combine, then cover and cook on low for 3 hours. If using mussels, add them for the last 20 minutes of cooking. Continue from step 4 above.

Chicken noodle soup with ponzu

Based on steamboats, in which food is cooked at the table in a simmering broth, this soup makes a satisfying main course. A sharp and savoury citrus sauce called ponzu adds a zing of flavour. We've included a recipe for ponzu, but to make this dish truly 'one pot', you can use bottled ponzu.

250 (8 oz) g fine rice noodles
2 cups (500 ml) salt-reduced chicken stock
500 g (1 lb) boneless, skinless chicken breasts, thinly sliced
250 g (8 oz) carrots, thinly sliced
200 g (7 oz) snow peas (mangetout)
250 g (8 oz) can sliced bamboo shoots, drained
125 g (4 oz) shiitake mushrooms, sliced
125 g (4 oz) Chinese cabbage (wombok), shredded

Ponzu

1/4 cup (60 ml) mirin (sweet rice wine)
juice of 1 lemon
juice of 1 1/2 limes
1/4 cup (60 ml) rice vinegar
1/3 cup (80 ml) salt-reduced soy sauce

- If you can't find fresh shiitake mushrooms, use about 8 dried ones. Soak in water to rehydrate them before adding to the soup.
- Replace the cabbage with the leaves from a bunch of watercress and 2 1/3 cups (125 g) baby English spinach leaves.
- For a vegetarian dish, use vegetable stock and replace the chicken with 500 g (1 lb) firm tofu, cut into cubes, adding it with the carrots.

PREPARATION 20 minutes **COOKING** 30 minutes **SERVES** 4

1 If making your own ponzu, you can prepare it a day or more in advance. Pour the mirin into a small saucepan, bring to a boil over high heat and boil for 30 seconds so that the alcohol evaporates. Stir in all the remaining sauce ingredients and remove from the heat. Pour into a dish, cover and set aside.

2 Place the noodles in a bowl and pour in cold water to cover. Leave to soak for 10 minutes, then drain and set aside.

3 Meanwhile, bring the stock to a boil in a large flameproof casserole dish. Reduce the heat so that the stock simmers, then add the chicken and simmer for 10 minutes.

4 Stir in the carrots, bring back to simmering point and cook for 5 minutes. Add the snow peas and bamboo shoots and simmer for a further 2–3 minutes. Stir in the mushrooms and cabbage, bring back to simmering point and cook for 2–3 minutes. Finally, stir in the noodles. Bring back to simmering point and cook for a few minutes, until the noodles are tender.

5 Divide the ponzu among four small serving bowls, for dipping bite-sized pieces into before eating. Ladle the soup into warm serving bowls and serve immediately.

PER SERVING 2072 kJ, 495 kcal, 36 g protein, 7 g fat (2 g saturated fat), 65 g carbohydrate (10 g sugars), 7 g fibre, 1388 mg sodium

Slow cooker

Place the stock, chicken and carrots in a slow cooker, then cover and cook on low for 4 hours. Meanwhile, prepare the ponzu as directed in step 1, if making your own.

Stir the snow peas, bamboo shoots, mushrooms and cabbage into the soup, then cover and cook for a further 20 minutes. Meanwhile, soak and drain the noodles, adding them for the last 5 minutes of cooking. Serve as directed in step 5.

Slow-cooker pea and ham soup

This ever-popular soup works brilliantly in the slow cooker, with the dried peas simmering to a smooth, velvety texture, infused with smoky ham. Add some crusty bread, and there's dinner taken care of — and lunch tomorrow, too!

2 cups (440 g) dried green split peas
1 large onion, finely chopped
2 carrots, finely chopped
2 celery stalks, finely chopped
2 cloves garlic, crushed
1 ham hock (about 750 g/1½ lb)
1 bay leaf
4 cups (1 litre) salt-reduced chicken or vegetable stock
grated parmesan, to serve
crusty bread, to serve

- For a smoother texture, use a hand-held stick blender to purée the soup before returning the shredded ham.
- Lightly sautéing the onion, carrots, celery and garlic first adds depth of flavour. If you have a slow cooker you can sauté in, or don't mind using another pot, heat 1 tablespoon olive oil in the slow cooker or pot and sauté the vegetables and garlic over medium heat for 5 minutes, or until softened. Proceed as directed.

PREPARATION 15 minutes **COOKING** 8 hours **SERVES** 6

1 Place the split peas in a sieve and rinse under running water. Drain, then place in a 5 litre (5 quart) slow cooker with the vegetables, garlic, ham hock, bay leaf, stock and 3 cups (750 ml) water. Cover and cook on low for 8 hours.

2 Remove the ham hock, allow to cool slightly, then pull all the meat from the bone. Discard the bone, rind and any fat. Shred the meat and return to the soup.

3 Season to taste with salt and freshly ground black pepper. Serve sprinkled with parmesan, with crusty bread on the side.

PER SERVING 1714 kJ, 409 kcal, 38 g protein, 12 g fat (3 g saturated fat), 40 g carbohydrate (6 g sugars), 9 g fibre, 1419 mg sodium

On the stove

HEAT 1 TABLESPOON OLIVE OIL in a large saucepan and sauté the onion, carrots, celery and garlic over medium heat for 5 minutes, or until softened. Add the rinsed and drained peas, ham hock, bay leaf, stock and 3 cups (750 ml) water, then cover and bring to a boil.

Reduce the heat and simmer for 1½ hours, or until the peas are tender. Continue from step 2 above.

- Instead of dried mushrooms, use 60 g (2 oz) sliced button mushrooms and add an extra 100 ml ($3^{1}/_{2}$ fl oz) stock.
- If you can't get fresh lime leaves, use 8 dried lime leaves. Remove and discard the dry stalks, then crush the leaves before using.
- Low-fat coconut milk is available in cans in supermarkets. If you can't find it, just use half the quantity of ordinary coconut milk.

Fragrant beef noodle soup

Replete with spices, but not fiery with chilli, this is definitely a main-course soup. You can eat the noodles, beef and vegetables with chopsticks, then enjoy the luscious soup with a spoon. For extra bite you can serve it with extra chopped chilli on the side.

- 15 g (1/2 oz) dried shiitake mushrooms
- 4 cups (1 litre) salt-reduced beef stock
- 4 fresh kaffir lime (makrut) leaves, torn
- 1 lemongrass stem, white part only, chopped into 3 pieces
- 1 clove garlic, crushed
- 1 red chilli, seeded and chopped
- 2.5 cm (1 inch) piece of fresh ginger, peeled and grated
- 1/2 bunch (45 g) coriander (cilantro)
- 1 large carrot, cut into thin strips
- 1 leek, white part only, cut into thin strips
- 2 celery stalks, cut into thin strips
- 100 ml (3 1/2 fl oz) low-fat coconut milk
- 250 g (8 oz) thin dried Chinese egg noodles
- 340 g (12 oz) lean rump steak, trimmed of fat, cut into thin strips about 1 cm (1/2 inch) wide
- 100 g (3 1/2 oz) sugar snap peas, sliced in half lengthwise
- 100 g (3 1/2 oz) Chinese cabbage (wombok), finely shredded
- finely grated zest and juice of 1 lime
- 1 tablespoon fish sauce, or to taste

Use any type of Asian noodles. Dried 'instant' noodles will cook quickly, but the wider flat rice noodles may need to be soaked first. Check the directions on your noodle packet.

PREPARATION 30 minutes **COOKING** 25 minutes **SERVES** 4

1 Put the mushrooms in a small bowl, add 100 ml (3 1/2 fl oz) boiling water and leave to soak for 20 minutes.

2 Meanwhile, pour the stock into a large saucepan and add the lime leaves, lemongrass, garlic, chilli and ginger. Separate the coriander leaves from the stalks and set the leaves aside. Chop the stalks and add them to the stock. Cover and bring just to a boil, then reduce the heat to very low. Leave to simmer gently for 10 minutes.

3 Drain the mushrooms, pouring the soaking liquid into the stock. Cut each mushroom in half lengthwise and set aside.

4 Remove the lemongrass and lime leaves from the stock. Bring the stock back to a boil, then add the carrot, leek and celery. Cover and simmer for 3 minutes.

5 Pour in the coconut milk and increase the heat. Just as the liquid comes to a boil, add the noodles, crushing them in your hands as you drop them into the pan. Stir in the mushrooms and beef, bring back to a simmer and cook, uncovered, for 1 minute.

6 Stir well, then add the peas and cabbage. Simmer for a further 3 minutes, or until the beef, noodles and vegetables are just tender. Add the lime zest and juice and fish sauce and stir well. Taste and add more fish sauce if you like.

7 Transfer the noodles, beef and vegetables to bowls using a slotted spoon. Ladle the coconut stock over, sprinkle with the coriander leaves and serve immediately.

PER SERVING 1916 kJ, 458 kcal, 36 g protein, 9 g fat (5 g saturated fat), 59 g carbohydrate (7 g sugars), 6 g fibre, 1557 mg sodium

Beefy mushroom barley soup

It's easy to see why robust one-pot dishes have withstood the test of time — they offer up lashings of flavour and are so easy to prepare. Perfect with warm bread and a wedge of cheddar, this soup is brimming with fibre and nutrients essential to good health.

- 1 tablespoon olive oil
- 350 g (12 oz) lean beef chuck steak, cut into 2.5 cm (1 inch) cubes
- 3 onions, chopped
- 300 g (10 oz) mushrooms, sliced
- 3 large carrots, sliced
- ½ cup (110 g) pearl barley
- 7 cups (1.75 litres) salt-reduced beef stock
- 1 cup (250 ml) dry red wine or no-salt-added tomato juice
- 1 cup (155 g) frozen green peas
- 2 teaspoons lemon juice

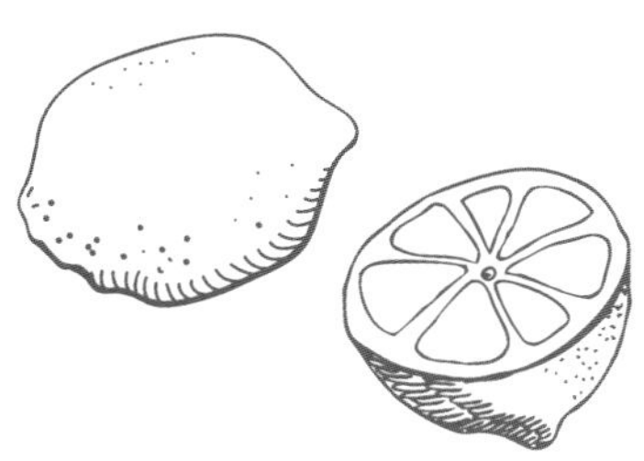

PREPARATION 20 minutes **COOKING** 1 hour **SERVES** 6

1 Heat the oil in a large heavy-based saucepan over medium–high heat until hot but not smoking. Add the beef and brown on all sides for about 5 minutes. Using a slotted spoon, transfer the beef to a double layer of paper towels to drain.

2 Sauté the onions and mushrooms in the pan drippings over medium heat for 7 minutes, or until the onions are golden.

3 Add the beef, carrots, barley, stock and wine. Season with salt and freshly ground black pepper and mix well. Bring to a boil, then reduce the heat to medium–low. Simmer, partially covered, for 45 minutes, or until the beef and barley are tender.

4 Stir in the peas and cook, uncovered, for 5 minutes. Remove from the heat, stir in the lemon juice and serve.

PER SERVING 1149 kJ, 274 kcal, 25 g protein, 7 g fat (2 g saturated fat), 21 g carbohydrate (7 g sugars), 5 g fibre, 1236 mg sodium

Slow cooker

If you have a slow cooker you can sauté in, or you don't mind using another pot, brown the beef and sauté the onions and mushrooms as directed in steps 1 and 2 above. (Alternatively, omit the oil and the browning and sautéing steps.) Transfer all the ingredients to the slow cooker, except the peas and lemon juice. Gently combine, then cover and cook on low for 8 hours.

Add the fully thawed peas, then cover and cook for a further 15 minutes. Stir in the lemon juice and serve.

Use a slotted spoon to transfer the browned beef to paper towels.

Add the peas to the soup during the last 5 minutes of cooking.

Remove the pan from the heat and add the lemon juice before serving.

Vegetable soup with pesto

The beauty of this garden-fresh soup is that you can showcase any vegetables in season. Pesto, however, is best made in summer when peppery green basil is at its sweetest.

2 tablespoons olive oil
1 small onion, finely chopped
2 cloves garlic, crushed
2 potatoes, peeled and diced
2 carrots, diced
2 celery stalks, finely diced
410 g (15 oz) can chopped tomatoes
6–8 cups (1.5–2 litres) salt-reduced beef or chicken stock
2 tablespoons chopped fresh basil
1 cup (150 g) small macaroni
125 g (4 oz) green beans, chopped
420 g (15 oz) can borlotti (cranberry) beans, drained and rinsed
420 g (15 oz) can cannellini beans, drained and rinsed
grated parmesan, to serve
good-quality ready-made pesto, or make your own (see below)

Pesto

2 cloves garlic, peeled
2 cups (100 g) fresh basil leaves
2 tablespoons pine nuts, toasted
1/3 cup (80 ml) olive oil
1/3 cup (35 g) grated parmesan

- 'Sweating' vegetables in olive oil or butter helps to start the cooking process and draw out the flavour. If you brown them too much at this stage it can affect the final colour of the finished soup.
- Pine nuts and other nuts are best bought in small quantities and used soon after purchase so their natural oils don't become rancid. Store in an airtight container in a cool place.

PREPARATION 25 minutes **COOKING** 20 minutes **SERVES** 6

1 Heat the oil in a large saucepan over medium heat and sauté the onion and garlic for a few minutes, until lightly golden.

2 Add the potatoes, carrots and celery and stir for 1 minute. Add the tomatoes with all their juice, along with the stock and basil. Increase the heat and bring to a boil, then stir in the macaroni. Cook for 10 minutes, or until the pasta is just tender.

3 Reduce the heat to medium, then add the green beans, borlotti and cannellini beans. Simmer for 2–3 minutes, then season well with salt and freshly ground black pepper.

4 Meanwhile, make the pesto. Put the garlic, basil and pine nuts in a food processor and blend until finely chopped. Work in the oil, then scoop the pesto into a bowl and stir the parmesan through.

5 Ladle the soup into warm bowls and sprinkle with a little grated parmesan. Pass the pesto around separately to spoon over the soup.

PER SERVING 1965 kJ, 469 kcal, 18 g protein, 25 g fat (4 g saturated fat), 43 g carbohydrate (8 g sugars), 10 g fibre, 1056 mg sodium

Slow cooker

If you have a slow cooker you can sauté in, or you don't mind using another pot, follow step 1 as above. (Alternatively, omit the oil and the sautéing step.) Transfer all the ingredients to the slow cooker, except the macaroni, parmesan and pesto. Gently combine, then cover and cook on low for 7 hours.

Stir in the macaroni, then cover and cook for a further 30 minutes. Just before serving, make the pesto. Serve the soup as directed in step 5.

Slow-cooker crab chowder

Chowders come in different forms, but usually contain some type of seafood. They are thickened with a starchy ingredient, quite often potatoes or crushed stale crackers, harking back to the days of thrifty peasant-style eating where nothing was wasted and dishes were adapted using ingredients on hand.

1 onion, finely chopped
2 cloves garlic, crushed
pinch of cayenne pepper
4 cups (1 litre) salt-reduced vegetable stock
2 potatoes, peeled and finely diced
420 g (15 oz) can creamed corn
310 g (10 oz) can corn kernels, drained
1 cup (175 g) crab meat
4 tablespoons sour cream (optional)
2 spring onions (scallions), finely sliced on the diagonal
crusty bread, to serve

- You can used canned, fresh or frozen crab meat in this soup. If using frozen, make sure to thaw it fully in the refrigerator before cooking.
- Choose baking (floury) potatoes and dice them quite small, so they break down and thicken the soup.

PREPARATION 15 minutes **COOKING** 6 hours **SERVES** 4

1 Place the onion and garlic in a 5 litre (5 quart) slow cooker. Add the cayenne pepper and stir to combine, then stir in the stock, potatoes, creamed corn, corn kernels and crab meat. Cover and cook on low for 6 hours.

2 Top with a dollop of sour cream, if desired, and garnish with the spring onions. Serve with crusty bread.

PER SERVING 1045 kJ, 250 kcal, 14 g protein, 3 g fat (<1 g saturated fat), 41 g carbohydrate (13 g sugars), 7 g fibre, 1613 mg sodium

On the stove

HEAT 1 TABLESPOON OLIVE OIL in a large saucepan and sauté the onion and garlic over medium heat for 5 minutes, or until softened but not browned. Add the stock, potatoes, creamed corn and corn kernels. Bring to a boil, reduce the heat slightly and cook, partially covered, for 20 minutes, or until the potatoes are tender. Stir in the crab and heat through. Serve as directed in step 2.

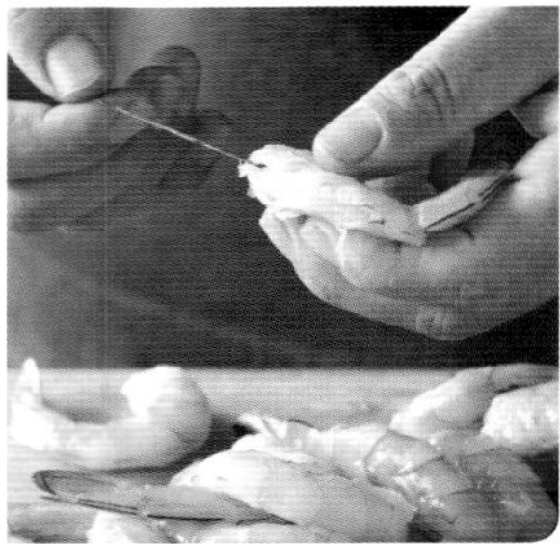

Peel the prawns, leaving the tail on, then pull out the intestinal vein.

Finely chop the white stem of the lemongrass. Discard the green leaves.

Remove the central vein from the lime leaves, then finely shred the leaves.

Seafood coconut noodle soup

This laksa-style soup is fragrant with the classic Thai ingredients lime leaves, galangal, lemongrass and chilli. When chopping the lemongrass, use only the tender white root end in the soup; save the stalky green leaves and steep them in boiling water to make a refreshing herbal tea.

- 8 large raw prawns (shrimp)
- 4 cups (1 litre) salt-reduced chicken stock
- 400 ml (14 fl oz) coconut milk
- 3 tablespoons finely chopped lemongrass, white part only
- 5 cm (2 inch) piece of galangal, peeled and thinly sliced
- 1 tablespoon chilli paste
- 2 tablespoons finely shredded kaffir lime (makrut) leaves
- 1 tablespoon shaved palm sugar (jaggery) or soft brown sugar
- $\frac{1}{4}$ cup (60 ml) fish sauce
- 100 g ($3\frac{1}{2}$ oz) flat fresh rice noodles, or other noodles of your choice
- 400 g (14 oz) firm white fish fillets, cut into bite-sized chunks
- 2 tablespoons lime juice
- coriander (cilantro) leaves, to garnish
- fresh Thai basil leaves, to garnish
- lime wedges, to serve (optional)

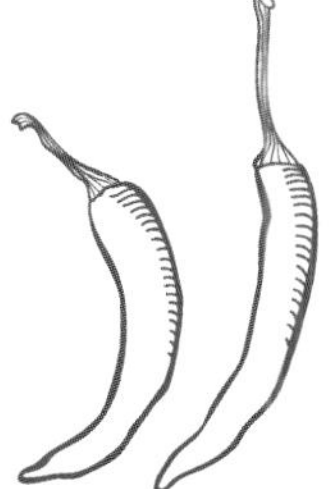

PREPARATION 20 minutes **COOKING** 20 minutes **SERVES** 4

1 Peel the prawns, leaving the tail on, then carefully pull out the intestinal vein. Butterfly the prawns by cutting an incision along the back, being careful not to cut all the way through. Set aside.

2 Place the stock, coconut milk, lemongrass, galangal, chilli paste, lime leaves, sugar and fish sauce in a large saucepan. Combine, bring to a boil, then reduce the heat and simmer for 10 minutes.

3 Meanwhile, prepare the noodles according to the packet instructions. Set aside.

4 Add the fish to the simmering stock and cook for 2 minutes. Add the prawns and cook for a further 1–2 minutes, or until the prawns turn pink. Remove from the heat and stir in the lime juice.

5 Divide the noodles among serving bowls and ladle the soup over. Serve topped with coriander and Thai basil leaves, with lime wedges on the side if desired.

PER SERVING 1387 kJ, 331 kcal, 24 g protein, 16 g fat (13 g saturated fat), 22 g carbohydrate (7 g sugars), 2 g fibre, 1483 mg sodium

---

Palm sugar is a dense, sticky sugar made from the sap of the palmyra, or sugar palm. It is sold in rounded cakes, cylinders, blocks or jars. If unavailable, use equal parts maple syrup and soft brown sugar. Galangal is a pink-skinned member of the ginger family with the characteristic heat of ginger plus a hint of sour lemon. If you can't obtain any, use ginger in this recipe instead.

Slow-cooker chicken and barley soup

Who wouldn't love to come home to a warming pot of soup on a cold winter's night? Full of nutrition, the barley helps thicken this nourishing soup, and is such a hearty carbohydrate you might find you don't even need to serve bread on the side.

- 350 g (12 oz) boneless, skinless chicken breasts
- 1 large carrot, diced
- 2 parsnips, peeled and diced
- 1 onion, chopped
- 2 cloves garlic, crushed
- 1/2 cup (110 g) pearl barley
- 5 cups (1.25 litres) salt-reduced chicken stock
- 2 tablespoons lemon juice
- fresh dill or parsley sprigs, to garnish

If you have a large slow cooker, make a double batch of this soup, and freeze half for another meal.

PREPARATION 20 minutes **COOKING** 7 hours **SERVES** 6

1 Cut the chicken breasts in half lengthwise, then cut into slices. Place in a 5 litre (5 quart) slow cooker with the vegetables and barley. Pour in the stock and stir to combine. Cover and cook on low for 7 hours.

2 Just before serving, stir in the lemon juice and season with freshly ground black pepper. Serve garnished with dill or parsley.

PER SERVING 781 kJ, 187 kcal, 18 g protein, 4 g fat (1 g saturated fat), 19 g carbohydrate (6 g sugars), 4 g fibre, 584 mg sodium

On the stove

Heat 1 tablespoon olive oil in a large saucepan and sauté the onion and garlic over medium heat for 5 minutes, or until softened and lightly golden. Add the stock and barley, then cover and simmer for 25 minutes.

Stir in the chicken and vegetables. Cover and simmer for a further 20 minutes, or until the chicken is cooked and the vegetables are tender. Serve as directed in step 2.

Beef, lamb and pork

Beef and potato hotpot

Bacon, red wine, thyme and bay leaves add flavour and richness to this simple beef stew. To retain its flavour and juices, the meat should be seared quickly over a very high heat.

1 kg (2 lb) piece of braising beef, such as chuck
100 g (3½ oz) bacon, diced
3–4 small onions, cut into wedges
4 sprigs fresh thyme, leaves separated
2 bay leaves
1 cup (250 ml) dry red wine
½ cup (125 ml) salt-reduced beef stock
750 g (1½ lb) small boiling (waxy) or all-purpose potatoes, peeled and sliced
4 carrots, sliced

The onions also need to be fried at quite a high temperature, but be careful not to burn them or they'll taste bitter. Stir them frequently to stop them catching on the bottom of the pan and charring.

PREPARATION 30 minutes **COOKING** 2 hours 15 minutes **SERVES** 4–6

1 Remove the sinews and fat from the beef. Pat dry with paper towels and rub on all sides with a little salt and freshly ground black pepper.

2 Fry the bacon in a large flameproof casserole dish or heavy-based saucepan over high heat without any oil. Add the beef and brown thoroughly on all sides. Add the onions and fry until well browned, stirring constantly. Sprinkle the thyme leaves over the beef and place the bay leaves on top.

3 Pour in the wine and stir to loosen the solids from the bottom of the dish. Add the stock and bring to a boil. Reduce the heat to low, then cover and simmer for 1½ hours, turning the beef occasionally. Season the sauce generously with salt and freshly ground black pepper.

4 Add the potatoes and carrots, then cover and simmer for a further 30 minutes, or until the vegetables are tender.

5 Discard the bay leaves. Remove the meat from the dish, carve into slices and place back in the dish with the vegetables. Season to taste and serve hot from the dish.

PER SERVING 2449 kJ, 585 kcal, 63 g protein, 19 g fat (8 g saturated fat), 30 g carbohydrate (5 g sugars), 5 g fibre, 780 mg sodium

Slow cooker

If you have a slow cooker you can sauté in, or you don't mind using another pot, follow steps 1 and 2 as above. (Alternatively, omit the oil and the browning step.) Reduce the red wine to ½ cup (125 ml).

Arrange the potatoes and carrots in the base of the slow cooker, then place the beef and all the remaining ingredients on top. Cover and cook on low for 8 hours.

Beef pot roast

A pot roast needs an attentive eye as it simmers so it doesn't boil dry or stick to the pan. Don't be tempted to add too much liquid, though, or the finished dish will have little flavour.

- 2 tablespoons plain (all-purpose) flour
- 2 teaspoons mustard powder
- 1.25 kg (2½ lb) piece of beef bolar blade, trimmed of excess fat
- 1 tablespoon olive oil
- 1 onion, diced
- 1 carrot, diced
- 2 celery stalks, diced
- 2 slices rindless bacon (bacon strips), finely chopped
- 2 bay leaves
- 1 cup (250 ml) salt-reduced beef stock, approximately
- 500 g (1 lb) broccolini, trimmed

A beef bolar blade comes from the shoulder and is a good choice for this dish — it's a very economical cut, it will cook beautifully and become quite tender after slow simmering, and is also easy to carve. You could also use a piece of (uncorned) rolled beef brisket.

Slow cooker

IF YOU HAVE A SLOW COOKER you can sauté in, or you don't mind using another pot, follow steps 1 to 3 as above. (Alternatively, omit the oil and the browning and sautéing steps.) Reduce the stock to ½ cup (125 ml). Arrange the vegetable and bacon mixture in the base of the slow cooker, and place the beef and all the remaining ingredients on top. Cover and cook on low for 8 hours. Continue from step 5.

PREPARATION 15 minutes **COOKING** 2 hours 20 minutes, plus 15 minutes resting **SERVES** 6

1 Mix the flour and mustard powder and season with salt and freshly ground black pepper. Rub the mixture over the beef.

2 Heat the oil in a large heavy-based saucepan over medium heat. Brown the beef on all sides, making sure the flour does not burn. Remove the beef and set aside.

3 Add the onion, carrot, celery and bacon to the pan and sauté for 5 minutes, or until the onion has softened. Add the bay leaves and stock and bring to a boil, then reduce the heat to low so the mixture is just simmering.

4 Place the beef over the vegetables. Cover and simmer for 2 hours, or until the beef is tender — a fork should easily penetrate the centre. During cooking, turn the beef occasionally, adding just a little extra liquid — about ⅓ cup (80 ml) at a time — as needed. It is important to keep the heat low during cooking, so check regularly and adjust the heat and the liquid as needed.

5 Remove the beef to a warm serving plate, cover loosely with foil and allow to rest for 15 minutes. Meanwhile, add the broccolini to the pan; cover and cook over medium heat for 5 minutes, or until tender.

6 Carve the beef into thin slices and spoon the warm vegetables and the pan juices over.

PER SERVING 1499 kJ, 358 kcal, 49 g protein, 14 g fat (5 g saturated fat), 10 g carbohydrate (3 g sugars), 2 g fibre, 527 mg sodium

Beef in beer

Braising the beef in beer with juniper and allspice adds an earthy richness to this mouth-watering casserole, packed with hearty winter vegetables. You can replace some of the beer with beef stock.

- 500 g (1 lb) lean beef stewing steak, cut into bite-sized chunks
- 2 tablespoons fine oatmeal (or oatmeal, roughly chopped)
- 2 tablespoons olive oil
- 2 onions, finely chopped
- 600 ml (21 fl oz) good-quality beer
- 3–4 sprigs fresh thyme
- 3 juniper berries, crushed
- 2 good pinches of ground allspice
- 200 g (7 oz) baby French shallots (eschalots) or small pickling onions, peeled
- 250 g (8 oz) baby carrots, scrubbed and trimmed
- 250 g (8 oz) baby parsnips or baby turnips, scrubbed and trimmed, or mature ones, peeled and diced
- 1 baguette

PREPARATION 30 minutes **COOKING** 1 hour 50 minutes **SERVES** 4

1 Preheat the oven to 160°C (320°F/Gas 2–3). Toss the steak pieces in the oatmeal to lightly coat them, then shake to remove any excess.

2 Heat the oil in a large flameproof casserole dish and briefly brown the beef over medium heat until lightly coloured. Transfer to a plate. Add the chopped onions to the casserole dish and gently sauté over low heat for 10 minutes, or until softened and golden.

3 Add the beer, thyme, juniper berries and allspice and stir to loosen any solids from the bottom of the dish. Season with salt and freshly ground black pepper and bring to a boil, stirring constantly.

4 Add the remaining vegetables, as well as the beef and any meat juices. Bring back to a boil, then cover the casserole dish and transfer to the oven. Cook for 1½ hours, or until the meat is very tender, stirring once or twice.

5 Towards the end of the cooking time, cut the bread into slices 2.5 cm (1 inch) thick and arrange on a baking tray. Bake for 15 minutes, or until lightly browned and crisp.

6 Remove the lid from the casserole dish, arrange the toasted bread over the stew and cook, uncovered, for a further 5 minutes. Serve hot, straight from the casserole dish.

PER SERVING 3006 kJ, 718 kcal, 41 g protein, 20 g fat (5 g saturated fat), 83 g carbohydrate (15 g sugars), 9 g fibre, 847 mg sodium

Slow cooker

If you have a slow cooker you can sauté in, or you don't mind using another pot, follow steps 1 and 2 as above. (Alternatively, omit the oil and the browning step.) Reduce the beer to 300 ml (10 fl oz) and add to the slow cooker with all the ingredients, except the bread. Cover and cook on low for 8 hours. Serve the toasted bread slices on the side.

- To prepare ahead, cook the stew up to the end of step 4. Allow to cool, then either refrigerate for up to 48 hours, or freeze in an airtight container. If frozen, allow to thaw first, then reheat thoroughly before topping with the toasted bread.
- French shallots and pickling onions are easy to peel if you make a small cut in the skin at the top and soak them in boiling water for 5 minutes.
- If parsnips or turnips aren't available, use swedes (rutabagas) instead.

Beef in red wine

Beef and red wine are perfect partners and the addition of potatoes and other vegetables makes this a complete, one-pot meal. Long, slow cooking gives this casserole its inimitable flavour. The cooking liquid is reduced by removing the casserole lid to produce an aromatic sauce.

2 tablespoons olive oil
1 large onion, sliced
500 g (1 lb) stewing beef or chuck steak, cut into bite-sized chunks
250 g (8 oz) baby carrots, scrubbed and trimmed
250 g (8 oz) baby parsnips, scrubbed and trimmed
250 g (8 oz) button mushrooms, trimmed
1 clove garlic, finely chopped
2 cups (500 ml) full-bodied red wine
grated zest and juice of 1 orange
2 sprigs fresh thyme
1 sprig fresh rosemary
1 bay leaf
8 small new potatoes
1 cup (185 g) shelled fresh broad (fava) beans, or thawed frozen ones
2 tablespoons chopped fresh parsley

- If you can't find baby carrots or parsnips, use large vegetables. Peel them, then cut into evenly sized chunks.
- Small broccoli florets or shelled peas can be added instead of the broad beans.
- For an everyday version, use 2 cups (500 ml) salt-reduced beef stock instead of wine.

PREPARATION 20 minutes **COOKING** 2 hours 40 minutes **SERVES** 4

1 Preheat the oven to 150°C (300°F/Gas 2). Heat the oil in a large flameproof casserole dish and sauté the onion over medium heat for 5 minutes, or until softened and beginning to brown. Add the beef and cook, stirring frequently, for 5 minutes, or until browned on all sides.

2 Add the carrots, parsnips, mushrooms and garlic. Pour in the wine, then stir in the orange zest, orange juice and herbs. Season with freshly ground black pepper and bring to a boil, then cover the casserole dish and transfer to the oven. Cook for 1½ hours.

3 Stir in the potatoes and cook for 30 minutes, stirring once or twice. Stir in the broad beans and cook, uncovered, for a further 30 minutes, again stirring once or twice.

4 Just before serving, stir in the parsley and season to taste with salt and freshly ground black pepper.

PER SERVING 2240 kJ, 535 kcal, 37 g protein, 16 g fat (3 g saturated fat), 40 g carbohydrate (11 g sugars), 11 g fibre, 321 mg sodium

Slow cooker

If you have a slow cooker you can sauté in, or you don't mind using another pot, follow step 1 as above. (Alternatively, omit the oil and the browning step.) Reduce the red wine to 1½ cups (375 ml) and add to the slow cooker with all the other ingredients, except the broad beans, parsley and brandy. Cover and cook on low for 7 hours.

Add the broad beans; if using frozen broad beans, ensure they are fully thawed first. Cook for a further 1 hour, then continue with step 4.

Pot-au-feu

The French often serve the broth from this dish as a clear soup, either before or with the beef and vegetables. Serve a generous dollop of dijon mustard on the side.

- 2 kg (4 lb) piece of uncorned, rolled beef brisket
- $^1/_2$ cup (30 g) roughly chopped fresh parsley
- 2 cloves garlic, crushed
- 500 g (1 lb) beef short ribs, trimmed of excess fat
- 8 cups (2 litres) salt-reduced beef stock
- 2 bay leaves
- 4 sprigs fresh thyme
- 6–8 black peppercorns
- 3 carrots, cut into 6 cm ($2^1/_2$ inch) lengths
- 2 leeks, white part only, cut into 6 cm ($2^1/_2$ inch) lengths
- 4 whole baby turnips, scrubbed and trimmed, or 1 large turnip, peeled and cut into 6 wedges
- 6 kipfler (fingerling) potatoes, scrubbed and cut in half lengthwise

---

- During cooking, check the heat now and then and adjust so the liquid is barely simmering — if the beef is cooked at boiling point it will be stringy and dry.
- Any leftover broth can be frozen and used as a flavoursome beef stock. For convenience, freeze it in 1 cup (250 ml) quantities.

PREPARATION 15 minutes **COOKING** 2 hours 30 minutes, plus 15 minutes resting **SERVES** 6

1 Unroll the brisket; if it has been rolled and tied by your butcher, you'll need to cut off the string. In a small bowl, combine the parsley, garlic and a little salt and freshly ground black pepper. Spread the mixture over the inside of the brisket, then roll the brisket up again and tie it in three or four places with kitchen string to hold its shape.

2 Put the brisket and ribs in a large heavy-based saucepan. Pour in the stock and slowly bring to a boil over medium heat. Use a large spoon to skim any froth from the surface, then reduce the heat to low — the liquid should be barely simmering, and should cover the beef by about 6 cm ($2^1/_2$ inches), so add a little water if needed.

3 Add the bay leaves, thyme and peppercorns. Keeping the liquid just at simmering point, cook the beef for $1^3/_4$ hours.

4 Add the carrots, leeks, turnips and potatoes and simmer for a further 30 minutes, or until the vegetables are just tender and the beef is also tender when tested with a fork — the fork should easily penetrate the centre of the meat.

5 Carefully remove the vegetables, brisket and ribs from the broth and arrange on a warm serving plate. Cover loosely with foil and allow the beef to rest for 15 minutes before carving.

6 Strain the liquid and serve as a broth, or ladle some of the broth over the sliced brisket, ribs and the vegetables.

PER SERVING 4174 kJ, 997 kcal, 127 g protein, 42 g fat (15 g saturated fat), 20 g carbohydrate (7 g sugars), 5 g fibre, 1779 mg sodium

Slow cooker

ARRANGE THE CARROTS, LEEKS, TURNIPS and potatoes in the base of the slow cooker. Fill, roll and tie the brisket as directed in step 1, then place in the slow cooker with the ribs. Reduce the stock to 4 cups (1 litre) and add to the slow cooker with the bay leaves, thyme and peppercorns. Cover and cook on low for 8 hours, then continue from step 5.

SALT

- You can substitute 250 g (8 oz) mushrooms for the carrots, and also add 100 g ($3^1/2$ oz) lean diced bacon. Before browning the beef, fry the bacon until crisp and remove with a slotted spoon; cut the mushrooms in half and sauté them in the bacon fat with the onions.
- Instead of serving the stew with the dumplings, offer crusty bread or mashed potato (see page 311) on the side.

Beef hotpot with potato dumplings

Potato dumplings are a good alternative to mashed or baked potatoes. This hotpot can be made ahead to the end of step 2; shape the dumplings near serving time and cook on the reheated stew.

- 2 tablespoons olive oil
- 2 large onions, finely chopped
- 800 g (1¾ lb) topside, round or stewing steak, cut into bite-sized chunks
- 1 tablespoon plain (all-purpose) flour
- 2 carrots, cut into 5 cm (2 inch) chunks
- 200 g (7 oz) baby or small turnips, scrubbed and trimmed, then quartered if necessary (optional)
- 1 cup (250 ml) salt-reduced beef stock

Potato dumplings

- 300 g (10 oz) baking (floury) potatoes, peeled and finely grated
- 1 egg, beaten
- 1¼ cups (125 g) dry breadcrumbs
- 1 tablespoon plain (all-purpose) flour, plus extra for dusting
- 1 tablespoon finely chopped fresh parsley

PREPARATION 25 minutes **COOKING** 2 hours 15 minutes **SERVES** 4

1 Heat the oil in a large heavy-based saucepan and sauté the onions over medium heat for 5 minutes, or until softened. Add the beef and brown on all sides. Season with salt and freshly ground black pepper and dust the flour over the meat, stirring well.

2 Add the carrots and turnips, if using. Pour in the stock and bring to a boil. Reduce the heat, cover and simmer for 1½ hours.

3 Meanwhile, make the dumplings. In a bowl, combine the potatoes, egg, breadcrumbs, flour and parsley until well combined. Season with salt and freshly ground black pepper. With flour-dusted hands, shape the mixture into small dumplings and sprinkle them with a little more flour.

4 Spread the dumplings over the stew. Cover and simmer for a final 30 minutes without lifting the lid. Serve hot.

PER SERVING 2563 kJ, 612 kcal, 53 g protein, 25 g fat (7 g saturated fat), 44 g carbohydrate (9 g sugars), 6 g fibre, 942 mg sodium

Slow cooker

If you have a slow cooker you can sauté in, or you don't mind using another pot, follow step 1 as above. (Alternatively, omit the oil and the browning step.) Reduce the stock to ½ cup (125 ml) and add to the slow cooker with all the hotpot ingredients. Gently combine, then cover and cook on low for 7½ hours.

Meanwhile, prepare the dumplings as directed in step 3. Spread the dumplings over the stew. Cover and simmer, without lifting the lid, for a final 30 minutes, or until the dumplings are cooked through.

Beef stew

A traditional beef stew is ideal for using up tougher meats that are suitable for slow cooking. Cooking at a low temperature allows the flavours to combine and the meat to become juicy and tender. Serve with some crusty bread to mop up the juices and a green salad alongside.

2 tablespoons vegetable oil
1.5 kg (3 lb) stewing beef, cut into 3 cm ($1\frac{1}{4}$ inch) cubes
1 large onion, chopped
2 tablespoons plain (all-purpose) flour
$1\frac{1}{2}$ cups (375 ml) beef stock
410 g (15 oz) can chopped tomatoes
2 carrots, halved and sliced
salt and freshly ground black pepper

PREPARATION 20 minutes **COOKING** 2 hours 30 minutes **SERVES** 8

1 Heat half the oil in a large flameproof casserole dish or heavy-based saucepan over high heat. Brown the beef in four batches, stirring often; the meat will at first stick to the pan, until it begins to sear, so add a little more oil between batches if necessary. Set the beef aside.

2 Reduce heat to medium and heat the rest of the oil. Fry the onion for 5 minutes, or until soft and golden. Sprinkle over the flour and stir for 30 seconds. (Alternatively, coat the pieces of meat with flour before searing.) Gradually stir in the stock, scraping the base of the pan to stop lumps forming.

3 Stir in the tomatoes and add the beef. Cover and bring to a boil, then reduce the heat as low as possible, so the liquid is only just simmering. Cook, covered, for 1 hour, stirring occasionally.

4 Add the carrots, cover and cook for 45 minutes, stirring occasionally. Remove the lid and cook, uncovered, for a further 10 minutes, or until the sauce is thickened and reduced slightly – you'll need to increase the heat a little to keep the liquid at a simmer. Season with salt and freshly ground black pepper.

5 To freeze, cool completely, then divide into portions for 1 or 2 and place in airtight containers or zip-lock bags. Label, date and freeze for up to 3 months. To use, thaw in the microwave, or overnight in the refrigerator.

PER SERVING 1415 kJ, 338 kcal, 41 g protein, 17 g fat (6 g saturated fat), 6 g carbohydrate (4 g sugars), 1 g fibre, 419 mg sodium

Slow cooker

If you have a slow cooker you can sauté in, or you don't mind using another pot, follow steps 1 and 2 as above. (Alternatively, omit the oil and the browning steps.) Reduce the stock to ½ cup (125 ml) and add to the slow cooker with all the other ingredients. Gently combine, then cover and cook on low for 7 hours.

- To make a Greek stifado version of this basic beef stew, replace the stock with red wine and follow steps 1 to 4. Add 2 crushed cloves garlic, ½ teaspoon ground cumin, ½ teaspoon ground cinnamon, 1 bay leaf and 350 g (12 oz) small new potatoes. In the final 5 minutes add 410 g (15 oz) can artichoke hearts, drained and halved, 1¼ cups (200 g) frozen broad (fava) beans, thawed, and ⅓ cup (50 g) kalamata olives, pitted and roughly chopped.
- You can make the whole stew up to 3 days ahead, leaving out the artichokes, broad beans and olives. Allow to cool, then cover and refrigerate. When ready to serve, allow to come to room temperature, then add the remaining ingredients and reheat gently over low heat until bubbling hot.

Braised oxtail with red wine

This recipe is best made at least a day ahead. Refrigerating the cooked oxtail and the sauce separately overnight lets you skim the excess fat from the sauce and deepens the dish's flavour.

1.3 kg (2¾ lb) beef oxtail
1 tablespoon olive oil
1 small onion, finely diced
2 cloves garlic, sliced
410 g (15 oz) can chopped tomatoes
2 cups (500 ml) salt-reduced beef stock, approximately
1 cup (250 ml) red wine
2 bay leaves
1 teaspoon sugar
1 teaspoon salt
hot cooked pasta (see page 311), such as pappardelle, to serve

---

You can substitute osso buco (veal shin) pieces for the oxtail. Osso buco is not quite as fatty as oxtail, but it, too, yields a rich, flavoursome sauce.

Slow cooker

If you have a slow cooker you can sauté in, or you don't mind using another pot, follow steps 1 to 3 as above. (This recipe particularly benefits by browning the beef, garlic and onions first to add colour and enhance the flavour.) Reduce the stock to 1 cup (250 ml) and the wine to ½ cup (125 ml). Transfer all the ingredients to the slow cooker, except the pasta. Gently combine, then cover and cook on low for 8 hours. Continue the recipe from step 5.

PREPARATION 15 minutes COOKING 2 hours 30 minutes, plus overnight refrigeration SERVES 4

1 Using a small sharp knife, cut and scrape away the outside fat sections from the larger oxtail pieces. Season the meat with salt and freshly ground black pepper.

2 Heat a large heavy-based saucepan over medium heat. Add the oxtail and brown each piece well on both sides (you won't need to oil the pan). Transfer to a plate and set aside.

3 Heat the oil in the same saucepan over medium heat. Add the onion and garlic and sauté for 5 minutes, or until the onion has softened.

4 Add the tomatoes, stock, wine, bay leaves, sugar, salt and a little freshly ground black pepper and bring to a boil. Reduce the heat to low and add the oxtail pieces. Simmer, uncovered, and stirring occasionally, for 2 hours, or until the oxtail is very tender — the meat should be nearly falling off the bone. Add a little more stock or water if needed during cooking to keep the oxtail just covered.

5 Remove the oxtail pieces from the sauce. Pour the sauce into a bowl and cover with plastic wrap. Use a fork to remove the meat from the oxtails, then lightly shred the meat with the fork. Discard the bones. Place the meat in a small bowl and cover. Refrigerate the sauce and meat separately overnight.

6 When ready to serve, carefully remove the layer of solidified fat from the top of the sauce. Spoon the sauce into a saucepan and bring to a boil, then reduce the heat to low and simmer for 3 minutes.

7 Add the oxtail meat and simmer, uncovered, for 5 minutes, or until the meat and sauce are heated through. Serve hot, spooned over hot cooked pasta.

PER SERVING 2629 kJ, 628 kcal, 32 g protein, 49 g fat (17 g saturated fat), 7 g carbohydrate (5 g sugars), 2 g fibre, 1310 mg sodium

Slow-cooker beef bourguignon

Long, slow cooking simmers this classic French dish to perfection. To enrich the flavours even more, follow the stovetop instructions at the bottom of the recipe, then transfer the ingredients to your slow cooker and simmer on low for 8 hours. Serve hot, with a crusty baguette.

4 sprigs fresh thyme, plus extra leaves for sprinkling
2 bay leaves
6 sprigs fresh flat-leaf (Italian) parsley
1 kg (2 lb) beef stewing steak (such as chuck), trimmed and cut into large chunks
2 slices rindless bacon (bacon strips), trimmed and sliced
300 g (10 oz) French shallots (eschalots) or pickling onions, peeled
200 g (7 oz) whole small button mushrooms, trimmed, or larger ones cut in half
2 cloves garlic, crushed
½ cup (125 ml) red wine
½ cup (125 ml) salt-reduced beef stock
1 tablespoon tomato paste (concentrated purée)
1 tablespoon cornflour (cornstarch)
1½ cups (70 g) baby English spinach leaves

- French shallots are also known as eschalots. They can be almost round, or shaped like two garlic cloves joined together. Small pickling onions are fine to use, or chop two regular onions instead.
- To peel French shallots or pickling onions, place in a heatproof bowl and cover with boiling water. Stand for 5 minutes, then drain. The skins will slip off much more easily.
- You can leave the little roots attached to pickling onions so they don't fall apart during cooking.

PREPARATION 20 minutes **COOKING** 8 hours 15 minutes **SERVES** 6

1 Using a piece of kitchen string, tie together the thyme, bay leaves and parsley to make a bouquet garni. Combine the beef, bacon, vegetables and garlic in a 5 litre (5 quart) slow cooker. Stir in the wine, stock and tomato paste. Nestle the bouquet garni into the top of the mixture. Cover and cook on low for 8 hours.

2 Discard the bouquet garni. Mix the cornflour with 1½ tablespoons cold water to make a smooth paste, then stir into the stew. Replace the lid, increase the heat to high and cook for a further 15 minutes, or until the sauce has thickened slightly.

3 Fold the spinach through until the leaves have just wilted but are still bright green. Season to taste with salt and freshly ground black pepper. Serve sprinkled with extra thyme leaves.

PER SERVING 1179 kJ, 282 kcal, 41 g protein, 9 g fat (4 g saturated fat), 5 g carbohydrate (2 g sugars), 2 g fibre, 482 mg sodium

On the stove

Heat 1 tablespoon olive oil in a large heavy-based saucepan and sauté the shallots and bacon over medium heat for 5 minutes, or until browned. Remove with a slotted spoon and set aside. Toss the beef in some plain (all-purpose) flour and shake off any excess. Brown the beef in batches over medium–high heat and set aside.

Sauté the garlic for 30 seconds, then stir in the tomato paste. Return the shallots, bacon and beef to the pan and add the mushrooms. Increase the wine to 1 cup (250 ml) and the stock to 1 cup (250 ml) and stir in well, scraping the bottom of the pan. Bring to a boil, then reduce the heat to low. Cover and simmer gently for 2 hours. Omit the cornflour and serve as directed in step 3.

Chilli con carne

This versatile family favourite can be served with rice or potatoes baked in their skins and topped with sour cream or yogurt, or spooned into taco shells with lettuce, grated cheddar and avocado.

1 tablespoon olive oil
1 large onion, diced
2 cloves garlic, crushed
500 g (1 lb) minced (ground) beef
35 g (1 oz) sachet taco seasoning mix
750 g (1½ lb) tomato passata (puréed tomatoes)
1 tablespoon tomato paste (concentrated purée)
420 g (15 oz) can red kidney beans, drained and rinsed

If you're out of taco seasoning, use 1 tablespoon ground cumin and 1 teaspoon mild chilli powder.

PREPARATION 10 minutes **COOKING** 40 minutes **SERVES** 4

1 Heat the oil in a large deep frying pan and sauté the onion and garlic over medium–high heat for 3–4 minutes, or until softened. Add the beef and cook for a further 3–4 minutes, or until browned, breaking up the lumps with a wooden spoon.

2 Reduce the heat to medium. Add the taco seasoning and stir for 30 seconds. Stir in the tomato passata, tomato paste and beans, mixing well.

3 Reduce the heat to low and simmer for 20–25 minutes, or until the meat is cooked and tender. Serve hot.

PER SERVING 1623 kJ, 388 kcal, 31 g protein, 17 g fat (6 g saturated fat), 26 g carbohydrate (14 g sugars), 9 g fibre, 1985 mg sodium

Slow cooker

If you have a slow cooker you can sauté in, or you don't mind using another pot, follow steps 1 and 2 as above. Transfer to the slow cooker, then cover and cook on low for 8 hours.

Sausages and beans

This quick and easy dish freezes well. Any leftovers will also keep well in the fridge for a few days for another meal. It is particularly good with sourdough toast as a warming winter breakfast.

1 tablespoon olive oil
8 thin beef sausages
1 onion, chopped
200 g (7 oz) button mushrooms, sliced
2 cloves garlic, crushed
800 g (28 oz) can chopped tomatoes
½ cup (125 ml) salt-reduced beef stock
2 x 420 g (15 oz) cans cannellini beans, drained and rinsed
3–4 tablespoons chopped fresh parsley
pinch of brown sugar
crusty bread, to serve

- Canned brown lentils are also great in this dish instead of beans.
- Add some chopped chilli if you like a bit of heat.
- For a vegetarian meal, omit the sausages and use a mixture of different beans. Use vegetable stock instead of beef stock.

PREPARATION 15 minutes **COOKING** 35 minutes **SERVES** 4

1 Heat half the oil in a large deep frying pan over medium–high heat. Brown the sausages, turning occasionally, for 5 minutes. Transfer to a board, cool slightly, then thickly slice.

2 Heat the remaining oil in the pan and sauté the onion over medium heat for 5 minutes, or until softened. Add the mushrooms and cook for a further 2 minutes, then add the garlic and cook for 1 minute.

3 Stir in the tomatoes, stock and sausages. Bring to a boil, then reduce the heat slightly. Simmer, partially covered, for 15 minutes, or until the sausages are cooked through.

4 Stir in the beans, parsley and sugar. Cook for a further 5 minutes, or until the beans are heated through. Season with salt and freshly ground black pepper and serve with crusty bread.

PER SERVING 2314 kJ, 553 kcal, 27 g protein, 36 g fat (15 g saturated fat), 32 g carbohydrate (8 g sugars), 16 g fibre, 1162 mg sodium

Quick massaman beef curry

Ready-made curry pastes are widely available these days. They keep well and are great to have on hand, so you can whip up a mouth-watering curry in a hurry when in need of a spicy flavour hit.

2 tablespoons peanut or vegetable oil
500 g (1 lb) beef rump, cut into thin strips across the grain
2–3 tablespoons massaman curry paste
400 ml (14 fl oz) can coconut milk
2 large potatoes, peeled and diced
roasted peanuts, for sprinkling
steamed rice (see page 310), to serve

- This curry is wonderful with steamed jasmine rice (Thai fragrant rice).
- Garnish the finished curry with a scattering of fresh basil leaves.
- Diced pork fillet is also good in this curry.
- Replace the massaman curry paste with 1–2 tablespoons Thai red or green curry paste, or an Indian-style curry paste like rogan josh.

PREPARATION 10 minutes **COOKING** 20 minutes **SERVES** 4

1 Heat a wok or large deep frying pan over high heat. Add half the oil and swirl to coat. Working in two batches, stir-fry the beef for 3 minutes each time, or until well browned and just cooked through, reheating the wok in between. Remove each batch to a plate.

2 Reheat the wok and add the remaining oil. Reduce the heat to low, add the curry paste and cook, stirring, for 1–2 minutes. Stir in the coconut milk and 1 cup (250 ml) water. Increase the heat to medium, add the potatoes and simmer for 10 minutes, or until the potatoes are just tender and the sauce has thickened slightly.

3 Return the beef to the wok and simmer for 1 minute to heat through — do not boil. Season to taste with salt and freshly ground black pepper and sprinkle with peanuts. Serve with steamed rice.

PER SERVING 2206 kJ, 527 kcal, 32 g protein, 37 g fat (22 g saturated fat), 17 g carbohydrate (5 g sugars), 3 g fibre, 686 mg sodium

Slow cooker

If you have a slow cooker you can sauté in, or you don't mind using another pot, follow step 1 as above. Reduce the coconut milk to 200 ml (7 fl oz) and the water to ½ cup (125 ml). Transfer all the ingredients to the slow cooker, except the peanuts and rice. Gently combine, then cover and cook on low for 6 hours.

Corned beef and creamy onion sauce

Corned beef is delicious served with baby carrots that have been simmered in the pickling liquid, and a helping of mashed potato. If you happen to have some, caramelised onion jam also pairs beautifully with the beef instead of the creamy onion sauce.

- 1 kg (2 lb) piece of corned beef or corned silverside
- 1/4 cup (60 ml) vinegar
- 1/4 cup (45 g) soft brown sugar
- 5–8 cloves
- 1 bay leaf
- 12 baby carrots, scrubbed and trimmed

Creamy onion sauce

- 1 large onion, diced
- 1 cup (250 ml) salt-reduced chicken stock
- 1 1/2 tablespoons butter
- 2 tablespoons plain (all-purpose) flour
- 3/4 cup (180 ml) milk
- 1/2 cup (125 ml) cream
- 2 tablespoons chopped fresh parsley (optional)

- If you'd like to draw some of the salt from the corned beef, soak it in a bowl of cold water overnight in the fridge.
- Cold leftover corned beef is great on sandwiches, or served with coleslaw and a green salad.

Slow cooker

COMBINE ALL THE INGREDIENTS, EXCEPT those for the creamy onion sauce, in a slow cooker. Cover and cook on low for 8 hours. Serve with the sauce.

PREPARATION 15 minutes **COOKING** 1 hour 20 minutes, plus 15 minutes resting **SERVES** 6

1 Rinse the corned beef in cold water to remove any surface brine. Place in a large saucepan, cover with cold water and bring slowly to a boil over medium heat. Use a large spoon to skim any froth from the surface, then reduce the heat to low — the liquid should be barely simmering and should cover the beef by about 6 cm (2 1/2 inches); add a little more water if needed.

2 Add the vinegar, sugar, cloves and bay leaf. Keeping the heat at simmering point, cook the beef for between 1 hour and 1 hour 10 minutes, or until it is tender when tested with a fork — the fork should easily penetrate the centre of the meat.

3 Remove the beef to a carving board, cover loosely with foil and leave to rest for 15 minutes. Add the carrots to the pickling liquid and cook for 10 minutes, or until tender.

4 While the beef is resting, make the onion sauce. Put the onion and stock in a small saucepan and cook over medium heat for 3 minutes, or until the onion is tender. Drain, reserving the stock and the onion separately. Melt the butter in a small saucepan over medium heat, then add the flour and stir for 1 minute, or until the flour is light golden. Remove from the heat and gradually add the milk and the reserved stock. Return to the heat and cook, stirring constantly, until the sauce boils and thickens. Stir in the cream, reserved onion and parsley, if using.

5 Carve the beef and drizzle with the onion sauce. Serve the simmered baby carrots on the side.

PER SERVING 1588 kJ, 379 kcal, 34 g protein, 19 g fat (11 g saturated fat), 19 g carbohydrate (15 g sugars), 3 g fibre, 2216 mg sodium

Slow-cooker spiced braised beef

Lamb is equally good in this savoury, slightly sweet and lightly spicy stew; use the leg or shoulder, which cooks to a beautifully tender result. Serve with couscous or steamed rice.

- 1 kg (2 lb) beef stewing steak (such as chuck), trimmed and cut into bite-sized chunks
- 1 onion, chopped
- 2 carrots, cut into chunks
- 410 g (15 oz) can chopped tomatoes
- 2 teaspoons sweet paprika
- 1 teaspoon ground cumin
- 1 teaspoon ground coriander
- 1/2 teaspoon cayenne pepper
- 1/2 cup (85 g) sultanas (golden raisins)
- 3/4 cup (180 ml) salt-reduced beef stock
- 3 teaspoons cornflour (cornstarch)

For added depth of flavour, you can prepare the stew using the stovetop instructions, then transfer all the ingredients to your slow cooker and cook as directed. In this case, omit the cornflour.

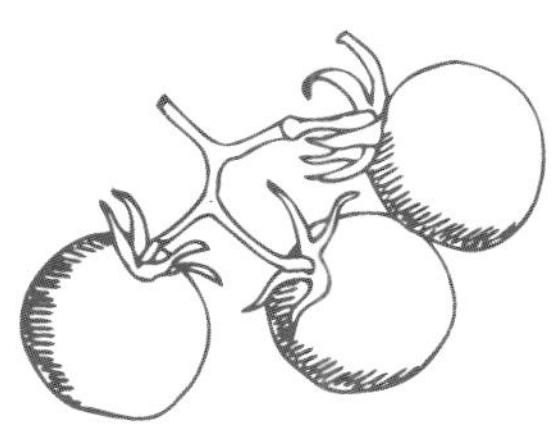

PREPARATION 20 minutes **COOKING** 8 hours **SERVES** 6

1 Combine the beef, onion, carrots, tomatoes, spices and sultanas in a 5 litre (5 quart) slow cooker. Stir in the stock. Cover and cook on low for 8 hours.

2 Mix the cornflour with 1 tablespoon cold water to make a smooth paste, then stir into the stew. Replace the lid, increase the heat to high and cook for a further 15 minutes, or until the sauce has thickened slightly.

PER SERVING 1208 kJ, 288 kcal, 37 g protein, 8 g fat (4 g saturated fat), 17 g carbohydrate (14 g sugars), 3 g fibre, 282 mg sodium

On the stove/In the oven

Toss the beef in plain (all-purpose) flour, then shake off any excess. Heat 1 tablespoon olive oil in a large heavy-based saucepan and brown the beef in batches over medium–high heat; set aside.

Reduce the heat to medium and sauté the onion and carrot for 5 minutes, or until the onion has softened and is lightly golden. Add the spices and cook for 30 seconds, then stir in the tomatoes and sultanas.

Increase the stock to 1 cup (250 ml) and stir in well, scraping the bottom of the pan. Bring to a boil, reduce the heat to low, then cover and gently simmer on the stovetop for 2 hours or transfer to a casserole dish and cook 2 hours in a preheated oven at 160°C (320°F/Gas 2–3). Omit the cornflour.

Pot roast with braised vegetables

Leaner ingredients and clever cooking techniques deliver all the flavour of a traditional pot roast, without all the fat. Add vegetables and you have a meal that is sure to satisfy all the meat-and-potato lovers at your table. Serve with lightly steamed greens.

- 2 slices prosciutto
- 1 boneless beef chuck pot roast (about 1.5–2 kg/3–4 lb), trimmed
- 1½ teaspoons salt
- 1½ teaspoons freshly ground black pepper
- 8 large carrots, cut into large chunks
- 2 onions, chopped
- 4 cloves garlic, crushed
- 800 g (28 oz) can chopped tomatoes
- 1 cup (60 g) chopped fresh basil
- 2 cups (500 ml) dry red wine or salt-reduced beef stock
- 1 kg (2 lb) small red-skinned potatoes, scrubbed
- 2 teaspoons cornflour (cornstarch)

Slow cooker

IF YOU HAVE A SLOW COOKER you can sauté in, or don't mind using another pot, fry the prosciutto as directed in step 1, and follow steps 2 and 3. (Alternatively, omit the browning steps for the beef and vegetables.) Arrange all the vegetables in the base of the slow cooker. Reduce the wine or stock to 1 cup (250 ml), and add to the slow cooker with the beef and all the remaining ingredients — but don't add any water. Cover and cook on low for 8 hours.

PREPARATION 30 minutes **COOKING** 2 hours 30 minutes **SERVES** 8

1 Preheat the oven to 160°C (320°F/Gas 2–3). Briefly fry the prosciutto slices in a large flameproof casserole dish over medium heat until crisp. Leave to dry on paper towels, then crumble and refrigerate in an airtight container.

2 Tie the beef at 5 cm (2 inch) intervals with kitchen string to hold its shape. Rub with 1 teaspoon of the salt and 1 teaspoon of the pepper. Sear in the casserole dish over medium–high heat for 8 minutes, or until browned on all sides. Transfer to a plate.

3 Sauté the carrots, onions and garlic in the pan drippings for 8 minutes, or until the onions are browned. Stir in the tomatoes, half the basil, and the remaining salt and pepper. Cook for 5 minutes.

4 Return the beef to the casserole dish. Add the wine and enough water to come 5 cm (2 inches) up the side of the dish. Bring to a boil. Cover with foil, then with the lid, creating a tight seal. Transfer to the oven and roast for 1 hour, turning the meat once.

5 Add the potatoes and remaining basil, and enough water (if needed) to come 5 cm (2 inches) up the side of the dish. Roast for a further 1 hour, or until the meat and vegetables are tender.

6 Reheat the reserved prosciutto. Remove the beef to a cutting board, cut the beef into chunks and arrange on a platter with the vegetables. Cover loosely with foil to keep warm.

7 Strain the braising liquid, return to the casserole dish and bring to a simmer. Mix the cornflour with 2 tablespoons cold water to make a smooth paste, then whisk into the liquid and bring to a boil. Cook for 1 minute, or until the sauce thickens.

8 Serve the roast and vegetables sprinkled with the prosciutto and drizzled with the gravy.

PER SERVING 1743 kJ, 416 kcal, 46 g protein, 9 g fat (4 g saturated fat), 26 g carbohydrate (9 g sugars), 7 g fibre, 709 mg sodium

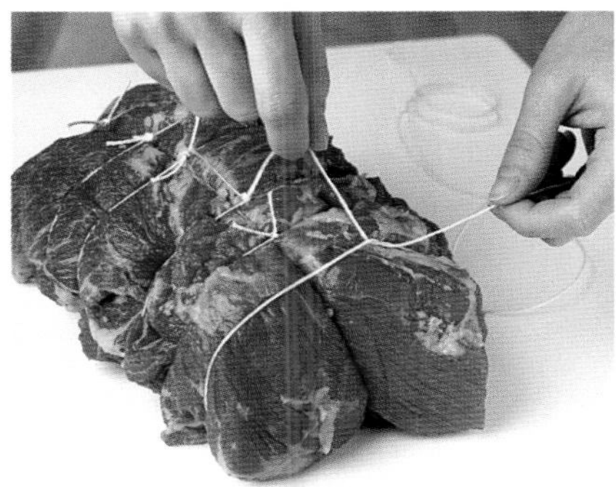

Tie the roast with kitchen string at 5 cm (2 inch) intervals.

Return the roast to the pot with the vegetables.

Whisk the dissolved cornflour into the sauce and cook until thickened.

Beef stroganoff

Using beef stir-fry strips makes this creamy classic even quicker to prepare. Traditionally it is served with fried potato straws, but it is also lovely over pasta or rice, with lightly steamed asparagus.

600 g ($1\frac{1}{4}$ lb) rump steak, cut into thin strips across the grain
$2\frac{1}{2}$ tablespoons olive oil
$1\frac{1}{2}$ tablespoons butter
1 small onion, finely chopped
2 cloves garlic, crushed
250 g (8 oz) mushrooms, thinly sliced
2 teaspoons sweet paprika
$\frac{3}{4}$ cup (180 ml) salt-reduced beef stock
2 tablespoons tomato paste (concentrated purée)
2 teaspoons cornflour (cornstarch)
1 cup (250 g) light sour cream
2 tablespoons finely chopped fresh chives or parsley
hot cooked egg noodles (see page 311), such as tagliatelle, to serve

---

For a richer and more traditional sauce, use full-fat sour cream.

PREPARATION 10 minutes **COOKING** 25 minutes **SERVES** 4

1 Place the beef in a bowl, add 2 tablespoons of the oil and mix well. Heat a large heavy-based frying pan over high heat. Cook the beef in two batches for about 2 minutes each time, or until just done, removing each batch to a plate.

2 Reduce the heat to medium and heat the butter and remaining oil in the pan. Sauté the onion for 5 minutes, or until softened. Add the garlic and mushrooms and sauté for 3 minutes, or until the mushrooms are tender. Stir in the paprika.

3 Stir in the stock and tomato paste and bring to a boil, then reduce the heat to low and simmer for 5 minutes.

4 Mix the cornflour through the sour cream; add to the mushroom mixture and stir until well combined. Simmer for 1 minute, then season to taste with salt and freshly ground black pepper.

5 Return the beef to the pan and simmer for 2 minutes to heat through. Stir in the chives or parsley and serve with hot cooked pasta.

PER SERVING 1998 kJ, 477 kcal, 38 g protein, 33 g fat (14 g saturated fat), 8 g carbohydrate (5 g sugars), 3 g fibre, 408 mg sodium

Pressure-cooker goulash

Paprika is the signature spice in this famed Hungarian dish, and is sold in various grades of heat and sweetness. If possible, use Hungarian paprika here. Using a pressure cooker brings the meat to tenderness in no time at all. Serve with rustic farmhouse bread and perhaps some sour cream.

- 1 tablespoon lard or vegetable oil
- 500 g (1 lb) veal shoulder, cut into small chunks
- 400 g (14 oz) large onions, cut in half, then sliced into half-rings
- 2 tablespoons sweet paprika (preferably Hungarian noble sweet paprika)
- 2 teaspoons hot paprika
- 1 teaspoon dried marjoram
- 1 teaspoon caraway seeds
- 2 tablespoons tomato paste (concentrated purée)
- 400 g (14 oz) waxy (boiling) potatoes
- 1 red capsicum (bell pepper)
- 1 yellow capsicum (bell pepper)
- 5 cups (1.25 litres) salt-reduced beef stock
- 2 cloves garlic
- grated zest of ½ lemon

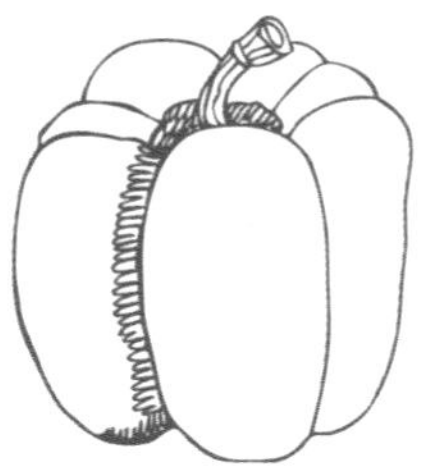

PREPARATION 30 minutes **COOKING** 15 minutes **SERVES** 4

1 Heat the lard or oil in a pressure cooker over medium–high heat. Add the veal and brown without the lid on for 2 minutes. Add the onions and cook for 3 minutes, stirring constantly.

2 Reduce the heat to low. Sprinkle with the spices and season with salt and freshly ground black pepper. Stir in the tomato paste and 150 ml (5 fl oz) water. Cover with the lid and leave to gently braise with the pressure off while preparing the vegetables.

3 Peel the potatoes and cut into 1 cm (½ inch) cubes. Quarter the capsicums lengthwise, remove the core and seeds, then cut the flesh into thin strips. Add the potatoes and capsicums to the pressure cooker and pour in the stock. Seal the lid in place and bring the cooker to high pressure (quick-cook setting) over high heat.

4 Once high pressure is reached, reduce the heat to stabilise the pressure and cook for 2 minutes. Remove the cooker from the heat. Allow the pressure to release naturally.

5 Meanwhile, peel and finely chop the garlic, then place on a chopping board and sprinkle with salt. Press to a fine purée using the back of a knife, transfer to a small serving dish and stir in the lemon zest.

6 Once the pressure has released itself from the pressure cooker, carefully open the lid. Transfer the goulash to a serving bowl and serve with the lemony garlic purée.

PER SERVING 1742 kJ, 416 kcal, 51 g protein, 11 g fat (3 g saturated fat), 29 g carbohydrate (10 g sugars), 7 g fibre, 1595 mg sodium

On the stove

Follow steps 1 to 3 as above, using a heavy-based saucepan instead of a pressure cooker. In step 4, cover the saucepan and increase the cooking time to 45 minutes. Prepare the lemony garlic purée as directed in step 5 and serve with the goulash.

Slow-cooker osso buco with gremolata

This is one dish that particularly benefits from browning the meat first. If you have the time, follow the directions for the stovetop version, then transfer all the ingredients (except the gremolata) to the slow cooker and finish the recipe as directed. Serve with steamed baby carrots.

1 onion, diced
1 large carrot, diced
2 celery stalks, diced
3 cloves garlic, crushed
8 veal osso buco pieces (about 1.25 kg/2½ lb in total)
410 g (15 oz) can chopped tomatoes
½ cup (125 ml) white wine
½ cup (125 ml) salt-reduced beef stock

Gremolata

4 tablespoons chopped fresh flat-leaf (Italian) parsley
1 tablespoon finely grated lemon zest
1 clove garlic, finely chopped

- Osso buco is traditionally served with risotto, but you could serve it with plain steamed rice or even soft polenta (see page 311).
- Veal osso buco or veal shanks come from the top of the thigh, which has a high proportion of bone to meat. The shank is then cross-cut into sections about 3 cm (1¼ inches) thick.

PREPARATION 25 minutes **COOKING** 6 hours **SERVES** 4–6

1 Combine the onion, carrot, celery and garlic in a 4–5 litre (4–5 quart) slow cooker. Combine, then place the veal pieces on top. Pour in the tomatoes, wine and stock.

2 Cover and cook on low for 5½ hours. Remove the lid and cook for a further 30 minutes to thicken the cooking juices slightly.

3 Meanwhile, combine the gremolata ingredients in a small bowl. Serve the gremolata separately, for sprinkling over the stew.

PER SERVING 921 kJ, 220 kcal, 34 g protein, 4 g fat (3 g saturated fat), 7 g carbohydrate (6 g sugars), 3 g fibre, 384 mg sodium

On the stove

Toss the veal pieces in plain (all-purpose) flour and shake off the excess. Heat 1 tablespoon olive oil in a heavy-based saucepan and brown the veal in batches over medium–high heat. Remove to a plate.

Sauté the vegetables and garlic in the pan over medium heat for 5 minutes, or until lightly browned. Stir in the tomatoes, wine and stock, increasing the stock to 1 cup (250 ml). Return the veal to the pan, cover and simmer for 1½ hours, until tender. Serve with the gremolata.

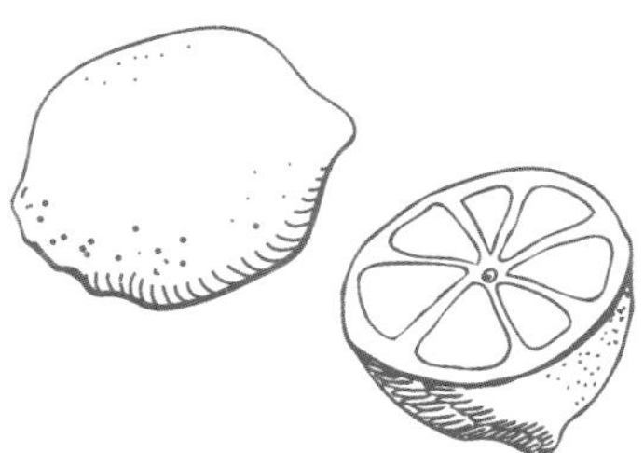

Beef stew with herb dumplings

Herb dumplings transform this simple stew into a substantial meal. Fresh lovage leaves, when available, can be used in the dumplings instead of the parsley for a bolder celery flavour.

1 tablespoon olive oil
1 onion, finely chopped
800 g (1¾ lb) beef blade steak, cut into bite-sized chunks
4 cloves garlic, crushed
1 teaspoon celery salt
1 tablespoon plain (all-purpose) flour
2 teaspoons sugar
800 g (28 oz) can chopped tomatoes
1 cup (250 ml) salt-reduced beef stock
1 tablespoon worcestershire sauce

Herb dumplings

1⅓ cups (200 g) self-raising flour, plus extra for dusting
½ teaspoon salt
60 g (2 oz) butter, chilled and diced
2 tablespoons grated parmesan
1 tablespoon finely snipped fresh chives
1 tablespoon finely chopped fresh parsley
½ cup (125 ml) milk

In France, lovage is called céleri bâtard, or false celery. It has a much stronger flavour than parsley when used raw, but its pungency diminishes in cooking. Try the leaves and stems in salads.

PREPARATION 20 minutes **COOKING** 2 hours 35 minutes **SERVES** 6

1 Heat the oil in a large heavy-based saucepan and sauté the onion over medium heat for 5 minutes, or until softened. Add the beef and brown on all sides. Add the garlic and cook for 1 minute. Sprinkle with the celery salt, season with freshly ground black pepper and dust the flour over the meat, stirring well.

2 Sprinkle with the sugar, then stir in the tomatoes, stock and worcestershire sauce. Bring to a boil, reduce the heat, then cover and simmer for 2 hours.

3 Meanwhile, make the dumplings. Sift the flour and salt into a bowl, then rub in the butter with your fingertips until the mixture resembles breadcrumbs. Using a wooden spoon or spatula, fold in the parmesan and herbs. Add the milk and use a flat-bladed knife to bring the dough together. Scoop out heaped teaspoons of the mixture and form into balls with floured hands.

4 Place the dumplings on top of the stew. Cover and simmer without lifting the lid for 15–20 minutes, or until the dumplings are cooked through. Serve immediately.

PER SERVING 1893 kJ, 452 kcal, 36 g protein, 19 g fat (9 g saturated fat), 34 g carbohydrate (8 g sugars), 4 g fibre, 1196 mg sodium

In the oven

Preheat the oven to 160°C (320°F/Gas 2–3). Brown the ingredients in a large flameproof casserole dish as directed in step 1. Increase the stock to 2 cups (500 ml) and add to the casserole with the other hotpot ingredients. Bring to a boil, then transfer to the oven and cook for 2 hours.

Meanwhile, prepare the dumplings as directed in step 3.

Increase the oven temperature to 180°C (350°F/Gas 4). Remove the lid, place the dumplings on top of the stew and bake, uncovered, for 15–20 minutes, or until the dumplings are cooked through.

Rub the butter and flour together until mixture resembles breadcrumbs.

Using a wooden spoon, lightly fold in the parmesan and herbs.

Roughly scoop into balls, then lightly shape using floured hands.

Lancashire hotpot

This modern version of the old British favourite is, like the original, slow-cooked for maximum flavour, but is quite a deal lighter, using lean lamb neck fillet and more vegetables than in days gone by. If you like, you can sprinkle the top with grated cheddar towards the end of cooking.

- 500 g (1 lb) lean lamb neck fillet, trimmed of all excess fat, then sliced
- 1 clove garlic, crushed
- 2 tablespoons worcestershire sauce
- 1 onion, thinly sliced
- 2 leeks, white part only, thinly sliced
- 3 carrots, thinly sliced
- 250 g (8 oz) button mushrooms, halved
- 1 bay leaf
- 4 sprigs fresh thyme
- 1 sprig fresh rosemary
- 500 g (1 lb) small new potatoes, scrubbed and sliced
- 2 tablespoons tomato paste (concentrated purée)
- 400 ml (14 fl oz) salt-reduced beef or chicken stock, heated
- grated cheddar, for sprinkling (optional)

- You can prepare the hotpot ahead of time up until the end of step 4 and leave it in the refrigerator for several hours, or overnight if more convenient.
- For a more traditional Lancashire hotpot, add a few cleaned, sliced lamb's kidneys with the lamb.
- Instead of sliced potatoes, top the stew with a layer of coarsely grated potato, or a mixture of grated potato and parsnip. Sprinkle with grated parmesan if desired and bake as directed in the main recipe.

PREPARATION 25 minutes **COOKING** 2 hours **SERVES** 4

1 Preheat the oven to 180°C (350°F/Gas 4). Combine the lamb, garlic and worcestershire sauce in a bowl and toss to coat the lamb.

2 Spread a layer of onion, leek and carrot in the bottom of a large casserole dish. Top with a layer of lamb and mushrooms and season lightly with salt and freshly ground black pepper. Repeat the layers until the ingredients are used up.

3 Make a bouquet garni by tying together the bay leaf, thyme and rosemary with kitchen string. Tuck it into the centre of the stew. Top with a thick layer of overlapping potato slices.

4 Mix the tomato paste into the stock and pour the mixture over the potatoes. Cover tightly, transfer to the oven and bake for 1½ hours, or until the lamb and potatoes are tender.

5 Remove the lid and sprinkle the cheese over the potatoes, if using. Increase the oven temperature to 230°C (450°F/Gas 8) and bake, uncovered, for a further 25–30 minutes, or until the topping is golden.

PER SERVING 1429 kJ, 341 kcal, 36 g protein, 9 g fat (4 g saturated fat), 28 g carbohydrate (10 g sugars), 8 g fibre, 731 mg sodium

Slow cooker

Assemble the ingredients in the slow cooker as directed in steps 1 to 3. Reduce the stock to 200 ml (7 fl oz), but don't worry about heating it. Mix the stock with the tomato paste and drizzle over the potatoes. Cover and cook on low for 8 hours. Omit the cheese.

Lamb with chickpeas and figs

Sweetened with figs and infused with spices, this luscious lamb tagine displays definite North African and Middle Eastern influences. Wholemeal couscous is the perfect accompaniment.

- 1 lamb shoulder (about 1 kg/2 lb), cut into bite-sized chunks
- 2 tablespoons olive oil
- 1 large onion, chopped
- 2 cloves garlic, chopped
- 2 teaspoons ground coriander
- 2 teaspoons ground cumin
- 1 teaspoon ground ginger
- 1 tablespoon plain (all-purpose) flour
- 3 cups (750 ml) salt-reduced beef stock
- 3 tomatoes, chopped
- 2 strips orange zest
- 1 cinnamon stick, broken
- ½ cup (90 g) chopped dried figs
- 300 g (10 oz) can chickpeas, drained and rinsed, or 1 cup (160 g) cooked chickpeas
- 3 tablespoons chopped fresh parsley or coriander (cilantro) leaves
- couscous (see page 310), to serve

Taking time to brown the lamb well in step 1 will result in a richly flavoured dish. Don't overcrowd the pan when you brown the meat, otherwise it will stew in its juices rather than turning a deep golden brown.

PREPARATION 20 minutes **COOKING** 1 hour 50 minutes **SERVES** 4

1 Preheat the oven to 180°C (350°F/Gas 4). Season the lamb with freshly ground black pepper. Heat half the oil in a large flameproof casserole dish over medium heat. Brown the lamb in two batches for 4–5 minutes each time, stirring frequently, and transferring each batch to a plate.

2 Heat the remaining oil in the casserole dish over medium–low heat. Sauté the onion and garlic for 5 minutes, or until the onion has softened. Add the ground spices and stir for 1 minute. Sprinkle with the flour and cook, stirring constantly, for 1 minute.

3 Stir in the stock and tomatoes. Add the orange zest and cinnamon, bring to a boil, then reduce the heat to low. Mix the lamb through. Cover the dish, transfer to the oven and bake for 1 hour.

4 Stir in the figs and chickpeas, then cover and cook for a further 30 minutes, or until the lamb is tender. Stir once or twice during cooking, and add a little water if needed to keep the lamb just covered.

5 Sprinkle with the parsley or coriander and serve with couscous.

PER SERVING 2452 kJ, 586 kcal, 61 g protein, 25 g fat (8 g saturated fat), 30 g carbohydrate (19 g sugars), 9 g fibre, 1134 mg sodium

Slow cooker

If you have a slow cooker you can sauté in, or you don't mind using another pot, follow steps 1 and 2 as above. Transfer the onion mixture and lamb to the slow cooker.

Reduce the stock to 1½ cups (375 ml) and add to the slow cooker with the remaining ingredients except the parsley and couscous. Gently combine, then cover and cook on low for 8 hours.

Sprinkle with the parsley or coriander and serve with couscous.

Pressure-cooker lamb, lentil and chickpea stew

This dish really benefits from being made a day ahead, to allow all the fragrant spices to soak into the lamb and legumes. Serve with warm soft flat bread or a rustic farmhouse loaf.

4 tablespoons olive oil
400 g (14 oz) lamb leg, cut into small chunks
1 onion, finely diced
1 clove garlic, finely chopped
1 teaspoon ground cumin
$1/2$ teaspoon ground coriander
$1/2$ teaspoon ground ginger
$1/4$ teaspoon ground cardamom
1 carrot, finely diced
$1\,2/3$ cups (300 g) brown lentils, drained and rinsed
410 g (15 oz) can chopped tomatoes
800 ml (28 fl oz) vegetable stock
150 g (5 oz) natural (plain) yogurt
1 tablespoon chopped fresh dill
420 g (15 oz) can chickpeas, drained and rinsed
cayenne pepper, to taste
2 tablespoons lemon juice

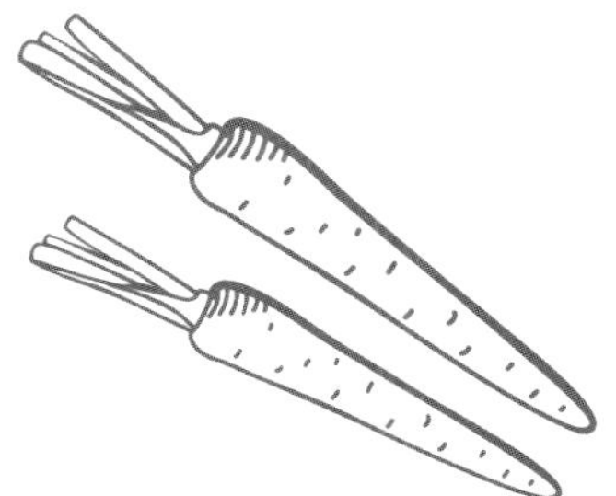

PREPARATION 20 minutes **COOKING** 15 minutes **SERVES** 4

1 Heat half the oil in a pressure cooker over medium–high heat. Add the lamb and brown without the lid on for 2 minutes. Add the onion and cook for 3 minutes, stirring constantly.

2 Stir in the garlic and ground spices until well combined. Add the carrot, lentils and tomatoes, then stir in the stock. Seal the lid in place and bring the cooker to high pressure (quick-cook setting) over high heat.

3 Once high pressure is reached, reduce the heat to stabilise the pressure and cook for 10 minutes. Remove the cooker from the heat. Allow the pressure to release naturally. As soon as the pressure has released itself, carefully open the lid.

4 Meanwhile, put the yogurt in a small bowl with the dill. Stir the yogurt to a creamy consistency and season to taste with salt and freshly ground black pepper.

5 Stir the chickpeas into the stew and allow to heat through over medium heat, without the lid on. Season with salt, freshly ground black pepper and cayenne pepper to taste.

6 Stir in the lemon juice and drizzle with the remaining 2 tablespoons oil. Serve with the dill yogurt.

PER SERVING 2748 kJ, 657 kcal, 49 g protein, 29 g fat (7 g saturated fat), 553 g carbohydrate (15 g sugars), 16 g fibre, 1308 mg sodium

On the stove

FOLLOW STEPS 1 AND 2 as above, using a heavy-based saucepan instead of a pressure cooker. In step 3, cover the saucepan and increase the cooking time to 45 minutes. Finish the recipe as directed in steps 4 to 6.

Mediterranean lamb stew

Lamb shoulder becomes mouth-wateringly tender in this slow-simmered stew. Just ensure the liquid doesn't boil, or the lamb will become tough. Crusty bread completes the meal.

- 1 large eggplant (aubergine), cut into large cubes
- 1 kg (2 lb) boneless lamb shoulder, trimmed and cut into large chunks
- ½ cup (125 ml) red wine
- 4–6 sprigs fresh thyme
- 2 cloves garlic, sliced
- ¼ cup (60 ml) olive oil
- 1 large red capsicum (bell pepper), cut into large chunks
- 1 large green capsicum (bell pepper), cut into large chunks
- 2 zucchini (courgettes), cut into thick rounds
- 1 onion, chopped
- 3 tomatoes, chopped
- 1 cup (250 ml) salt-reduced beef stock
- crusty bread, to serve

This is a great dish to cook ahead and reheat. As soon as the steam has evaporated, transfer the cooked stew to a casserole dish, cover and refrigerate for up to 3 days. Scrape off any solidified fat, then cover and reheat in a preheated 160°C (320°F/Gas 2–3) oven for 30 minutes, or until thoroughly heated through.

PREPARATION 20 minutes, plus 10 minutes standing
COOKING 1 hour 10 minutes **SERVES** 4

1 Spread the eggplant in a colander, sprinkle generously with salt and leave to stand for 10 minutes.

2 Meanwhile, place the lamb in a large bowl. Add the wine, thyme, garlic and 1 tablespoon of the oil. Toss well to coat, then leave to marinate while sautéing the vegetables.

3 Rinse the eggplant and pat dry with paper towels. Heat another 1 tablespoon of the oil in a large heavy-based saucepan over medium heat. Brown the eggplant all over, then remove to a large plate. Heat the remaining tablespoon of oil and sauté the capsicums for 2 minutes, then add to the eggplant. Sauté the zucchini and onion for 2 minutes.

4 Return all the vegetables to the pan. Add the lamb and its marinade and season with salt and freshly ground black pepper. Stir in the tomatoes and stock and slowly bring to a boil.

5 Reduce the heat to medium–low, then cover and slowly simmer for 50 minutes, or until the lamb is just tender, stirring occasionally and adding a little more stock or water if needed to keep the lamb and vegetables just covered.

6 Remove the lid and simmer, uncovered, for a further 10 minutes, or until the liquid has reduced slightly. Serve with crusty bread.

PER SERVING 2233 kJ, 534 kcal, 55 g protein, 29 g fat (9 g saturated fat), 8 g carbohydrate (8 g sugars), 5 g fibre, 516 mg sodium

Slow cooker

Reduce the wine to ¼ cup (60 ml) and the stock to ½ cup (125 ml). Place in a slow cooker with all the ingredients except the bread. Gently combine, then cover and cook on low for 8 hours.

- To French-trim lamb shanks, cut the meat and fat away from the end of the shank to expose the bone. Alternatively, ask your butcher to do this for you.
- Tagines such as this are usually high in fibre as they feature legumes and dried fruit such as prunes or figs. These ingredients also lower the glycaemic index of this dish, which is helpful for those needing to regulate their blood-glucose levels.

Moroccan-style lamb shanks

Rich with flavours savoury and sweet, this dish couldn't be simpler to prepare. For a spicy kick, add fresh or dried chilli or harissa paste. Sprinkle with fresh parsley and serve with a green salad.

1 apple, peeled, cored and diced
1 onion, finely chopped
410 g (15 oz) can chopped tomatoes
1 carrot, finely diced
420 g (15 oz) can chickpeas, drained and rinsed
8 kalamata olives
8 pitted prunes
2 tablespoons chopped preserved lemon rind
1 cinnamon stick
1/4 teaspoon ground ginger
1/4 teaspoon ground cumin
1/4 teaspoon ground turmeric
4 lamb shanks (about 1 kg/2 lb), French trimmed

PREPARATION 10 minutes **COOKING** 4 hours **SERVES** 4

1 Preheat the oven to 150°C (300°F/Gas 2). Place the apple, onion, tomatoes, carrot and chickpeas in a large casserole dish with a tight-fitting lid, or a tagine if you have one.

2 Add the olives, prunes, preserved lemon, cinnamon stick and ground spices and mix until well combined.

3 Add the lamb shanks and turn them about to coat in the mixture. Cover and bake for 4 hours, or until the lamb is very tender.

PER SERVING 1610 kJ, 385 kcal, 36 g protein, 16 g fat (6 g saturated fat), 25 g carbohydrate (13 g sugars), 7 g fibre, 896 mg sodium

Slow cooker

COMBINE ALL THE INGREDIENTS IN a slow cooker. Cover and cook on low for 8 hours.

Classic braised lamb shanks

Serve these meaty melt-in-the-mouth shanks and their rich tomato sauce with mashed potato or creamy polenta to soak up all the juices. Add some steamed greens or a leafy salad on the side.

4 lamb shanks (about 1 kg/2 lb), French trimmed
1 tablespoon plain (all-purpose) flour
2 tablespoons olive oil
1 small onion, finely diced
800 g (28 oz) can chopped tomatoes
1½ cups (375 ml) beef stock
½ cup (125 ml) red wine
3 tablespoons chopped fresh parsley

- 'Frenched' lamb shanks have been trimmed of tendons and excess fat. The knuckle joint from each end is removed so the shanks are much neater, and fit more easily into baking dishes.
- Build on this classic flavour base by adding black olives, a strip of orange zest and a few bay leaves. Thyme or rosemary also work well, as do chopped red or green capsicums (bell peppers), carrot and celery.

PREPARATION 10 minutes **COOKING** 2 hours 15 minutes **SERVES** 4

1 Season the shanks with salt and freshly ground black pepper, then dust with the flour.

2 Heat the oil in a large deep saucepan over medium heat. Add the lamb shanks and brown well on all sides, then remove and set aside. Sauté the onion in the pan for 5 minutes, or until softened.

3 Pour in the tomatoes, stock and wine. Bring to a boil, then reduce the heat to low. Add the shanks and parsley.

4 Simmer, uncovered, for 2 hours, or until the lamb is very tender, stirring now and then and adding a little more stock or water if needed to keep the shanks just covered.

PER SERVING 1685 kJ, 403 kcal, 34 g protein, 23 g fat (7 g saturated fat), 10 g carbohydrate (7 g sugars), 3 g fibre, 643 mg sodium

Slow cooker

If you have a slow cooker you can sauté in, or you don't mind using another pot, follow steps 1 and 2 as above. (Alternatively, omit the oil and the browning step.)

Reduce the stock to ¾ cup (180 ml) and the wine to ¼ cup (60 ml). Add to the slow cooker with all the other ingredients, then cover and cook on low for 8 hours.

- Packed with protein, lamb is also a good source of vitamin B_{12}, thiamin and iron. Trim off as much fat as you can before cooking.
- Spinach adds extra nutrients to this dish, including vitamins C, E and K, the B vitamins, beta-carotene and iron.
- A beautifully fragrant spice, cardamom is traditionally used to help relieve problems such as indigestion, flatulence and stomach cramps.

Fragrant lamb with spinach

Yogurt adds creaminess to this spice-infused dish. Serve with naan bread, and a salsa of finely diced tomato and avocado, tossed with a little lemon juice and finely chopped coriander.

- 2 tablespoons vegetable oil
- 2 onions, finely chopped
- 4 cloves garlic, crushed
- 2.5 cm (1 inch) piece of fresh ginger, peeled and chopped
- 1 red chilli, seeded and sliced
- 2 teaspoons paprika
- 2 teaspoons ground cumin
- 2 teaspoons ground coriander
- 1 teaspoon ground white pepper
- ½ teaspoon ground cinnamon
- seeds from 8 green cardamom pods, crushed
- 2 bay leaves
- 200 g (7 oz) thick (Greek-style) yogurt
- 500 g (1 lb) boneless lamb, trimmed and cut into chunks
- 2 large tomatoes, chopped
- 200 g (7 oz) baby English spinach leaves
- 4 tablespoons chopped fresh coriander (cilantro), plus extra sprigs to garnish
- steamed rice (see page 310), to serve

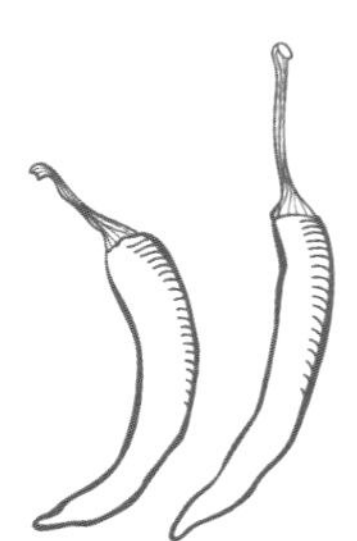

PREPARATION 25 minutes **COOKING** 1 hour 40 minutes **SERVES** 4

1 Heat the oil in a large heavy-based saucepan and sauté the onions, garlic and ginger over medium heat for 15 minutes, or until the onions are golden, stirring frequently.

2 Stir in the chilli, ground spices, crushed cardamom seeds and bay leaves and cook for 30 seconds. Stir in the yogurt and 150 ml (5 fl oz) water. Add the lamb, mix well and bring to a boil. Reduce the heat, then cover and simmer gently for 1¼ hours, or until the lamb is tender.

3 Stir in the tomatoes, spinach and coriander. Cook for 2–3 minutes, stirring often, until the tomatoes have softened slightly and all the spinach has wilted.

4 Remove the bay leaf and season as needed with salt and freshly ground black pepper. Garnish with coriander sprigs and serve with steamed rice.

PER SERVING 1613 kJ, 385 kcal, 34 g protein, 23 g fat (7 g saturated fat), 14 g carbohydrate (8 g sugars), 5 g fibre, 146 mg sodium

Lamb, pumpkin and barley stew

Pearl barley is a robust and highly nutritious grain that soaks up flavour and adds a lovely, slightly nutty texture to this warming hotpot. Serve some steamed broccoli or other greens on the side.

- 1 tablespoon olive oil
- 4 lamb chops (about 500 g/1 lb in total), trimmed
- 2 onions, quartered lengthwise
- 2 large leeks, white part only, thickly sliced
- 1 butternut pumpkin (squash), about 600 g (1¼ lb), peeled and cut into 2.5 cm (1 inch) chunks
- 2 turnips, peeled and quartered lengthwise
- ½ cup (110 g) pearl barley
- 4 cups (1 litre) salt-reduced lamb stock
- 2 bay leaves
- 2 large sprigs fresh thyme
- chopped fresh parsley, to garnish

- For extra piquancy, add a good dash or two of worcestershire sauce or a few crushed garlic cloves with the herbs in step 3.
- Try diced carrots and swedes (rutabagas) instead of the butternut pumpkin and turnips.

PREPARATION 20 minutes, plus 10 minutes standing
COOKING 1 hour 30 minutes **SERVES** 4

1 Preheat the oven to 160°C (320°F/Gas 2–3). Heat the oil in a large flameproof casserole dish over medium heat, add the lamb chops and brown them on both sides. Remove to a plate.

2 Sauté the onions in the dish for 5 minutes, or until softened. Stir in the leeks, pumpkin and turnips, then cover and sweat gently for 5 minutes, stirring occasionally.

3 Add the barley and stir for 1 minute, then pour in the stock and allow to warm through. Tuck the chops in with the vegetables. Add the bay leaves and thyme, season with salt and freshly ground black pepper and bring to a boil.

4 Cover the casserole dish and transfer to the oven. Bake for 1¼ hours, or until the meat and vegetables are very tender.

5 Remove the casserole from the oven and leave to stand for about 10 minutes, to allow the barley to soak up more of the stock. Adjust the seasoning if needed. Serve sprinkled with parsley.

PER SERVING 1564 kJ, 374 kcal, 29 g protein, 12 g fat (4 g saturated fat), 40 g carbohydrate (10 g sugars), 9 g fibre, 999 mg sodium

Slow cooker

IF YOU HAVE A SLOW COOKER you can sauté in, or you don't mind using another pot, follow steps 1 and 2 as above. (Alternatively, omit the oil and the browning steps.) Transfer all the ingredients to the slow cooker, except the parsley. Gently combine, then cover and cook on low for 8 hours. Serve sprinkled with the parsley.

Irish-style casserole

This simple recipe is based on Irish stew, which is enjoyed well beyond the Emerald Isle. In this version tender lamb plays a starring role. Serve with Irish soda bread or crusty white bread.

- 2 large onions, thickly sliced
- 6 large potatoes (about 800 g/1¾ lb), peeled
- 1 kg (2 lb) lamb neck chops, trimmed
- 3 carrots, cut into chunks
- 1 small swede (rutabaga), peeled and cut into chunks
- 6 sprigs fresh thyme, plus extra to garnish
- 2 cups (500 ml) hot salt-reduced beef stock, approximately

For a more traditional Irish stew, stir 2 tablespoons chopped fresh parsley into the stew at the end of step 1 instead of the thyme, and garnish the finished dish with extra parsley.

PREPARATION 15 minutes **COOKING** 2 hours **SERVES** 6

1 Preheat the oven to 160°C (320°F/Gas 2–3). Spread the onions in a large baking dish or casserole dish.

2 Slice four of the potatoes and cut the others into large chunks. Place half the sliced potatoes over the onions, then all the lamb chops. Add the carrots, swede and chopped potatoes. Season well with salt and freshly ground black pepper and add the thyme sprigs.

3 Top with the remaining sliced potatoes, then gently pour the hot stock over — it should cover the vegetables by about 3 cm (1¼ inches), so add a little more if needed. Cover the dish with a sheet of foil, then the lid (or another sheet of foil if it doesn't have one).

4 Transfer to the oven and bake for 2 hours, or until the lamb is very tender. During cooking, carefully lift the lid and foil from time to time to check the liquid hasn't evaporated and the onions are not catching on the bottom of the dish — add just a little stock or water to the dish as needed. Serve garnished with extra thyme.

PER SERVING 1609 kJ, 384 kcal, 42 g protein, 12 g fat (6 g saturated fat), 26 g carbohydrate (7 g sugars), 5 g fibre, 493 mg sodium

Slow cooker

Arrange the vegetables in the base of a slow cooker. Place the lamb on top and sprinkle with thyme. Reduce the stock to 1½ cups (375 ml), but don't worry about heating it. Pour the stock over the lamb, then cover and cook on low for 8 hours.

Lamb shanks with figs and lentils

Roasting the lamb shanks before slowly braising them removes much of the excess fat and helps develop a wonderful flavour. Pomegranate molasses adds a sweetly tart tang to this dish.

- 2 lamb shanks (about 350 g/12 oz each)
- 2 tablespoons olive oil
- 6 French shallots (eschalots), peeled and quartered
- 3 garlic cloves, chopped
- 2 sprigs fresh rosemary
- 1 bay leaf
- 500 g (1 lb) tomatoes, peeled and quartered
- 1½ cups (300 g) green lentils
- 2 tablespoons pomegranate molasses
- 1 tablespoon honey
- 4 cups (1 litre) salt-reduced beef or vegetable stock, approximately
- 8 dried figs, quartered
- 2 zucchini (courgettes), thickly sliced
- roughly chopped coriander (cilantro) leaves, to garnish

PREPARATION 25 minutes **COOKING** 2 hours **SERVES** 4

1 Preheat the oven to 220°C (425°F/Gas 7). Roast the lamb shanks in a large flameproof casserole dish for 25 minutes, or until richly browned. Remove from the dish and drain on paper towels. Reduce the oven temperature to 160°C (320°F/Gas 2–3).

2 Heat the oil in the casserole dish on the stovetop over medium heat. Add the shallots and cook for 5 minutes, stirring until lightly browned. Stir in the garlic, rosemary, bay leaf and tomatoes and cook for 1 minute. Stir in the lentils, then add the lamb shanks, pushing them down into the vegetable mixture.

3 Stir the pomegranate molasses and honey into the stock, then pour over the lamb. Slowly bring to a boil. Cover the casserole dish with a tight-fitting lid, transfer to the oven and bake for 45 minutes.

4 Remove the casserole from the oven. Remove the lid and check the liquid level, adding a little more stock if needed. Remove the lamb shanks to a plate, stir the figs and zucchini into the stew, then push the shanks back in.

5 Cover and bake for a further 45 minutes, or until the lamb is very tender. Lift out the shanks to a chopping board. Carve the meat from the shanks and discard the bones. Gently mix the meat through the casserole and serve garnished with coriander.

PER SERVING 2621 kJ, 626 kcal, 43 g protein, 19 g fat (5 g saturated fat), 76 g carbohydrate (36 g sugars), 19 g fibre, 960 mg sodium

Slow cooker

If you have a slow cooker you can sauté in, or you don't mind using another pot, fry the shanks in the oil, turning often until browned. Reduce the stock to 400 ml (14 fl oz) and transfer all the ingredients to the slow cooker, except the coriander. Cover and cook on low for 8 hours.

Take the meat from the bones, mix the lamb back into the stew and serve garnished with coriander.

- Pomegranate molasses is made with concentrated pomegranate juice. It really is worth seeking out for this recipe as it adds an exquisite flavour. If your local supermarket doesn't stock it, try a delicatessen or gourmet food store.
- To peel tomatoes, cut a shallow cross in the base of each tomato. Place them in a heatproof bowl and cover with boiling water. Leave for about 30 seconds, then drain and rinse under cold water. Leave until cool enough to handle, then simply peel the skin away from the cross.

- You can prepare the tagine ahead up to the end of step 4. Leave to cool, then refrigerate or freeze. If the tagine has been frozen, allow to thaw first, then reheat gently until piping hot throughout, adding a little extra stock if necessary.
- To vary the recipe, replace the pickling onions, dates and apricots with 2 tablespoons raisins, 1 large diced zucchini (courgette), 1 chopped tomato and some diced pumpkin (winter squash).

Lamb tagine with saffron

Available from spice shops and larger supermarkets, harissa is a fiery North African chilli paste, tempered in this aromatic stew by the sweetness of honey, dried dates and apricots, nutty chickpeas and the warm spicy notes of saffron, ground ginger and cinnamon.

- 2 cups (500 ml) salt-reduced vegetable stock
- 1/4 teaspoon saffron threads
- 2 tablespoons olive oil
- 500 g (1 lb) lean boneless lamb, such as from the leg, cut into bite-sized chunks
- 1 onion, chopped
- 1 tablespoon tomato paste (concentrated purée)
- zest of 1 orange, cut into strips
- 1/4 teaspoon ground ginger
- 1 teaspoon ground cinnamon
- 1/2 teaspoon ground coriander
- 1/2 teaspoon harissa, or to taste, plus extra harissa, to serve
- 1 tablespoon honey
- 16 pickling onions or small French shallots (eschalots), peeled
- 2/3 cup (125 g) pitted dried dates
- 1 cup (180 g) dried apricots
- 2 x 420 g (15 oz) cans chickpeas, drained and rinsed
- 2 tablespoons chopped walnuts

PREPARATION 30 minutes **COOKING** 2 hours **SERVES** 4

1 Heat the stock until hot, add the saffron threads and leave to infuse while browning the lamb.

2 Heat the oil in a large saucepan or flameproof casserole dish with a tight-fitting lid, or a tagine if you have one. Add the lamb and fry over medium heat until lightly browned all over. Push the meat to one side of the pan and sauté the chopped onion for 5 minutes, or until golden.

3 Stir the saffron stock to dissolve the saffron, then pour into the pan. Add the tomato paste, orange zest strips and ground spices. Stir well, then bring to a boil. Reduce the heat, cover and leave to simmer gently for 1½ hours.

4 Remove the lid and scoop out about 1 cup (250 ml) of the sauce. Stir the harissa and honey into the reserved sauce, then stir the mixture back into the pan. Stir in the pickling onions, dates, apricots and chickpeas. Simmer gently, uncovered, for a further 20 minutes, stirring occasionally.

5 Season to taste with salt and freshly ground black pepper, then scatter the walnuts over the top. Serve with a little extra harissa on the table for those who like more heat.

PER SERVING 2805 kJ, 670 kcal, 41 g protein, 23 g fat (6 g saturated fat), 78 g carbohydrate (44 g sugars), 13 g fibre, 948 mg sodium

Slow cooker

If you have a slow cooker you can sauté in, or you don't mind using another pot, follow steps 1 and 2 above. (Alternatively, omit the oil and browning step.) Transfer to the slow cooker and stir in the saffron stock, tomato paste, orange zest and spices. Cover and cook on low for 6 hours.

Add the harissa and honey as directed in step 4, then the onions, fruit and chickpeas. Cover and cook for a further 2 hours.

Slow-cooker lamb biryani

Variations of this aromatic, spice-infused rice dish abound throughout the Indian subcontinent. In this simple version, a slow cooker gently steams the rice and lamb to perfection.

- 750 g (1½ lb) lamb leg or shoulder, trimmed and cut into small chunks
- 3 cloves garlic, crushed
- 1 teaspoon grated fresh ginger
- 2 teaspoons garam masala
- ½ teaspoon ground coriander
- ½ teaspoon ground cumin
- ½ teaspoon cayenne pepper
- ½ teaspoon ground turmeric
- ½ cup (125 g) natural (plain) yogurt, plus extra to serve
- 1 onion, thinly sliced
- 2 tablespoons vegetable oil
- 1½ cups (300 g) basmati rice, rinsed and drained
- 3 cups (750 ml) salt-reduced chicken stock, hot
- coriander (cilantro) leaves, to garnish
- Indian chutney, to serve

If you are short on time, you can brown the onions in a frying pan first, or just eliminate this step.

PREPARATION 20 minutes **COOKING** 4 hours 30 minutes **SERVES** 4–6

1 Put the lamb in a large bowl. Mix the garlic, ginger and ground spices through the yogurt, then drizzle it over the lamb and gently combine until the lamb is well coated. Cover and set aside for the spices to infuse the meat.

2 Heat the slow cooker on high. If your slow cooker has a browning option, fry the onion in the oil until golden. Otherwise, add the oil and onion to the slow cooker and leave to cook for 1–1½ hours, or until the onion is golden, stirring occasionally. (Spreading the onion slices up the side of the cooker in a thin layer will help caramelise the onion.) Remove the onion from the cooker and set aside.

3 Spoon half the lamb mixture into the slow cooker and spread to cover the base. Top with half the rice, then half the onion. Repeat the layers with the remaining lamb, rice and onion. Pour in the hot stock.

4 Cover and cook on high for 2½–3 hours, or until all the liquid has been absorbed.

5 Serve garnished with coriander leaves, with some extra yogurt and a small bowl of Indian chutney.

PER SERVING 2813 kJ, 672 kcal, 51 g protein, 22 g fat (7 g saturated fat), 66 g carbohydrate (5 g sugars), 2 g fibre, 621 mg sodium

In the oven

Preheat the oven to 150°C (300°F/Gas 2). Heat 2 tablespoons vegetable oil in a large flameproof casserole dish on the stovetop. Sauté the onion over medium–high heat for 5 minutes, or until golden.

Remove from the heat, then layer the ingredients as directed in step 3. Cover, transfer to the oven and bake for 2–3 hours, or until the liquid has been absorbed. Serve as directed in step 5.

Slow-cooker lamb with apricots

This recipe draws upon the Moroccan method of stewing meat with fruit. The unusual addition of dark beer in the marinade yields a subtle yet intriguing depth of flavour.

4 sprigs fresh thyme
2 bay leaves
1 kg (2 lb) lamb leg or shoulder, cut into bite-sized chunks
1 onion, halved and thinly sliced
2 carrots, thinly sliced
2 celery stalks, thinly sliced
2 cloves garlic, crushed
150 g (5 oz) dried apricots, halved
1/4 teaspoon grated nutmeg
1 cup (250 ml) dark beer or brown ale
410 g (15 oz) can chopped tomatoes
1/2 cup (125 ml) salt-reduced chicken stock
torn fresh parsley leaves, to garnish

- Serve with couscous (see page 310).
- If you prefer not to use beer, increase the chicken stock to 1 1/2 cups (375 ml).

PREPARATION 20 minutes **COOKING** 8 hours **SERVES** 6

1 Using a piece of kitchen string, tie together the thyme and bay leaves to make a bouquet garni.

2 Combine the lamb, vegetables, garlic and apricots in a 4–5 litre (4–5 quart) slow cooker and gently combine. Sprinkle the nutmeg over, and stir in the beer, tomatoes and stock. Nestle the bouquet garni into the top of the mixture.

3 Cover and cook on low for 8 hours. Discard the bouquet garni and season to taste with salt and freshly ground black pepper. Serve sprinkled with parsley.

PER SERVING 1379 kJ, 329 kcal, 39 g protein, 10 g fat (5 g saturated fat), 17 g carbohydrate (14 g sugars), 4 g fibre, 235 mg sodium

In the oven

Combine the bouquet garni, lamb, vegetables, garlic, apricots, nutmeg and beer in a large bowl. Combine well, then cover and refrigerate overnight to marinate.

Preheat the oven to 160°C (320°F/Gas 2–3). Transfer the lamb mixture to a large casserole dish, then stir in the tomatoes and stock. Cover and bake for 2 hours.

Lamb and eggplant curry

Surprisingly low in fat, and thickened with red lentils, this highly satisfying curry pairs plenty of vegetables with lean, tender lamb. Serve with sliced tomatoes and chapattis or naan breads.

1 teaspoon cumin seeds
1 teaspoon coriander seeds
1 teaspoon fennel seeds
½ teaspoon black mustard seeds
seeds from 4 green cardamom pods, crushed
1 teaspoon dried red chilli flakes
400 g (14 oz) lean lamb leg, cut into bite-sized chunks
1 tablespoon vegetable oil
1 onion, sliced
2 red capsicums (bell peppers), cut into chunks
1 eggplant (aubergine), cut into chunks
½ cup (125 g) split red lentils
1 cinnamon stick
400 ml (14 fl oz) salt-reduced beef stock
¼ cup (25 g) flaked almonds, toasted

Curries improve in flavour if made ahead, allowing the flavours to develop and mingle. Refrigerate the curry for a few hours or overnight, then reheat gently until thoroughly heated through. This curry also freezes well.

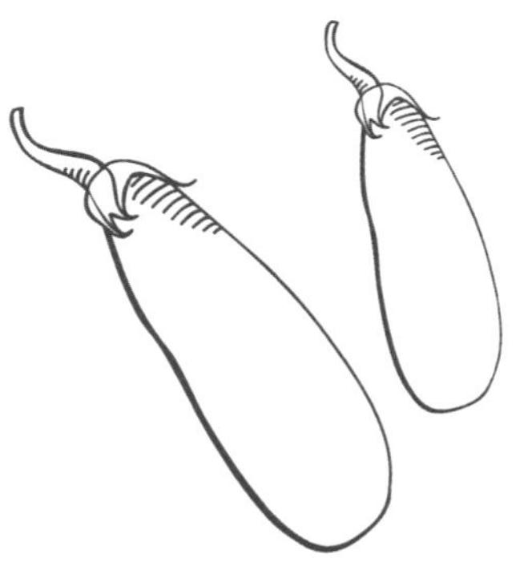

PREPARATION 30 minutes, plus at least 2 hours marinating
COOKING 45 minutes **SERVES** 4

1 Place the cumin, coriander, fennel, mustard and cardamom seeds in a mortar and crush with a pestle. Add the chilli flakes.

2 Place the lamb in a bowl, add the crushed spice mixture and toss to coat evenly. Cover and refrigerate for 2 hours, or overnight if possible.

3 Heat the oil in a large deep saucepan or flameproof casserole dish. Sauté the onion, capsicums and eggplant over medium heat for 10 minutes, or until softened.

4 Add the spiced lamb, lentils and cinnamon stick, then stir in the stock. Bring to a boil, stir again and reduce the heat. Cover and simmer gently for 30 minutes, or until the lamb is tender. Serve scattered with the almonds.

PER SERVING 1443 kJ, 345 kcal, 34 g protein, 16 g fat (4 g saturated fat), 18 g carbohydrate (6 g sugars), 7 g fibre, 473 mg sodium

Slow cooker

If you have a slow cooker you can sauté in, or you don't mind using another pot, sauté the onion in the vegetable oil to develop the flavour, but don't worry about sautéing the capsicums and eggplant. (Alternatively, omit the oil and sautéing step.)

Place all the ingredients except the almonds in the slow cooker. Gently combine, then cover and cook on low for 8 hours. Serve scattered with the almonds.

Slow-cooker pork, olive and sweet potato hotpot

Ras el hanout is an aromatic blend of as many as 30 spices and herbs that adds complexity to a dish. If you're in a hurry, you can cook this dish on the high setting of the slow cooker for 4 hours.

- 1 kg (2 lb) pork, cut into bite-sized chunks
- 1 onion, sliced
- 3 cloves garlic, crushed
- 1½ tablespoons ras el hanout or Moroccan spice mix
- 500 g (1 lb) sweet potato, peeled and cut into 7.5 cm (3 inch) chunks
- 1 red capsicum (bell pepper), diced
- 1 cup (250 ml) salt-reduced chicken stock
- 410 g (15 oz) can chopped tomatoes
- 1 tablespoon honey
- ½ cinnamon stick
- 8 large green pitted olives
- 2–3 teaspoons cornflour (cornstarch)
- 175 g (6 oz) baby English spinach leaves

PREPARATION 20 minutes **COOKING** 8 hours 15 minutes **SERVES** 4–6

1 Place all the ingredients except the cornflour and spinach in the slow cooker. Combine, then cover and cook on low for 8 hours.

2 Mix the cornflour with enough cold water to make a smooth paste, then stir into the stew. Replace the lid, increase the heat to high and cook for a further 15 minutes, or until the sauce has thickened slightly.

3 Season to taste with salt and freshly ground black pepper. Stir the spinach leaves through and serve.

PER SERVING 2107 kJ, 503 kcal, 59 g protein, 15 g fat (5 g saturated fat), 34 g carbohydrate (19 g sugars), 6 g fibre, 406 mg sodium

---

You can also cook this dish in a pressure cooker. Simply cook all the ingredients except the cornflour and spinach under high pressure for 40 minutes, then allow the pressure to release naturally. Follow step 2 and simmer the stew on the stovetop without the lid on until the sauce has thickened slightly. Stir in the spinach and serve.

On the stove/In the oven

Increase the stock to 2 cups (500 ml). Combine all the ingredients except the cornflour and spinach in a large flameproof casserole dish. Bring to a gentle boil, then cover and cook over low heat on the stovetop or in a preheated 170°C (340°F/Gas 3) oven for 2 hours, or until the pork is very tender. Continue as directed in steps 2 and 3.

Pork korma with potatoes and spinach

Thickened with ground almonds and yogurt, this dish is rich and creamy, yet not as indulgent as traditional Indian korma curries that are full of cream and ghee (clarified butter). Serve with warm chapattis or naan breads to mop up all that aromatic sauce.

- 1 tablespoon vegetable oil
- 2 large onions, sliced
- 500 g (1 lb) lean minced (ground) pork
- 2 garlic cloves, crushed
- seeds from 8 green cardamom pods, crushed
- 1 tablespoon cumin seeds
- 600 ml (21 fl oz) salt-reduced chicken stock
- 750 g (1½ lb) small new potatoes, scrubbed and halved
- 2 teaspoons cornflour (cornstarch)
- ¾ cup (80 g) almond meal (ground almonds)
- 300 g (10 oz) low-fat natural (plain) yogurt
- 250 g (8 oz) baby English spinach leaves
- ¼ cup (25 g) flaked almonds, lightly toasted

PREPARATION 10 minutes **COOKING** 1 hour **SERVES** 4

1 Heat the oil in a large heavy-based saucepan or flameproof casserole dish and sauté the onions over medium heat for 10 minutes. Transfer the onions to a bowl.

2 Add the pork, garlic, cardamom and cumin seeds to the pan. Cook for 5 minutes, or until the meat has changed colour, breaking up the lumps with a wooden spoon. Return half the onions to the pan, pour in the stock and bring back to a boil. Reduce the heat, then cover and simmer for 15 minutes.

3 Stir in the potatoes and bring back to simmering point. Cover and cook for 20 minutes, or until the potatoes are tender.

4 Blend the cornflour with the almond meal and ½ cup (125 g) of the yogurt to make a paste. Stir the mixture into the curry and bring just to a boil, stirring constantly. Reduce the heat and simmer for 1 minute, or until the sauce has thickened slightly. Season to taste with salt and freshly ground black pepper.

5 Reserving a few small leaves for garnishing, fold the spinach through, until the leaves are just wilted but still bright green.

6 Drizzle the curry with the remaining yogurt. Combine the almonds and remaining onions and scatter over the top. Garnish with the reserved spinach and serve.

PER SERVING 2653 kJ, 634 kcal, 44 g protein, 32 g fat (7 g saturated fat), 42 g carbohydrate (12 g sugars), 8 g fibre, 556 mg sodium

- The korma can be made with beef, lamb or chicken. Instead of potatoes, you could also use chunks of peeled orange sweet potato (kumara) or pumpkin (winter squash).
- This dish is even better if made ahead of time, then reheated. Prepare the korma up to the end of step 4, then cool and refrigerate. Reheat gently, then complete the dish as directed in steps 5 and 6.

Slow-cooker pork casserole

Chorizo, sherry and paprika add a Spanish accent to this simple but satisfying dish. To reduce the cooking time, you can simmer the stew on the slow cooker's high setting for 3–4 hours.

700 g (1 lb 9 oz) pork neck, cut into bite-sized chunks
1 chorizo or other spicy sausage, sliced
1 onion, diced
3 cloves garlic, crushed
2–3 sprigs fresh thyme, plus extra to garnish
1 tablespoon smoked paprika
⅓ cup (80 ml) sweet sherry
1 red capsicum (bell pepper), cut into thin strips
410 g (15 oz) can chopped tomatoes
¾ cup (180 ml) salt-reduced chicken stock

Herb scone topping
1 cup (150 g) self-raising flour
50 g (1¾ oz) butter, diced
1 teaspoon fresh or dried thyme leaves
½ cup (60 g) grated cheddar
½ cup (125 g) sour cream
2 tablespoons milk

The final flavour of the stew will be enhanced if you have time to brown the meat and onion first.

PREPARATION 20 minutes **COOKING** 8 hours 25 minutes **SERVES** 4–6

1 Place all the casserole ingredients in the slow cooker and gently combine. Cover and cook on low for 6–8 hours, or until the pork is very tender.

2 Near serving time, prepare the herb scone topping. Sift the flour into a bowl, then rub in the butter with your fingertips until the mixture resembles breadcrumbs. Add the remaining ingredients and mix until just combined. Divide the mixture into eight balls.

3 Place the scones on top of the stew. Cover and cook without lifting the lid for 20–25 minutes, or until the scones are cooked through. Garnish with extra thyme sprigs and serve immediately.

PER SERVING 2858 kJ, 683 kcal, 34 g protein, 42 g fat (24 g saturated fat), 38 g carbohydrate (10 g sugars), 5 g fibre, 749 mg sodium

On the stove/In the oven

Heat 1 tablespoon olive oil in a large flameproof casserole dish over medium–high heat. Brown the pork all over and remove to a plate. Sauté the onion for 5 minutes, or until golden. Increase the stock to 1¾ cups (435 ml) and stir in with all the remaining casserole ingredients.

Cover and cook over low heat or in a preheated 160°C (320°F/Gas 2–3) oven for 2–2½ hours, or until the pork is very tender. Check the liquid from time to time and add more stock if necessary.

Prepare the scones as directed in step 3 and place on top of the stew. Cover and cook without lifting the lid for 20–25 minutes, or until the scones are cooked through.

Pork with plums and five-spice

All the family will love this sweet and sour casserole that makes the most of fresh juicy plums. Flavours of ginger, five-spice, vinegar and soy sauce predominate, while the addition of water chestnuts and diced sweet potatoes turns this easy dish into a substantial meal.

- 2 tablespoons vegetable oil
- 4 lean pork loin steaks
- 800 g (1¾ lb) plums, halved, stoned and roughly chopped
- 4 spring onions (scallions), cut into 2.5 cm (1 inch) lengths
- 4 orange sweet potatoes (kumara), peeled and cut into 1 cm (½ inch) cubes
- 230 g (8 oz) can water chestnuts, drained and rinsed, then sliced
- 3 cm (1¼ inch) piece of fresh ginger, peeled and grated
- 2 cloves garlic, crushed
- 1 red chilli, seeded and finely chopped (optional)
- 2 teaspoons sugar
- 1 tablespoon salt-reduced soy sauce
- 1 tablespoon cider vinegar
- 2 tablespoons Chinese rice wine or dry sherry
- ¼ teaspoon five-spice
- 2 tablespoons chopped fresh coriander (cilantro)

- Five-spice is a blend of ground spices, typically cloves, star anise, sichuan pepper, cinnamon and fennel seeds. You'll find it in the Asian section of large supermarkets, along with Chinese rice wine.
- This dish can be prepared a day ahead and refrigerated. Reheat gently before sprinkling with the coriander.
- This recipe works equally well with skinless chicken thighs.

PREPARATION 30 minutes **COOKING** 50 minutes **SERVES** 4

1 Preheat the oven to 180°C (350°F/Gas 4). Heat the oil in a large flameproof casserole dish and briefly fry the pork steaks on both sides until lightly browned. Add the plums, spring onions, sweet potatoes and water chestnuts to the casserole dish, then combine everything.

2 In a small bowl, combine the ginger, garlic, chilli if using, sugar, soy sauce, vinegar, rice wine and five-spice. Spoon the mixture over the casserole ingredients.

3 Cover the dish and transfer to the oven. Bake, stirring occasionally, for 45 minutes, or until the pork is tender.

4 Taste the sauce and add more sugar or vinegar if needed, depending on the flavour of the plums, to give a good balance of sweet and sour flavours. Scatter the coriander over the top and serve.

PER SERVING 2065 kJ, 493 kcal, 38 g protein, 13 g fat (2 g saturated fat), 50 g carbohydrate (29 g sugars), 10 g fibre, 295 mg sodium

Slow cooker

If you have a slow cooker you can sauté in, or you don't mind using another pot, brown the pork as directed in step 1. (Alternatively, omit the oil and browning step.) Make up the sauce mixture as directed in step 2, then add to the slow cooker with all the ingredients except the coriander. Cover and cook on low for 6 hours. Serve sprinkled with the coriander.

Cut two of the spring onions into fine shreds. Place in a bowl of iced water and leave to curl.

Bring the stock to a gentle simmer and baste the pork occasionally, adding more liquid as needed.

Add the soaked noodles and gently turn them about to coat them with the juices.

Chinese-style slow-cooked pork

Simmered in a flavoursome broth with shallots, carrots, mushrooms, star anise and ginger, a prime piece of pork becomes succulently sweet, while slippery rice noodles absorb those heady juices.

- 25 g (1 oz) dried Chinese mushrooms
- 6 spring onions (scallions)
- 500 g (1 lb) lean, boneless loin of pork with skin, tied firmly
- 400 ml (14 fl oz) salt-reduced chicken stock
- 2 tablespoons salt-reduced soy sauce
- 2 tablespoons Chinese rice wine or dry sherry
- 2 tablespoons honey
- 2 garlic cloves, crushed
- 3 cm (1¼ inch) piece of fresh ginger, peeled and finely chopped
- 3 star anise
- 4 red Asian shallots, halved, or 1 small red onion, quartered
- 2 large carrots, sliced on the diagonal
- 125 g (4 oz) oyster mushrooms, either sliced or halved
- 250 g (8 oz) dried flat rice noodles

- The soaking liquid from the dried mushrooms makes a tasty stock, but needs to be strained through a fine sieve to remove any gritty bits.
- Omit the spring onions and instead stir 75 g (2½ oz) bean sprouts into the hot broth just before adding the noodles. Garnish with chopped coriander (cilantro) instead of spring onion curls.

PREPARATION 25 minutes, plus 20 minutes soaking
COOKING 1 hour 30 minutes **SERVES** 4

1 Put the mushrooms in a heatproof bowl, cover with boiling water and leave to soak for 20 minutes so they rehydrate. Cut two of the spring onions into long lengths, then lengthwise into fine shreds. Place the spring onion shreds in a bowl of iced water and leave to curl.

2 Place the pork in a large flameproof casserole dish and cover with boiling water. Bring to a boil on the stovetop, then pour off the water.

3 Pour in the stock, soy sauce and rice wine. Add the honey, garlic, ginger, star anise, shallots and carrots and bring back to a boil. Thickly slice the remaining four spring onions and add to the dish. Drain the dried mushrooms, reserving the soaking liquid, then roughly chop them and add to the dish.

4 Cover and simmer gently over very low heat for 1–1¼ hours, or until the pork is tender, basting it occasionally. Add the oyster mushrooms during the last 20 minutes of cooking. If necessary, top up the liquid level using the reserved mushroom soaking liquid, or more stock or water.

5 Soak the noodles in a bowl of boiling water for 4 minutes, or until soft; drain well. Remove the pork from the dish with a slotted spoon and keep hot. Bring the juices back to a boil, then add the noodles and remove from the heat. Turn and stir the noodles to coat with the juices.

6 Slice the pork thinly. Lift the noodles from the dish using a slotted spoon and spread on a large shallow serving platter. Arrange the pork and vegetables on top, then spoon the juices over. Garnish with the spring onion curls and serve.

PER SERVING 2087 kJ, 499 kcal, 36 g protein, 4 g fat (1 g saturated fat), 76 g carbohydrate (17 g sugars), 6 g fibre, 943 mg sodium

Slow cooker

Follow steps 1 and 2 above. Reduce the stock to 200 ml (7 fl oz) and add to the slow cooker with the ingredients in step 3. Cover and cook on low for 8 hours. Remove the pork, stir in the oyster mushrooms and soaked noodles, then cover and cook for 15 minutes. Serve as directed in step 6.

Quick cassoulet

Cassoulet has its origins in French peasant cuisine. A hearty repast of slow-simmered beans, sausages and whatever meats were available, cassoulet was traditionally cooked for many hours in an earthenware pot. With this easy version you'll have a simple French feast in no time at all.

- 1 tablespoon vegetable oil
- 8 large pork sausages, cut into bite-sized pieces
- 125 g (4 oz) rindless bacon (bacon strips), diced
- 1 large onion, halved and sliced
- 2 cloves garlic, crushed
- 410 g (15 oz) can chopped tomatoes
- 1–2 teaspoons mixed dried herbs
- 1 tablespoon wholegrain mustard
- 2 tablespoons tomato paste (concentrated purée)
- $1\frac{1}{2}$ x 200 g (7 oz) cans butterbeans (lima beans), drained and rinsed
- 420 g (15 oz) can cannellini beans, drained and rinsed
- chopped fresh parsley, to garnish (optional)
- crusty baguette, to serve

PREPARATION 20 minutes **COOKING** 30 minutes **SERVES** 4

1 Heat the oil in a large flameproof casserole dish or large heavy-based saucepan. Fry the sausages and bacon over medium–high heat for 8 minutes, or until the sausages are golden on all sides and the bacon is cooked. Transfer the sausages and bacon to a plate lined with paper towels and leave to drain.

2 Pour off all but 2 tablespoons of fat from the dish. Add the onion and garlic and sauté over medium heat for 5 minutes, or until softened.

3 Stir in the tomatoes, then add the dried herbs, mustard and tomato paste. Fill the tomato can one-third full of water, mix well and add the liquid to the dish. Bring to a boil, stirring, then add the butterbeans and cannellini beans.

4 Return the sausages and bacon to the dish and season to taste with salt and freshly ground black pepper. Reduce the heat, cover and simmer gently for 10 minutes, or until the sausages are cooked through. Garnish with parsley if desired and serve with a crusty baguette.

PER SERVING 2839 kJ, 678 kcal, 36 g protein, 50 g fat (19 g saturated fat), 22 g carbohydrate (8 g sugars), 10 g fibre, 2204 mg sodium

- This dish can be made a day ahead to allow the flavours to develop. Leftovers are especially tasty, so make a little extra to hold aside.
- The cassoulet could also be served with a green salad and mashed potato (see page 311) instead of a baguette.
- Replace one of the cans of beans with 250 g (8 oz) frozen corn kernels, peas or broad (fava) beans.

Speedy bean and sausage hotpot

Super quick to throw together, this one-pot marvel is equally good as a simple weeknight dinner or a hearty weekend breakfast. Serve with thick toasted slices of Italian-style bread.

- 1 tablespoon olive oil
- 1 large green capsicum (bell pepper), diced
- 8 thin Italian-style pork sausages, or other good-flavoured thin pork sausages
- 2 cloves garlic, sliced
- 420 g (15 oz) can tomato passata (puréed tomatoes)
- 1/2 cup (125 ml) beef stock
- 420 g (15 oz) can cannellini beans, drained and rinsed
- 3 tablespoons shredded fresh basil

We've used thin sausages as they pan-fry easily and absorb all those lovely tomato and basil flavours; beef sausages are good here too. For extra zing, add a little chopped fresh chilli.

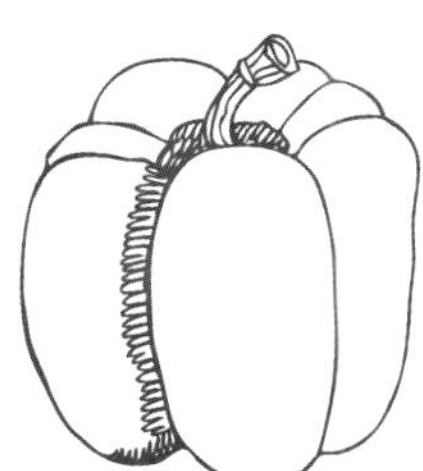

PREPARATION 5 minutes **COOKING** 20 minutes **SERVES** 4

1 Heat the oil in large heavy-based frying pan over medium heat and sauté the capsicum for 1–2 minutes. Push the capsicum to one side and add the sausages. Cook, turning, until golden brown and cooked through. Remove the sausages and set aside.

2 Add the garlic, passata and stock to the frying pan. Bring to a boil, then reduce the heat to low and simmer, stirring occasionally, until the mixture has thickened slightly.

3 Stir in the beans and most of the basil and simmer for 1 minute to warm the beans through. Return the sausages to the pan and stir gently until the sausages are heated through. Scatter with the remaining basil and serve.

PER SERVING 1774 kJ, 424 kcal, 20 g protein, 31 g fat (11 g saturated fat), 17 g carbohydrate (7 g sugars), 8 g fibre, 1460 mg sodium

Pork and mango curry

Using ready-made curry pastes makes cooking curries almost a one-step affair. Canned mango pulp gives all the sweetness and texture of mango when fresh mangoes are not in season. Serve with steamed rice and your choice of stir-fried greens.

2 tablespoons vegetable oil
750 g ($1\frac{1}{2}$ lb) lean pork stir-fry strips
2–3 tablespoons mild curry paste, such as korma or rendang
$\frac{3}{4}$ cup (180 ml) coconut cream
420 g (15 oz) can mango slices, drained
coriander (cilantro) leaves, to garnish

- Check that the stir-fry pork strips are from a tender cut of pork.
- Instead of ready-cut pork strips, you could use pork leg, loin or fillet and simply cut the pork thinly across the grain into thin strips.
- For a special touch, add some toasted flaked coconut as an additional garnish.

PREPARATION 5 minutes **COOKING** 20 minutes **SERVES** 4

1 Heat the oil in a large heavy-based frying pan or wok over high heat. Working in three batches, fry the pork for 2–3 minutes, or until just cooked. Remove each batch to a plate.

2 Reduce the heat to medium and add the curry paste to the pan. Cook, stirring, for 1 minute, or until fragrant. Add the coconut milk and simmer, stirring, for 3–4 minutes.

3 Return the pork to the pan and stir in the mango. Simmer for 2 minutes to heat through. Season to taste with salt and freshly ground black pepper and serve garnished with coriander.

PER SERVING 1978 kJ, 472 kcal, 42 g protein, 30 g fat (12 g saturated fat), 9 g carbohydrate (9 g sugars), 1 g fibre, 125 mg sodium

Slow cooker

If you have a slow cooker you can sauté in, or you don't mind using another pot, brown the pork as directed in step 1. (Alternatively, omit the oil and browning step.) Transfer all the ingredients to the slow cooker except the mango and coriander. Gently combine, then cover and cook on low for $5\frac{1}{2}$ hours.

Stir in the mango, then cover and cook for a further 30 minutes. Serve garnished with coriander.

Slow-cooker pulled pork

Pork is rendered pull-apart tender with slow, patient simmering — but if you don't have quite enough time you can cook the pork on high for 4 hours. This enticingly spicy mixture is also delicious served on tortillas, with diced avocados and tomatoes and a dollop of sour cream.

1.5 kg (3 lb) pork shoulder, cut into bite-sized chunks
1 onion, sliced
3 cloves garlic, sliced
410 g (15 oz) can chopped tomatoes
1/2 cup (125 ml) tomato sauce (ketchup)
1/4 cup (60 ml) apple cider vinegar
1 tablespoon soft brown sugar
1 teaspoon dried oregano
1 teaspoon ground cumin
1 teaspoon cayenne pepper or chipotle chilli powder
1 tablespoon worcestershire sauce
shredded lettuce, to serve
crusty rolls, to serve
coriander (cilantro) leaves, to garnish

PREPARATION 20 minutes **COOKING** 8 hours **SERVES** 6–8

1 Place the pork, onion and garlic in the slow cooker. Combine the tomatoes, tomato sauce, vinegar, sugar, spices and worcestershire sauce and add to the slow cooker.

2 Gently mix the ingredients until well combined. Cover and cook cook on low for 8 hours.

3 Shred the pork with two forks. Divide some lettuce among the rolls. Add a generous amount of pulled pork, drizzle with the sauce and garnish with coriander. Serve with a small bowl of the remaining sauce on the side.

PER SERVING 1767 kJ, 422 kcal, 51 g protein, 18 g fat (5 g saturated fat), 12 g carbohydrate (11 g sugars), 2 g fibre, 299 mg sodium

---

You can also cook this dish in a pressure cooker. Simply combine all the ingredients as directed in step 1. Cook under high pressure for 40 minutes, then allow the pressure to release naturally. Serve as directed in step 3.

On the stove/In the oven

HEAT 2 TEASPOONS OLIVE OIL in a flameproof casserole dish. Brown the pork all over and set aside. Sauté the onion for 5 minutes, then stir in the garlic and spices and cook for 30 seconds. Stir in the tomatoes, tomato sauce, vinegar, sugar and worcestershire sauce, then mix the pork through.

Cover and cook over low heat or in a preheated 150°C (300°F/Gas 2) oven for 2½ hours, or until the pork is very tender, turning the pork once during cooking. Serve as directed in step 3.

Slow-cooker sweet and sour pork

The classic combination of sweet and sour has proved an enduring winner. If it's more convenient you can cook this dish on high and reduce the cooking time to 3 hours. Serve with steamed rice.

- 600 g (1¼ lb) lean pork, cut into bite-sized chunks
- 3 tablespoons cornflour (cornstarch)
- 2.5 cm (1 inch) piece of fresh ginger, peeled and thinly sliced
- 3 spring onions (scallions), thinly sliced on the diagonal, plus extra to serve
- 2 small carrots, thinly sliced
- 2 celery stalks, thinly sliced on the diagonal
- 420 g (15 oz) can pineapple pieces in unsweetened juice
- 1 tablespoon tomato sauce (ketchup)
- 3 tablespoons caster (superfine) sugar
- ⅓ cup (80 ml) vinegar
- 2 tablespoons light soy sauce
- ½ cup (125 ml) salt-reduced chicken stock
- ½ red capsicum (bell pepper), diced
- coriander (cilantro) leaves, to garnish

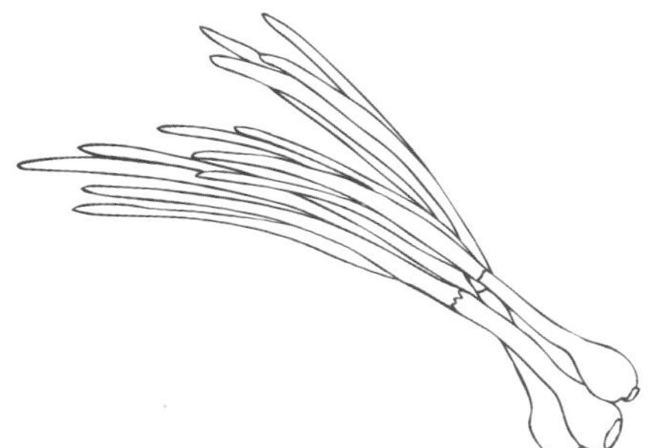

PREPARATION 20 minutes **COOKING** 6 hours **SERVES** 4

1 Toss the pork with the cornflour to lightly coat. Add to the slow cooker with the ginger, spring onions, carrots, celery and pineapple, including the pineapple juice.

2 In a bowl, combine the tomato sauce, sugar, vinegar, soy sauce and stock. Stir until the sugar has dissolved, then drizzle over the pork mixture and gently combine.

3 Cover and cook on low for 5½ hours. Stir in the capsicum, then cover and cook for a further 30 minutes, removing the lid and allowing the liquid to reduce if necessary.

4 Season to taste with salt and freshly ground black pepper. Serve garnished with coriander and extra spring onion slices.

PER SERVING 1419 kJ, 339 kcal, 34 g protein, 6 g fat (2 g saturated fat), 36 g carbohydrate (28 g sugars), 3 g fibre, 626 mg sodium

---

You can also use a pressure cooker. Combine all the ingredients except the coriander and cook under high pressure for 25 minutes, then allow the pressure to release naturally. Serve as directed in step 4.

On the stove

Follow steps 1 and 2 as directed above, placing the ingredients in a heavy-based saucepan. Gently bring to a boil, then reduce the heat, cover and simmer for 1 hour, or until the pork is tender. Check the liquid regularly and add more stock if necessary.

Place the dried beans in a bowl, cover with plenty of water and leave to soak overnight.

Place the drained beans in a pan with fresh water. Add the onion, capsicum, garlic and bay leaf.

Discard the bay leaf and drain the beans in a colander, over a bowl, to reserve some of the cooking liquid.

Spicy pork and beans

Traditionally made with 'fatback' — pork fat laced with a tiny bit of lean meat — this slimmed-down version of a homey American hotpot uses pork tenderloin instead. It's fabulous with cornbread.

- 1 cup (220 g) dried small red beans, picked over and rinsed
- 1 large onion, finely chopped
- 1 bay leaf
- 2 green capsicums (bell peppers), diced
- 6 cloves garlic, crushed
- 2 teaspoons olive oil
- 300 g (10 oz) pork tenderloin, cut into 1 cm (1/2 inch) chunks
- 1 cup (250 g) canned chopped tomatoes
- 2 tablespoons light molasses
- 1 tablespoon light brown sugar
- 3/4 teaspoon salt
- 3/4 teaspoon ground cinnamon
- 3/4 teaspoon ground ginger
- 1/4 teaspoon ground allspice

This recipe can be made ahead and gently reheated in the oven. You can save a lot of time by using canned beans in this recipe. Use two 420 g (15 oz) cans of drained pinto beans and skip steps 1 and 2. Use only 1 capsicum and 3 garlic cloves and omit the bay leaf. In step 3, add the onion along with the capsicum. In step 4, instead of the bean cooking liquid, use 3/4 cup (180 ml) water or chicken stock.

PREPARATION 20 minutes, plus overnight soaking
COOKING 2 hours 15 minutes **SERVES** 4

1 Put the beans in a bowl, cover with plenty of cold water and leave to soak overnight.

2 Drain the beans, place in a large heavy-based saucepan and pour in enough fresh water to cover by 5 cm (2 inches). Bring to a boil, then reduce the heat to a simmer. Add the onion, bay leaf, half the capsicum and half the garlic. Partially cover and cook for 1½ hours, or until the beans are tender.

3 Discard the bay leaf. Drain the beans, reserving 3/4 cup (180 ml) of the cooking liquid. (The beans can be cooked ahead and refrigerated at this point until required.)

4 Clean out the saucepan and heat the oil over medium–high heat. Add the pork and fry for 5 minutes, or until richly browned. Reduce the heat to medium. Stir in the remaining capsicum and garlic, along with the tomatoes, molasses, sugar, salt and ground spices.

5 Add the beans and reserved cooking liquid and bring to a boil. Reduce the heat, then cover and simmer for 30 minutes, or until the pork is tender. Season to taste with salt and freshly ground black pepper and serve.

PER SERVING 1473 kJ, 352 kcal, 30 g protein, 5 g fat (1 g saturated fat), 39 g carbohydrate (20 g sugars), 15 g fibre, 547 mg sodium

Slow cooker

Prepare the beans as directed in steps 1 and 2 above. (It is important that the soaked beans are fully cooked before adding them to the slow cooker. Alternatively, used canned beans.)

If you have a slow cooker you can sauté in, or you don't mind using another pot, brown the pork as directed in step 4. Transfer all the ingredients to the slow cooker. Gently combine, then cover and cook on low for 8 hours.

Slow-cooker pork cutlets with apples

Apples, cider and sage are lovely counterpoints to the richness of the pork. Browning the pork cutlets before assembling the other ingredients greatly enhances the flavour of the finished dish.

1 tablespoon olive oil
4 pork cutlets, trimmed
1 leek, white part only, sliced
2 cloves garlic, crushed
2 firm green apples, such as granny smith, peeled, cored and quartered
200 ml (7 fl oz) apple cider
$^1/_3$ cup (80 ml) salt-reduced chicken stock
1 teaspoon sugar
$^1/_4$ teaspoon fennel seeds
4 fresh sage leaves
1 sprig fresh thyme, plus extra sprigs to garnish
1–2 tablespoons cream
3 teaspoons cornflour (cornstarch), approximately

You can also make this dish in a pressure cooker. Brown the pork and leek in the pressure cooker as directed in step 1, then add all the ingredients except the cream, cornflour and parsley. Cook under high pressure for 25 minutes, then allow the pressure to release naturally.

Continue as directed in step 3, leaving the lid off. Serve as directed in step 4.

PREPARATION 20 minutes **COOKING** 6 hours 20 minutes **SERVES** 4

1 Heat the oil over medium–high heat and sear the pork cutlets on both sides, either in your slow cooker, if it has a browning option, or in a large frying pan. Remove the pork to a plate. Sauté the leek over medium heat for 5 minutes, or until softened.

2 If using a frying pan, transfer the leek to the slow cooker. Add the garlic, apples, cider, stock, sugar, fennel seeds, sage and thyme. Gently combine and nestle the cutlets into the mixture. Cover and cook on low for 6 hours.

3 Remove the pork and apples from the cooker and keep warm. Mix the cornflour with enough cold water to make a smooth paste, then whisk into the liquid with the cream. Replace the lid, increase the heat to high and cook for a further 5–10 minutes, or until the sauce has thickened, adding a little more cornflour if necessary.

4 Season the sauce with salt and freshly ground black pepper to taste. Transfer the pork and apples to warm serving plates. Drizzle the sauce over and serve sprinkled with extra thyme sprigs.

PER SERVING 1141 kJ, 273 kcal, 27 g protein, 9 g fat (3 g saturated fat), 15 g carbohydrate (13 g sugars), 2 g fibre, 129 mg sodium

On the stove/In the oven

Heat the oil in a flameproof casserole dish. Sear the pork cutlets and sauté the leek as directed in step 1. Assemble the ingredients as directed in step 2, adding extra stock if necessary to cover the cutlets. Bring to a simmer, then cover and cook over low heat or in a preheated oven at 170°C (340°F/Gas 3) for $1^1/_2$ hours.

Remove the pork and apples. Mix the cornflour to a smooth paste with a little water, then whisk into the liquid with the cream, stirring until thickened. Serve as directed in step 4.

Poultry and game

Slow-cooker whole chicken

To enhance its appearance, the chicken can be quartered and browned in a non-stick pan after it has been cooked, giving you a succulent chicken with crispy skin. Serve with brussels sprouts.

1.5 kg (3 lb) whole chicken
1 lemon
30 g (1 oz) butter, softened
2 cloves garlic, crushed
1–2 tablespoons chopped flat-leaf (Italian) parsley
2 carrots, cut into 4 cm (1½ inch) chunks
400 g (14 oz) small new potatoes, scrubbed
¼ cup (60 ml) salt-reduced chicken stock
¼ cup (60 ml) white wine or verjuice
1 bay leaf
3 teaspoons cornflour (cornstarch)

- You can also cook the chicken in the slow cooker on high, reducing the cooking time to 3–4 hours.
- If using a pressure cooker, the same method can be used, but the chicken can be browned prior to cooking. Cook under high pressure for 25 minutes and allow the pressure to release naturally.

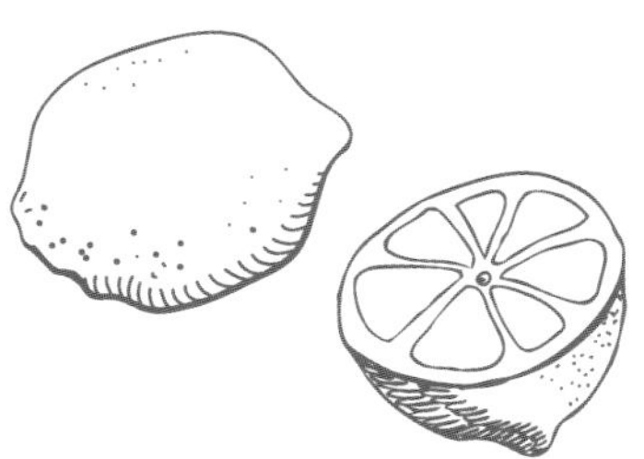

PREPARATION 10 minutes **COOKING** 6–8 hours **SERVES** 4

1 Wash the chicken inside and out. Pat dry with paper towels and trim off any excess fat.

2 Finely grate ½ teaspoon of zest from the lemon. Place in a small bowl with the butter, garlic and parsley and mix until well combined. Cut the lemon in half and place in the chicken cavity.

3 Loosen the skin on the chicken and carefully push the butter mixture under the skin, taking care not to break the skin. Season the chicken well with salt and freshly ground black pepper and tie the legs together with kitchen string.

4 Place the carrots and potatoes in the base of the slow cooker. Sit the chicken on top and add the stock, wine and bay leaf. Cover and cook on low for 6–8 hours, or until the chicken is cooked through and very tender.

5 Remove the chicken and vegetables to a serving platter. Cover loosely with foil and keep warm.

6 Mix the cornflour with enough cold water to make a smooth paste, then stir into the cooking juices. Replace the lid, increase the heat to high and cook for a further 10–15 minutes, or until the sauce has thickened slightly.

7 Transfer the sauce to a gravy jug. Carve the chicken and serve with the vegetables and the sauce.

PER SERVING 2932 kJ, 700 kcal, 57 g protein, 44 g fat (15 g saturated fat), 18 g carbohydrate (3 g sugars), 4 g fibre, 317 mg sodium

In the oven

PREHEAT THE OVEN TO 180°C (350°F/GAS 4). Follow steps 1 to 3 as directed above. Place the chicken and vegetables in a baking dish with the bay leaf. Pour in the stock and wine and bake for 1¼–1½ hours, or until the juices run clear when a skewer is inserted into the thickest part of the chicken. Continue from step 5, thickening the juices in a small saucepan on the stovetop.

Chicken and couscous

This quick recipe uses meat from a rotisseried chicken, making a super-easy midweek meal. It's also a great way to make a fresh new meal from any leftover roasted or cooked chicken.

- 1/3 cup (80 ml) olive oil
- 1 onion, diced
- 2 cloves garlic, finely chopped
- 500 g (1 lb) zucchini (courgettes), thinly sliced
- 2 celery stalks, thinly sliced
- 2 red capsicums (bell peppers), cut into strips
- 2 tablespoons tomato paste (concentrated purée)
- 1 tablespoon harissa powder or paste
- 2 teaspoons ground cumin
- 1/4 teaspoon ground cinnamon
- 2 cups (500 ml) salt-reduced vegetable stock
- 1 1/3 cups (250 g) instant couscous
- 400 g (14 oz) roasted chicken breast or other cooked chicken, without the skin, cut into small chunks
- 2 tablespoons lemon juice
- 3 sprigs fresh flat-leaf (Italian) parsley, leaves chopped
- 1 sprig fresh mint, small leaves picked, larger ones chopped

---

Harissa is a hot spice blend from northern Africa, available as a powder or paste. Offer some extra harissa paste or harissa powder on the side, with a little olive oil and a squeeze of lemon juice stirred in, so people can add extra if they prefer a bit more heat.

PREPARATION 30 minutes COOKING 25 minutes SERVES 4

1 Heat half the oil in a large saucepan and sauté the onion and garlic over medium heat for 5 minutes, or until softened. Add the zucchini, celery and capsicums and sauté for 2 minutes.

2 Stir in the tomato paste, harissa, cumin and cinnamon. Pour in the stock and bring to a boil. Reduce the heat, then cover and simmer for 10 minutes.

3 Meanwhile, place the couscous in a heatproof bowl. Stir in 2 cups (500 ml) boiling water, then cover and leave for 5 minutes for the liquid to absorb.

4 Stir the couscous and chicken through the vegetable mixture. Cook, stirring now and then, for 5 minutes to heat through.

5 Season to taste with salt and freshly ground black pepper. Stir in the lemon juice and remaining 2 tablespoons oil. Sprinkle with the parsley and mint and serve.

PER SERVING 2477 kJ, 592 kcal, 37 g protein, 29 g fat (5 g saturated fat), 40 g carbohydrate (26 g sugars), 21 g fibre, 860 mg sodium

Slow cooker

If you have a slow cooker you can sauté in, or you don't mind using another pot, follow step 1 as above. (Alternatively, omit the oil and the sautéing step.) Transfer to the slow cooker and stir in the tomato paste, harissa, cumin and cinnamon. Pour in the stock, then cover and cook on low for 4 hours.

Stir in the couscous and chicken, then cover and cook for a further 30 minutes to heat through. Finish as directed in step 5.

Chicken and vegetable stew

This versatile hotpot lends itself to whatever vegetables are in season — good candidates include corn, turnip, sweet potato or green beans. It goes well with mashed potato or crusty bread.

- 2 tablespoons olive oil
- 700 g (1 lb 7 oz) boneless, skinless chicken thighs, cut into bite-sized chunks
- 1 large onion, finely chopped
- 2 cloves garlic, crushed
- 2 celery stalks, diced
- 2 carrots, diced
- 1 tablespoon tomato paste (concentrated purée)
- 2 potatoes, peeled and diced
- 2 cups (500 ml) salt-reduced chicken stock
- ½ teaspoon dried oregano or mixed herbs
- 1 tablespoon worcestershire sauce
- 1 zucchini (courgette), diced
- ½ cup (80 g) frozen peas
- 1–1½ tablespoons cornflour (cornstarch) (optional)
- 2–3 tablespoons chopped fresh parsley

- If you have herbs growing at home, use them instead of the dried herbs. Increase the quantity and stir them through at the end.
- Leftovers can be frozen for another meal. You can also use leftover cooked chicken in this dish — just add it to the stew for the last 5 minutes to heat through.

PREPARATION 20 minutes **COOKING** 40 minutes **SERVES** 6

1 Heat the oil in a large saucepan over medium–high heat. Fry the chicken in two batches for 2–3 minutes each time, or until lightly browned, removing each batch to a plate.

2 Sauté the onion, garlic, celery and carrots in the pan for 5 minutes, or until softened. Stir the tomato paste through, then add the potatoes, stock, herbs, worcestershire sauce and chicken. Bring to a boil, then reduce the heat, cover and simmer for 15 minutes.

3 Add the zucchini and peas and cook for a further 10 minutes, or until all the vegetables are soft.

4 If you wish to thicken the sauce, mix the cornflour with a little water until smooth, then add to the saucepan and stir for 2 minutes, or until thickened.

5 Season to taste with salt and freshly ground black pepper, then stir in the parsley and serve.

PER SERVING 1190 kJ, 284 kcal, 26 g protein, 15 g fat (4 g saturated fat), 12 g carbohydrate (5 g sugars), 3 g fibre, 632 mg sodium

Slow cooker

If you have a slow cooker you can sauté in, or you don't mind using another pot, brown the chicken as directed in step 1, then the onion, garlic, celery and carrots as directed in step 2. (Alternatively, omit the oil and the browning and sautéing steps.)

Transfer all the ingredients to the slow cooker, except the zucchini and peas, cornflour and parsley. Gently combine, then cover and cook on low for 7 hours.

Add the zucchini and the fully thawed peas and cook for a further 1 hour. Omit the cornflour and serve as directed in step 5.

Quick green chicken curry

Frozen vegetables are just as nutritious as fresh ones, and make this recipe so easy and speedy to prepare. This dish also works well with a Thai red curry paste. Simply serve with steamed rice.

- 300 g (10 oz) frozen mixed vegetables, such as baby corn, baby green beans and carrots
- 500 g (1 lb) boneless, skinless chicken thighs
- 2 tablespoons green curry paste
- 400 ml (14 fl oz) coconut cream
- 1 cup (250 ml) salt-reduced chicken stock

- Commercial curry pastes can vary in heat, so if you don't like your curries too hot, use a little less than suggested. If a curry is too hot, adding some fresh lemon or lime juice will help cool it down.
- You can replace the chicken thighs with chicken pieces — you'll just need to cook them for an extra 10 minutes or so.

PREPARATION 10 minutes **COOKING** 15 minutes **SERVES** 4

1. Set the frozen vegetables out to thaw. Cut the chicken into 2.5 cm (1 inch) cubes.

2. Heat a wok or deep frying pan over medium heat, then add the curry paste and stir briefly. Add the chicken and stir-fry for 1–2 minutes, tossing to ensure the curry paste doesn't burn.

3. Add the coconut cream and stock and bring to a boil, then reduce the heat to low and simmer for 6 minutes.

4. Stir in the thawed vegetables and simmer for a further 2 minutes, or until the chicken is cooked. Serve immediately.

PER SERVING 1791 kJ, 428 kcal, 28 g protein, 32 g fat (21 g saturated fat), 8 g carbohydrate (7 g sugars), 2 g fibre, 659 mg sodium

Slow-cooker chicken-stuffed capsicums

Red capsicums have a lovely sweet flavour, but you can use a mixture of yellow, green and red if you like. Serve with a mixed leaf salad with a dijon dressing for a light summer meal.

PREPARATION 20 minutes **COOKING** 6 hours **SERVES** 6

6 red capsicums (bell peppers)
350 g (12 oz) minced (ground) chicken
½ cup (100 g) raw long-grain white rice
1 small onion, finely chopped
2 cloves garlic, crushed
2 tablespoons chopped fresh dill, plus extra sprigs to garnish
3 teaspoons finely grated lemon zest
1 cup (250 g) tomato passata (puréed tomatoes)
1 cup (250 ml) salt-reduced chicken stock
100 g (3½ oz) fetta, crumbled
2 tablespoons chopped fresh mint

1 Cut the tops from the capsicums and reserve them. Scoop out the membrane and seeds from inside the capsicums.

2 Place the chicken in a bowl with the rice, onion, garlic, dill and lemon zest. Season with salt and freshly ground black pepper, then combine using your hands until evenly combined. Spoon the mixture into the capsicums, filling them only three-quarters full to allow room for the rice to expand.

3 Spoon the passata over the rice mixture in the capsicums, then replace the tops. Place the capsicums in a 5 litre (5 quart) slow cooker and pour the stock around them.

4 Cover and cook on low for 6 hours, or until the capsicums are tender and the rice cooked.

5 Lift off the capsicum tops. Sprinkle the filling with the fetta and mint, then replace the tops. Serve garnished with extra dill sprigs.

PER SERVING 1006 kJ, 240 kcal, 18 g protein, 9 g fat (4 g saturated fat), 21 g carbohydrate (7 g sugars), 3 g fibre, 490 mg sodium

In the oven

PREHEAT THE OVEN TO 180°C (350°F/Gas 4). Cook the rice in a saucepan of boiling water until just tender; drain well.

Heat 1 tablespoon olive oil in a large frying pan and sauté the chicken, onion and garlic for 5 minutes, breaking up any lumps with a wooden spoon.

Transfer to a mixing bowl, add the cooked rice, dill, lemon zest, fetta and mint. Season to taste with salt and freshly ground black pepper.

Prepare and fill the capsicums as directed. Arrange in a lightly oiled baking dish, but omit the chicken stock. Bake for 30 minutes, or until the capsicums are tender and the rice is cooked. Serve as directed in step 5.

Chicken with olives and chorizo

When things feel a bit dreary, here's a smoky, richly flavoured dish reminiscent of sunny Spain. All you need with it is some rustic bread and perhaps a green salad.

- 2 tablespoons olive oil
- 8 boneless, skinless chicken thighs (about 750 g/$1\frac{1}{2}$ lb in total), halved
- 1 red onion, thinly sliced
- 1 clove garlic, crushed
- 1 large red capsicum (bell pepper), cut into strips
- 1 large yellow capsicum (bell pepper), cut into strips
- 410 g (15 oz) can chopped tomatoes, drained
- $\frac{2}{3}$ cup (160 ml) dry white wine
- 1 tablespoon paprika
- 100 g ($3\frac{1}{2}$ oz) chorizo sausage, thickly sliced
- 2 tablespoons pitted black olives, halved
- 3 tablespoons chopped fresh flat-leaf (Italian) parsley

PREPARATION 20 minutes **COOKING** 30 minutes **SERVES** 4

1 Heat the oil in a large flameproof casserole dish or heavy-based saucepan and fry the chicken over high heat for 4–5 minutes, turning frequently, until golden all over.

2 Add the onion, garlic and capsicums and sauté for 5 minutes, or until lightly browned and slightly softened.

3 Stir in the tomatoes, wine and paprika and bring to a boil. Add the chorizo, reduce the heat and simmer for 15 minutes, or until the chicken is cooked through.

4 Add the olives, season to taste with salt and freshly ground black pepper and stir to heat through. Sprinkle with the parsley and serve.

PER SERVING 1950 kJ, 466 kcal, 40 g protein, 28 g fat (8 g saturated fat), 8 g carbohydrate (5 g sugars), 3 g fibre, 665 mg sodium

Slow cooker

If you have a slow cooker you can sauté in, or you don't mind using another pot, follow steps 1 and 2 above. (Alternatively, omit the oil and the browning steps.) Transfer to the slow cooker and stir in the tomatoes, chorizo and wine — you can reduce the wine to $\frac{1}{4}$ cup (60 ml), or leave out if you prefer. Gently combine, then cover and cook on low for 7 hours. Stir in the olives and heat through for 5 minutes. Season to taste, sprinkle with the parsley and serve.

One-pot chicken casserole with creamy sherry sauce

Including baby leeks, turnips, potatoes and button mushrooms, and brightened with a squeeze of lemon and a splash of sherry, this elegantly comforting dish is full of wonderful ingredients.

- 2 tablespoons olive oil
- 8 boneless, skinless chicken thighs (about 650 g/1 lb 7 oz in total)
- 250 g (8 oz) button mushrooms
- 175 g (6 oz) baby leeks, white part only
- 4 small turnips, scrubbed and quartered
- 500 g (1 lb) small new potatoes, scrubbed
- 2½ cups (625 ml) salt-reduced chicken stock
- ⅓ cup (80 ml) sherry
- 200 g (7 oz) green beans
- 1 tablespoon cornflour (cornstarch)
- ¾ cup (180 g) low-fat natural (plain) yogurt
- grated zest of 1 lemon

Slow cooker

If you have a slow cooker you can sauté in, or you don't mind using another pot, follow step 1 above. (Alternatively, omit the oil and the browning step.) Place all the vegetables except the beans in a slow cooker and lay the chicken on top. Reduce the stock to 1 cup (250 ml) and the sherry to 2 tablespoons, and add to the cooker. Cover and cook on low for 6½ hours.

Add the beans, cover and cook for a further 30 minutes. Turn off the slow cooker. Drain the liquid into a small saucepan, keeping the chicken and vegetables covered to keep warm. Continue from step 5.

PREPARATION 20 minutes **COOKING** 30 minutes **SERVES** 4

1 Heat the oil in a large saucepan or flameproof casserole dish. Add the chicken, season lightly with salt and freshly ground black pepper and cook over high heat for 2 minutes, turning to brown both sides. Remove to a plate.

2 Sauté the mushrooms over high heat for 1 minute. Reduce the heat, move the mushrooms to the side of the pan and lay the leeks across the middle. Add the turnips and potatoes in an even layer.

3 Pour in the stock and sherry and bring to a boil. Place the chicken on top of the vegetables, adding any juices from the plate. Reduce the heat so that the stock bubbles steadily, without boiling too fiercely. Cover and cook for 10 minutes.

4 Add the beans, then cover and cook for a further 5 minutes, or until the chicken and vegetables are cooked. Using a slotted spoon, divide the ingredients among four warm plates or bowls, or transfer to a serving dish. Keep warm while finishing the sauce.

5 Boil the cooking juices over high heat, uncovered, for 5 minutes, to reduce slightly and concentrate the flavour. Meanwhile, mix the cornflour, yogurt and lemon zest to a smooth paste in a heatproof bowl. (The cornflour stabilises the yogurt and stops it curdling when added to the hot liquid.)

6 Gradually stir some of the reduced stock into the yogurt mixture, then gradually stir in the remaining stock. Pour the mixture back into the pan and bring to a boil to thicken the sauce slightly, stirring frequently. Taste for seasoning.

7 Drizzle some of the sauce over the chicken and vegetables. Serve the remaining sauce in a gravy boat.

PER SERVING 2180 kJ, 521 kcal, 43 g protein, 22 g fat (5 g saturated fat), 33 g carbohydrate (13 g sugars), 8 g fibre, 772 mg sodium

- Semolina or fine oatmeal can be used to thicken the casserole instead of cornflour; use 1 tablespoon of either ingredient. Blend the oatmeal to a smooth paste with cold water and add as for the cornflour; sprinkle the semolina into the casserole and continue stirring until the sauce boils and thickens.
- This recipe uses vegetables to extend a modest amount of chicken. Served with a starchy (complex) carbohydrate, such as rice, it makes a well-balanced meal.

Chicken and vegetable casserole

This healthy casserole makes an easy midweek meal. To make it even quicker, you could use frozen or pre-prepared vegetables ready to go straight from the packet to the pan. For a touch of gourmet, serve with some mixed wild and long-grain rice on the side.

- 2 tablespoons olive oil
- 350 g (12 oz) boneless, skinless chicken breasts, cut into small chunks
- 1 small onion, chopped
- 250 g (8 oz) button mushrooms
- grated zest of 1 lemon
- 1 bay leaf
- 2 large sprigs fresh thyme, or ½ teaspoon dried thyme
- 3 large sprigs fresh tarragon, or ½ teaspoon dried tarragon (optional)
- 150 ml (5 fl oz) dry sherry
- 250 g (8 oz) baby carrots, scrubbed
- 4 cups (240 g) broccoli florets
- 1 tablespoon cornflour (cornstarch)
- 3 tablespoons chopped fresh flat-leaf (Italian) parsley

Slow cooker

If you have a slow cooker you can sauté in, or you don't mind using another pot, follow steps 1 and 2 above. (Alternatively, omit the oil and the browning and sautéing steps.) Transfer all the ingredients to the slow cooker, except the broccoli, cornflour and parsley, reducing the sherry to ⅓ cup (80 ml) and the water to 150 ml (5 fl oz). Gently combine, then cover and cook on low for 6½ hours.

Add the broccoli, then cover and cook for a further 30 minutes. Stir in the cornflour paste; cover and cook for a final 20 minutes. Check the seasoning, stir in the parsley and serve.

PREPARATION 10 minutes **COOKING** 25 minutes **SERVES** 4

1 Heat the oil in a large saucepan, or a deep frying pan with a lid. Add the chicken and brown over high heat for 3 minutes, stirring constantly. Reduce the heat to medium.

2 Add the onion, mushrooms, lemon zest, bay leaf, thyme and tarragon, if using. Sauté for 4 minutes, or until the onion and mushrooms are beginning to soften.

3 Pour in the sherry and 300 ml (10 fl oz) water. Add the carrots, season with salt and freshly ground black pepper and gently combine. Bring to a boil, reduce the heat, then cover and simmer for 5 minutes.

4 Stir in the broccoli. Increase the heat to bring the liquid back to a steady simmer. Cover and cook for a further 5 minutes, or until the chicken is tender and the vegetables are just cooked. Discard the bay leaf and herb sprigs.

5 Blend the cornflour to a smooth paste with 2 tablespoons cold water, then stir into the casserole. Simmer for 2 minutes, stirring constantly, until the sauce has thickened and is smooth.

6 Season with a little more salt and freshly ground black pepper if needed, then stir in the parsley and serve.

PER SERVING 1240 kJ, 296 kcal, 25 g protein, 14 g fat (3 g saturated fat), 8 g carbohydrate (4 g sugars), 6 g fibre, 258 mg sodium

Chicken with 40 cloves of garlic

This fabled recipe is an impressive dinner party piece. Don't be put off by the thought of using 40 garlic cloves here, as the garlic's raw pungency mellows into soft butteriness during cooking. The cooked garlic cloves are delicious squeezed out of their skins onto bread or toast.

- 500 g (1 lb) small boiling potatoes, peeled and quartered if large
- 3 celery stalks, thickly sliced
- 2 carrots, halved lengthwise, then cut crosswise into 4 cm ($1\frac{1}{2}$ inch) lengths
- 40 cloves garlic, unpeeled
- $\frac{3}{4}$ teaspoon chopped fresh tarragon
- $\frac{1}{2}$ teaspoon chopped fresh rosemary
- $\frac{3}{4}$ teaspoon salt
- 2 teaspoons olive oil
- 1 cup (250 ml) salt-reduced chicken stock
- $\frac{1}{2}$ cup (125 ml) dry vermouth
- 4 x 150 g (5 oz) boneless, skinless chicken thighs
- 3 tablespoons chopped fresh parsley
- crusty bread, to serve

If you don't have any vermouth, you can replace it with extra chicken stock.

PREPARATION 20 minutes **COOKING** 45 minutes **SERVES** 4

1 Preheat the oven to 180°C (350°F/Gas 4). Place the potatoes in a large flameproof casserole dish with the celery, carrots, garlic, tarragon, rosemary and salt. Drizzle with the oil and toss to combine. Pour in the stock and vermouth.

2 Bring to a boil over medium heat, then reduce the heat to a simmer. Cover and cook for 10 minutes.

3 Add the chicken thighs. Replace the lid, transfer to the oven and bake for 30 minutes, or until the chicken is cooked through and the potatoes and garlic are tender.

4 Just before serving, stir in the parsley. Serve with crusty bread and perhaps a tossed salad dressed with a red wine vinaigrette.

PER SERVING 1631 kJ, 390 kcal, 34 g protein, 14 g fat (4 g saturated fat), 23 g carbohydrate (5 g sugars), 9 g fibre, 796 mg sodium

Slow cooker

Arrange the potatoes, celery and carrots in the base of a slow cooker. Sprinkle with the tarragon, rosemary and salt, but omit the oil. Place the chicken on top. Reduce the stock to $\frac{1}{2}$ cup (125 ml) and the vermouth to $\frac{1}{4}$ cup (60 ml). Place the garlic cloves over the chicken.

Cover and cook on low for 6 hours, or until the vegetables are tender. Serve as directed in step 4.

Toss the vegetables and garlic to coat them with the oil, herbs and salt.

Pour in the stock and vermouth, then bring to a boil.

Simmer for 10 minutes, then add the chicken and transfer to the oven.

Creamy chicken korma

Indian-style korma curries are loved the world over. This version is quite mild, so add more korma paste if you like a bit more heat, or experiment by using another Indian curry paste. Serve with a warm Indian bread, such as wholemeal (whole-wheat) naan bread or chapattis.

1 tablespoon vegetable oil
1 onion, chopped
1 teaspoon finely chopped fresh ginger
2 tablespoons korma paste or powder
600 g (1¼ lb) boneless, skinless chicken breasts, thickly sliced
⅔ cup (160 ml) chicken stock
400 ml (14 fl oz) coconut milk
50 g (1¾ oz) almond meal (ground almonds)
2 tablespoons chopped fresh coriander (cilantro) leaves

PREPARATION 15 minutes **COOKING** 30 minutes **SERVES** 4

1 Heat the oil in a heavy-based saucepan or flameproof casserole dish and sauté the onion and ginger over medium heat for 5 minutes, or until softened. Stir in the korma paste or powder and cook over low heat for 1 minute, taking care that it does not burn.

2 Add the chicken, stirring to coat in the spicy onions. Stir in the stock and coconut milk, season with salt and freshly ground black pepper and bring to a boil. Reduce the heat and simmer for 20 minutes.

3 Stir in the almond meal to thicken the sauce. Scatter the coriander on top and serve.

PER SERVING 2431 kJ, 581 kcal, 38 g protein, 44 g fat (22 g saturated fat), 7 g carbohydrate (7 g sugars), 3 g fibre, 363 mg sodium

Slow cooker

If you have a slow cooker you can sauté in, or you don't mind using another pot, follow step 1 above. (Alternatively, omit the oil and the sautéing step.)

Transfer all the ingredients to the slow cooker, except the almond meal and coriander, reducing the stock to ⅓ cup (80 ml) and the coconut milk to 200 ml (7 fl oz). Gently combine, then cover and cook on low for 6 hours.

Season to taste, stir in the almond meal and serve sprinkled with the coriander.

In the oven

Preheat the oven to 180°C (350°F/Gas 4). Follow step 1 above, sautéing the ingredients in a flameproof casserole dish. Continue with step 2. After seasoning the mixture, bring to a boil, then cover the dish and transfer to the oven. Bake for 45 minutes, or until the chicken is tender. Stir in the almond meal, sprinkle with the coriander and serve.

Chicken à la king

Here's a lighter version of a big dinner-party classic from the 1970s. Despite its regal name, it's an absolute cinch to make — but thoroughly delicious all the same.

1 tablespoon butter
¼ cup (60 ml) olive oil
1 small green capsicum (bell pepper), diced
125 g (4 oz) button mushrooms, sliced
600 g (1¼ lb) boneless, skinless chicken breasts, cut into small chunks
1½ cups (375 ml) salt-reduced chicken stock
2 tablespoons plain (all-purpose) flour
1 cup (250 g) light sour cream
1 tablespoon sherry
fresh parsley leaves, to garnish
steamed rice (see page 310), to serve

- The original recipe uses just butter instead of olive oil, and regular sour cream rather than light sour cream.
- Leftovers can be used as a filling for crepes, or in mini pies. You could even mix them through leftover cooked pasta and gently reheat.

PREPARATION 10 minutes **COOKING** 15 minutes **SERVES** 4

1 Heat the butter and 1 tablespoon of the oil in a large frying pan over medium heat. Add the capsicum and mushrooms and sauté for a few minutes, or until starting to soften. Remove to a plate.

2 Reduce the heat slightly and gently sauté the chicken for 3–4 minutes, or until lightly browned and almost cooked. Pour in ½ cup (125 ml) of the stock and cook until the liquid has evaporated. Remove the chicken to a plate.

3 Heat the remaining oil in the pan. Stir in the flour until smooth, then cook for 1 minute, stirring constantly. Remove from the heat and whisk in the remaining stock.

4 Return the saucepan to the heat and whisk for 2 minutes, or until the sauce has thickened. Whisk in the sour cream.

5 Return the chicken and vegetables to the pan. Stir in the sherry and season to taste with salt and freshly ground black pepper. Bring to a simmer for 2–3 minutes to heat the chicken through. Garnish with parsley and serve with steamed rice.

PER SERVING 2246 kJ, 537 kcal, 38 g protein, 38 g fat (15 g saturated fat), 9 g carbohydrate (5 g sugars), 1 g fibre, 396 mg sodium

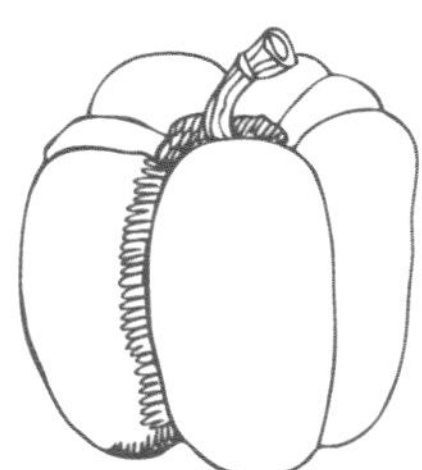

Chicken in red wine sauce

This contemporary version of the great French classic coq au vin (see page 164) is lower in fat and includes more vegetables. It just needs some crusty, rustic-style bread and perhaps a light green salad alongside. This dish is even better if made a full day ahead, so the flavours can mature.

- 8 large skinless chicken thighs (about 700 g/1 lb 7 oz in total)
- 8 thin slices pancetta or lean, thinly cut streaky bacon
- 2 tablespoons olive oil
- 3 large cloves garlic, chopped
- 1 large red onion, halved and sliced
- 2 carrots, thickly sliced
- 1 fennel bulb or 3 celery stalks, thinly sliced
- 1 turnip, peeled and cut into chunks
- 2 bay leaves
- 3–4 sprigs fresh thyme
- 1½ cups (375 ml) red wine
- 1 tablespoon redcurrant jelly
- 2 tablespoons brandy (optional)
- 2 cups (500 ml) salt-reduced chicken or vegetable stock
- 8 French shallots (eschalots) or pickling onions, peeled
- 250 g (8 oz) button mushrooms
- ¼ cup (30 g) cornflour (cornstarch)
- 2 tablespoons chopped fresh flat-leaf (Italian) parsley

- If preparing the dish a day ahead, simply reheat the casserole over medium heat before serving.
- To freeze the casserole, prepare it up until the end of step 3. Continue from step 4 when reheating the dish.

PREPARATION 25 minutes, plus 10 minutes cooling **COOKING** 1 hour **SERVES** 4

1 Trim any excess fat from the chicken thighs, then wrap each one in pancetta or bacon, securing with cocktail sticks if necessary. Heat half the oil in a large flameproof casserole dish, then add the chicken, join-side down, and brown over medium–low heat for 2–3 minutes. Turn the chicken to brown the other side, then remove to a plate.

2 Heat the remaining oil and gently sauté the garlic, onion, carrots, fennel and turnip for 5 minutes, or until softened. If you need to moisten the mixture, add 2–3 tablespoons water, rather than extra oil.

3 Stir in the herbs, wine, redcurrant jelly and brandy, if using. Simmer for 5 minutes, then stir in the stock and bring to a boil. Add the shallots and the chicken. Season with salt and freshly ground black pepper, then cover and simmer for 30 minutes.

4 Stir in the mushrooms, cover and simmer for a further 15 minutes. Blend the cornflour to a smooth paste with ½ cup (125 ml) cold water, then stir into the casserole and simmer for 2 minutes, or until the sauce has thickened slightly.

5 Remove from the heat and allow to cool for 10 minutes. Remove any cocktail sticks, sprinkle with the parsley and serve.

PER SERVING 2222 kJ, 531 kcal, 42 g protein, 25 g fat (6 g saturated fat), 22 g carbohydrate (12 g sugars), 6 g fibre, 771 mg sodium

Slow cooker

If you have a slow cooker you can sauté in, or you don't mind using another pot, follow steps 1 and 2 above. (Alternatively, omit the oil and the browning step.) Transfer to the slow cooker with the herbs, redcurrant jelly, shallots and mushrooms. Stir in ¾ cup (180 ml) red wine and 1 tablespoon brandy, then cover and cook on low for 6 hours.

Mix 1 tablespoon cornflour to a smooth paste with 2 tablespoons water and stir into the sauce. Cover and cook for a further 20 minutes. Remove any cocktail sticks and serve sprinkled with parsley.

Coq au vin

French peasants devised this dish to deal with a tough old rooster — they slowly simmered it with onions, herbs and good red wine to render the gamey meat flavoursome and tender. If you don't have fresh thyme, use a good pinch of dried mixed herbs. Chopped parsley can be stirred into the sauce just before serving.

2 kg (4 lb) chicken, jointed
1/4 cup (60 ml) olive oil
150 g (5 oz) rindless bacon, diced
12 pickling onions, peeled
2 celery stalks, finely diced
2 cloves garlic, crushed
200 g (7 oz) whole button mushrooms
2 tablespoons brandy
3 cups (750 ml) red wine
2 bay leaves
3 sprigs fresh thyme, plus extra to garnish
1 tablespoon butter, softened
1 tablespoon plain (all-purpose) flour
chopped fresh parsley, to serve

For maximum flavour, prepare the casserole a day ahead. Reheat over medium heat before serving.

PREPARATION 10 minutes **COOKING** 1 hour 30 minutes **SERVES** 6

1 Season the chicken with salt and freshly ground black pepper. Heat the oil in a flameproof casserole dish over medium–high heat. Brown the chicken in two batches for 3 minutes on each side, removing each batch to a plate.

2 Fry the bacon for 3 minutes, or until crisp; remove to a plate. Sauté the onions, celery and garlic for 3 minutes, then add the mushrooms and sauté for 2 minutes, or until softened.

3 Pour in the brandy, then the wine, stirring to loosen the solids from the bottom of the dish. Add the chicken, bacon, bay leaves and thyme. Bring to a gentle boil, then reduce the heat. Cover and simmer for 1 hour.

4 Mix the butter and flour to a smooth paste, then stir into the sauce, 1 teaspoon at a time. Simmer for another few minutes, or until the sauce has thickened. Garnish with extra thyme sprigs and serve.

PER SERVING 2993 kJ, 715 kcal, 45 g protein, 44 g fat (13 g saturated fat), 13 g carbohydrate (<1 g sugars), 1 g fibre, 568 mg sodium

Slow cooker

If you have a slow cooker you can sauté in, or you don't mind using another pot, follow steps 1 and 2 above, then deglaze the pan with the brandy and wine, reducing the wine to 1½ cups (375 ml). (Alternatively, omit the oil and the browning and sautéing steps.)

Transfer all the ingredients to the slow cooker, except the butter, flour and parsley. Gently combine, then cover and cook on low for 8 hours.

Omit the butter and flour. Mix 1 tablespoon cornflour (cornstarch) with 2 tablespoons cold water to make a smooth paste, then stir into the sauce. Cover and cook for a further 20 minutes, or until thickened. Serve garnished with extra thyme sprigs.

- The combination of capsicum, onion and celery is called the 'holy trinity' by Creole and Cajun cooks, and is used to flavour many dishes; red or yellow capsicums can be substituted for the green.
- Okra is thought to have originated in Africa. When cut, it releases a sticky substance that has thickening properties, which makes it popular in this kind of dish. Fresh okra can now be found in many supermarkets and grocery stores.

Chicken and prawn gumbo

From the American 'Deep South' comes this piquant gumbo starring rice, chicken, prawns and vegetables. A cross between a soup and a stew, it is truly a feast in a bowl.

- 100 g ($3\frac{1}{2}$ oz) chorizo sausage, skinned and finely diced
- 2 tablespoons vegetable oil
- $3\frac{1}{2}$ tablespoons plain (all-purpose) flour
- 2 celery stalks, finely chopped, leaves reserved for garnishing
- 2 onions, finely chopped
- 2 green capsicums (bell peppers), chopped
- 3 garlic cloves, crushed
- 410 g (15 oz) can chopped no-added-salt tomatoes
- 4 cups (1 litre) salt-reduced chicken or vegetable stock
- 200 g (7 oz) fresh okra, thinly sliced
- 2 tablespoons chopped fresh parsley
- 1 teaspoon dried thyme
- 1 bay leaf
- pinch of cayenne pepper
- 1 cup (185 g) basmati and wild rice, rinsed
- 3 boneless, skinless chicken thighs, cut into bite-sized pieces
- 250 g (8 oz) large raw prawns (uncooked shrimp), peeled and deveined, tails left on
- Tabasco sauce, to serve (optional)

PREPARATION 30 minutes **COOKING** 1 hour **SERVES** 4

1 Heat a heavy-based saucepan or flameproof casserole dish over medium heat. Sauté the chorizo for 3 minutes, or until it has rendered some fat and is crisp at the edges. Remove and drain on paper towels.

2 Add the oil to the chorizo fat remaining in the pan. Reduce the heat to low and sprinkle in the flour, stirring constantly, until well blended. Cook very gently, stirring occasionally, for 5 minutes, or until the mixture turns a rich brown.

3 Increase the heat slightly. Stir in the celery, onions, capsicums and garlic and sauté for 5 minutes, or until softened. Add the tomatoes, stock, okra, parsley, thyme, bay leaf and cayenne pepper. Bring to a boil, then reduce the heat, partially cover the pan and simmer for 30 minutes, or until the okra thickens the soup, stirring frequently.

4 Increase the heat and bring the liquid to a boil. Stir in the rice, then reduce the heat to low. Add the chicken and simmer for 15–20 minutes, or until the rice is tender and the chicken is cooked through. During this time, add a little extra stock or water if needed.

5 Add the prawns and chorizo and simmer for 2 minutes, or until the prawns turn pink and the sausage is heated through.

6 Remove the bay leaf and season to taste with salt and freshly ground black pepper. Ladle into bowls, garnish with the reserved celery leaves and serve with Tabasco sauce, if desired.

PER SERVING 3016 kJ, 721 kcal, 61 g protein, 28 g fat (7 g saturated fat), 57 g carbohydrate (10 g sugars), 5 g fibre, 1387 mg sodium

Slow-cooker honey ginger chicken

Honey, soy and ginger are a classic flavour triad and are spectacular with succulent chicken. The pineapple adds a sweet-and-sour tingle, but can be omitted if you prefer.

- ½ cup (175 g) honey
- ⅓ cup (80 ml) light soy sauce
- ¼ cup (60 ml) no-added-salt tomato sauce (ketchup)
- 440 g (15 oz) can pineapple pieces, drained, reserving the juice
- 2 cloves garlic, crushed
- 1 tablespoon grated fresh ginger
- 8 boneless, skinless chicken thighs
- 2 tablespoons cornflour (cornstarch)
- steamed rice (see page 310), to serve
- coriander (cilantro) leaves, to garnish

Browning the chicken enhances the flavour of this dish. If you have a slow cooker you can sauté in, or you don't mind using another pot, heat 1 tablespoon vegetable oil in a large frying pan over medium heat. Add the chicken and fry for 4 minutes on each side, or until golden brown. Add the chicken to the slow cooker and proceed from step 1.

PREPARATION 20 minutes **COOKING** 4 hours 15 minutes **SERVES** 4

1 Pour the honey, soy sauce, tomato sauce and reserved pineapple juice into a slow cooker. Add the garlic and ginger and mix well. Add the chicken and turn to coat all over.

2 Cover and cook on high for 4 hours, stirring in the pineapple during the final 20 minutes of cooking. Remove the chicken and keep warm.

3 Mix the cornflour to a smooth paste with ⅓ cup (80 ml) cold water, then stir into the sauce remaining in the slow cooker. Cover and cook for a further 10–15 minutes, or until the sauce thickens.

4 Serve the chicken on a bed of steamed rice, drizzled with the sauce and garnished with coriander.

PER SERVING 3691 kJ, 882 kcal, 89 g protein, 34 g fat (10 g saturated fat), 57 g carbohydrate (51 g sugars), 2 g fibre, 1166 mg sodium

On the stove

HEAT 1 TABLESPOON VEGETABLE OIL in a large deep frying pan and fry the chicken over medium heat for 4 minutes on each side, or until golden. Remove to a plate.

Pour the honey, soy sauce, tomato sauce, pineapple and pineapple juice into the pan. Add the garlic and ginger and mix well. Return the chicken to the pan. Cover and bring to a boil, then reduce the heat and simmer for 15 minutes, or until the chicken is cooked. Continue from step 3, reducing the cooking time slightly.

Chicken stew with butterbeans

Most stews and casseroles benefit by being prepared ahead and then refrigerated overnight, allowing the flavours to develop and blend. If making this stew ahead of time, leave out the corn and parsley and instead add them after the stew has been gently reheated on the stovetop.

- 125 g (4 oz) rindless bacon slices (bacon strips), cut crosswise into thick strips
- 4 chicken leg quarters, about 1.25 kg (2½ lb) in total, cut into drumsticks and thighs, skin removed
- ¼ cup (35 g) plain (all-purpose) flour
- 1 large onion, diced
- 500 g (1 lb) small red-skinned potatoes, such as desiree or pontiac, scrubbed and thinly sliced
- ¾ cup (180 ml) salt-reduced chicken stock
- 410 g (15 oz) can chopped tomatoes
- 420 g (15 oz) can butterbeans (lima beans), drained and rinsed
- 1 cup (150 g) frozen corn kernels, thawed, or 1 cup (200 g) fresh corn kernels
- 3 tablespoons chopped fresh flat-leaf (Italian) parsley

PREPARATION 25 minutes **COOKING** 1 hour 15 minutes **SERVES** 4

1 Preheat the oven to 180°C (350°F/Gas 4). Heat a flameproof casserole dish over low heat and fry the bacon for 7 minutes, or until crisp. Remove and drain on paper towels. Remove all but 2 tablespoons of the bacon drippings from the dish.

2 Dredge the chicken in the flour, shaking off the excess. Increase the heat to medium–high and fry the chicken in batches for 4 minutes on each side, or until golden brown, transferring each batch to a plate.

3 Reduce the heat to medium and sauté the onion for 5 minutes, or until softened. Add the potato slices and stir to coat. Add the stock, tomatoes, beans and bacon and bring to a boil. Cover, transfer to the oven and cook for 35 minutes, or until the chicken is tender.

4 Place the dish back on the stovetop and remove the lid. Stir in the corn and parsley and cook over medium heat for 3 minutes, or until the corn is heated through. Serve hot.

PER SERVING 2116 kJ, 506 kcal, 49 g protein, 15 g fat (5 g saturated fat), 40 g carbohydrate (8 g sugars), 10 g fibre, 952 mg sodium

Slow cooker

If you have a slow cooker you can sauté in, or you don't mind using another pot, brown the bacon, chicken and onion as directed in steps 1 to 3. Place in a slow cooker with the potatoes, stock, tomatoes, beans and corn and gently combine. Cover and cook on low for 8 hours. Stir in the parsley before serving.

Slow-cooker lemon chicken and vegetables

This dish proves that slow cookers aren't just for wintery stews — this lovely hotpot has springtime written all over it! All it needs is some fresh crusty bread or steamed white rice to go with it.

- 1 teaspoon dried oregano
- 1/2 teaspoon salt
- 1/4 teaspoon freshly ground black pepper
- 6 small boneless, skinless chicken breasts, about 115 g (4 oz) each
- 250 g (8 oz) baby carrots, scrubbed and trimmed
- 10 small new potatoes (400 g/14 oz), scrubbed and quartered
- 1/4 cup (60 ml) lemon juice
- 1/4 cup (60 ml) salt-reduced chicken stock
- 2 cloves garlic, crushed
- 1 cup (155 g) frozen peas, thawed
- 30 g (1 oz) butter, chopped
- 2 teaspoons chopped fresh flat-leaf (Italian) parsley

Make sure the peas are fully thawed before adding them to the slow cooker.

PREPARATION 20 minutes **COOKING** 6 hours 20 minutes **SERVES** 6

1 In a small bowl, combine the oregano, salt and pepper. Rub the mixture into each chicken breast.

2 Arrange the carrots and potatoes in the base of a 5 litre (5 quart) slow cooker. Lay the chicken breasts on top. Combine the lemon juice, stock and garlic and drizzle over the chicken.

3 Cover and cook on low for 6 hours. Add the peas, replace the lid and increase the heat to high. Cook for a further 20 minutes.

4 Dot the chicken with the butter to melt over the top. Sprinkle with the parsley and serve.

PER SERVING 1110 kJ, 265 kcal, 28 g protein, 11 g fat (5 g saturated fat), 13 g carbohydrate (3 g sugars), 3 g fibre, 353 mg sodium

In the oven

Preheat the oven to 180°C (350°F/Gas 4). Arrange the potatoes and carrots in a baking dish. Add the combined lemon juice, stock and garlic. Cover with foil and bake for 20 minutes.

Add the chicken to the dish, on top of the vegetables. Cover with the foil and bake for a further 15 minutes.

Add the peas, then cover with the foil and bake for a final 10 minutes. Serve as directed in step 4.

Slow-cooker Cajun chicken

Take a shortcut to the Deep South by adding a sprinkling of Cajun seasoning to this simplest of stews, which you essentially just combine and forget all about. If it suits you better, you can use the high setting on your slow cooker and reduce the cooking time to 4–5 hours.

- 1/2 teaspoon salt
- 1/4 teaspoon freshly ground black pepper
- 1–2 teaspoons cajun seasoning, or to taste
- 4 boneless, skinless chicken breasts
- 410 g (15 oz) can chopped tomatoes
- 1 celery stalk, diced
- 1 green capsicum (bell pepper), diced
- 3 cloves garlic, crushed
- 1 onion, diced
- 1 1/3 cups (125 g) sliced button mushrooms
- 1 fresh green chilli, seeded and chopped, plus extra to garnish
- steamed white rice (see page 310), to serve

PREPARATION 15 minutes **COOKING** 8 hours **SERVES** 4

1 Combine the salt, pepper and cajun seasoning. Rub the mixture over each side of each chicken breast.

2 Add the remaining ingredients, except the rice, to the slow cooker and gently combine. Nestle the chicken breasts into the mixture, ensuring they are covered.

3 Cover and cook on low for 8 hours. Check the seasoning, sprinkle with extra chopped chilli and serve with steamed white rice.

PER SERVING 2134 kJ, 510 kcal, 76 g protein, 19 g fat (6 g saturated fat), 7 g carbohydrate (5 g sugars), 3 g fibre, 771 mg sodium

---

Cajun seasoning is a combination of salt, garlic powder, onion powder, paprika, cayenne pepper, dried oregano and dried thyme. There can be slight variations to this basic mix. Most supermarkets stock a Cajun spice blend, or for a more authentic spice mix, try specialty food shops.

Chicken, pumpkin and lentil stew

To cut up the butternut pumpkin, you'll need a large, sturdy chef's knife. To make the procedure easier, first cut off the 'neck' of the pumpkin, then halve the thicker bottom part.

- 2 tablespoons olive oil
- 1 onion, finely chopped
- 3 cloves garlic, crushed
- ½ cup (95 g) brown lentils, rinsed and picked over
- 1 small (600 g/1¼ lb) butternut pumpkin (squash), peeled and diced
- 1 cup (250 g) canned chopped tomatoes
- ½ teaspoon salt
- 2 teaspoons chilli powder
- 1 teaspoon ground coriander
- tiny pinch of ground cloves
- 750 g (1½ lb) boneless, skinless chicken thighs, cut into large chunks
- 1½ cups (70 g) baby English spinach leaves

To save time, use 500 g (1 lb) shredded cooked chicken instead of cooking the chicken. Stir the chicken into the stew for the last 15 minutes of cooking.

PREPARATION 15 minutes **COOKING** 55 minutes **SERVES** 4

1 Preheat the oven to 180°C (350°F/Gas 4). Heat the oil in a large flameproof casserole dish and sauté the onion and garlic over medium heat for 5 minutes, or until the onion has softened.

2 Stir in the lentils, pumpkin, tomatoes, salt and spices. Add ½ cup (125 ml) water and bring to a boil.

3 Add the chicken thighs. Cover with the lid, transfer to the oven and bake for 45 minutes, or until the chicken is cooked through and the pumpkin and lentils are tender.

4 Fold the spinach through, until the leaves have just wilted but are still bright green. Serve hot.

PER SERVING 2024 kJ, 483 kcal, 43 g protein, 24 g fat (6 g saturated fat), 27 g carbohydrate (6 g sugars), 8 g fibre, 534 mg sodium

Slow cooker

If you have a slow cooker you can sauté in, or you don't mind using another pot, follow step 1 above. (Alternatively, omit the oil and the sautéing step.) Place all the ingredients in the slow cooker, except the spinach leaves, and increasing the water to 1 cup (250 ml).

Gently combine, then cover and cook on low for 6 hours. Stir in the spinach leaves just before serving.

Mediterranean chicken

This is a dish of vivid colour and bold flavours. Onions, tomatoes and capsicums make a chunky vegetable sauce for the chicken, with spicy chorizo sausage, sun-dried tomatoes, rosemary and olives adding tastes of the Mediterranean. Serve with crusty bread or steamed rice.

- 2 tablespoons olive oil
- 2 onions, roughly chopped
- 2 cloves garlic, crushed
- 1 tablespoon chopped fresh rosemary
- 40 g (1½ oz) chorizo sausage, skinned and diced
- 2 large red capsicums (bell peppers), roughly chopped
- ⅓ cup (50 g) sun-dried tomatoes, roughly chopped
- 410 g (15 oz) can chopped tomatoes
- ¼ cup (60 ml) dry white wine
- 4 boneless, skinless chicken breasts or large thighs (about 500 g/1 lb in total)
- ⅓ cup (50 g) pitted olives (black, green or a mixture)

You can prepare the dish ahead until the end of step 4. Keep refrigerated or frozen, then thaw and reheat gently. Add the olives before serving.

PREPARATION 15 minutes **COOKING** 50 minutes **SERVES** 4

1 Heat the oil in a large flameproof casserole dish or deep frying pan with a lid. Sauté the onions, garlic and rosemary over low heat for 15 minutes, or until soft and golden.

2 Increase the heat to medium. Add the chorizo and capsicums and sauté for a few minutes, until the sausage turns slightly golden.

3 Add the sun-dried tomatoes, canned tomatoes and wine. Season with freshly ground black pepper, but avoid adding salt at this stage (the olives will be very salty). Stir well and bring to a simmer.

4 Add the chicken and stir to coat with the sauce. Bring to a boil, then reduce the heat so the sauce simmers. Cover and cook for 25–30 minutes, or until the chicken is tender and the sauce is thick.

5 Just before serving, stir in the olives. Cook for just long enough to heat the olives through. Serve hot.

PER SERVING 1556 kJ, 372 kcal, 32 g protein, 19 g fat (5 g saturated fat), 15 g carbohydrate (12 g sugars), 5 g fibre, 421 mg sodium

Slow cooker

THIS DISH NEEDS TO BE started in a deep frying pan to develop the flavours. Prepare up to the end of step 3, then transfer to the slow cooker. Add the chicken, then cover and cook on low for 6 hours. Stir in the olives, replace the lid and cook for 5 minutes to heat them through.

Quick turkey curry

Vary this versatile recipe to suit: use your favourite curry paste instead of curry powder, add some diced pineapple or apple, and use whatever chutney you fancy. Serve with steamed rice, naan bread and extra chutney and maybe banana pieces tossed in desiccated coconut.

- 2 tablespoons butter
- 1 onion, finely chopped
- 2 celery stalks, finely diced
- 1 small red capsicum (bell pepper), finely diced
- 1 clove garlic, crushed
- 1 tablespoon curry powder
- 1 cup (250 ml) chicken stock
- ½ cup (125 ml) coconut milk
- 500 g (1 lb) boneless, skinless turkey breast, cut into small chunks
- 1 teaspoon garam masala
- 2 tablespoons mango chutney (optional)
- 1–2 teaspoons lime or lemon juice
- coriander (cilantro) leaves, to garnish

PREPARATION 10 minutes **COOKING** 30 minutes **SERVES** 4

1 Melt the butter in a saucepan over medium heat. Sauté the onion, celery, capsicum and garlic for 5 minutes, or until starting to colour.

2 Add the curry powder and cook, stirring, for 30 seconds, or until fragrant. Add the stock and coconut milk and simmer for 15 minutes.

3 Stir in the turkey, garam masala and chutney, if using. Simmer for 5–10 minutes, or until the turkey is cooked through.

4 Add lime or lemon juice to taste and season with salt and freshly ground black pepper. Garnish with coriander leaves and serve.

PER SERVING 1756 kJ, 419 kcal, 38 g protein, 24 g fat (13 g saturated fat), 12 g carbohydrate (10 g sugars), 3 g fibre, 599 mg sodium

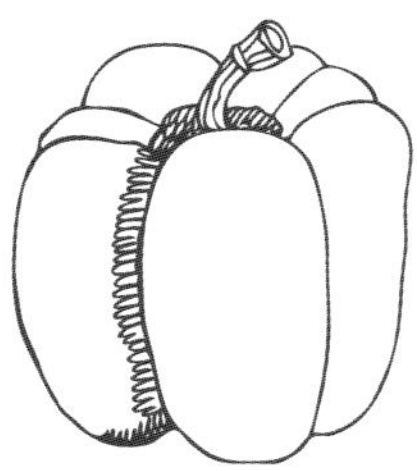

Slow cooker

If you have a slow cooker you can sauté in, or you don't mind using another pot, follow step 1 above. (Alternatively, omit the butter and the sautéing step.) Reduce the chicken stock to ½ cup (125 ml) and add to the slow cooker with all the other ingredients except the lime juice.

Gently combine, then cover and cook on low for 6–8 hours. Finish as directed in step 4.

Turkey and black bean chilli

With chunks of lean turkey and sweet potato, hearty black beans and a mild chilli hit, this splendid dish offers a healthy gourmet alternative to the regular beef chilli bowl. Serve with warm corn tortillas and perhaps an avocado salsa and a squeeze of lime.

- 1½ tablespoons olive oil
- 500 g (1 lb) boneless, skinless turkey breast, cut into 1 cm (½ inch) chunks
- 1 large onion, cut into 1 cm (½ inch) chunks
- 3 cloves garlic, crushed
- 1 green capsicum (bell pepper), chopped
- 1 tablespoon chilli powder
- 1 teaspoon ground coriander
- ½ teaspoon ground oregano
- ½ teaspoon salt
- 500 g (1 lb) orange sweet potatoes (kumara), peeled and cut into 1 cm (½ inch) chunks
- 410 g (15 oz) can chopped tomatoes
- 420 g (15 oz) can black beans, drained and rinsed

PREPARATION 15 minutes **COOKING** 30 minutes **SERVES** 4

1 Heat 1 tablespoon of the oil in a large heavy-based saucepan. Add the turkey and sauté over medium–high heat for 5 minutes, or until lightly browned all over. Remove to a plate.

2 Heat the remaining oil and sauté the onion and garlic for 5 minutes, or until the onion has softened. Add the capsicum and cook for 4 minutes, or until it is crisp but tender.

3 Add the chilli powder, coriander, oregano and salt. Mix well, then stir in the sweet potatoes and 1½ cups (375 ml) water. Bring to a boil, then reduce the heat to a simmer. Cover and cook for 5 minutes.

4 Stir in the tomatoes and beans, then cover and simmer for a further 5 minutes, or until the sweet potatoes are tender.

5 Return the turkey to the pan. Cover and cook for a further 3 minutes, or until the turkey is cooked through.

PER SERVING 1622 kJ, 388 kcal, 36 g protein, 13 g fat (2 g saturated fat), 34 g carbohydrate (12 g sugars), 8 g fibre, 610 mg sodium

Slow cooker

If you have a slow cooker you can sauté in, or you don't mind using another pot, follow steps 1 and 2 above. (Alternatively, omit the oil and the browning and sautéing steps.) Place all the ingredients in the slow cooker, reducing the water to ¾ cup (180 ml). Gently combine, then cover and cook on low for 6 hours.

Slow-cooker red duck curry

Duck becomes even more succulent bathed in coconut milk with Thai herbs and spices. Instead of a quartered duck, you could also use four duck pieces — breasts, leg quarters or a mix of both.

2 teaspoons vegetable oil
1 duck, cut into quarters
4 tablespoons red curry paste
1 tablespoon soft brown sugar
2 tablespoons fish sauce
400 ml (14 fl oz) coconut milk
3 cm (1¼ inch) piece of fresh ginger, peeled and grated
1 lemongrass stem, bruised
2 kaffir lime (makrut) leaves
100 g (3½ oz) snake beans or green beans, trimmed and cut into 4 cm (1½ inch) lengths
juice of 1 lime
coriander (cilantro) leaves, to garnish
steamed rice (see page 310), to serve

- When following the slow-cooker, stovetop or oven methods, the beans can be added for only the last 30 minutes of cooking if you prefer a firmer texture.
- If using a pressure cooker, follow the same method as for the slow cooker, browning the duck in the pressure cooker without the lid on. Cook under low pressure for 35–40 minutes and allow the pressure to release naturally.

PREPARATION 10 minutes **COOKING** 6–8 hours **SERVES** 4

1 Heat the oil over medium–high heat and brown the duck all over, either in your slow cooker, if it has a browning option, or in a large frying pan. Discard the fat. (Browning the duck isn't essential, but helps render off some of the excess fat so the finished dish isn't too rich in fat.)

2 Place the duck in the slow cooker. In a bowl, combine the curry paste, sugar and fish sauce. Stir in the coconut milk and ginger, then pour the mixture over the duck. Add the lemongrass, lime leaves and beans to the slow cooker.

3 Cover and cook on low for 6–8 hours. Stir the lime juice through, garnish with coriander and serve with steamed rice.

PER SERVING 3429 kJ, 819 kcal, 74 g protein, 53 g fat (27 g saturated fat), 13 g carbohydrate (9 g sugars), 3 g fibre, 1213 mg sodium

On the stove/In the oven

Heat 2 teaspoons vegetable oil in a flameproof casserole dish on the stovetop. Brown the duck pieces to render off the fat, then discard the fat from the dish. Add the other ingredients as directed in step 2, along with enough salt-reduced chicken stock to just cover the duck.

Bring the mixture to a simmer. Cover and cook over low heat on the stovetop or in a preheated 170°C (340°F/Gas 3) oven for 1½ hours, or until the duck is tender. Stir in the lime juice, garnish with coriander and serve with steamed rice.

Slow-cooker duck with orange

It isn't absolutely essential to brown the duck first, but taking this extra step does develop the flavour and renders off some of the excess fat. Alternatively, you could cook the duck to the end of step 2, then cut it into quarters and brown them in a non-stick pan. Serve with a mixed leaf salad.

2 kg (4 lb) duck
2 teaspoons olive oil
1 onion, finely diced
3 cloves garlic, crushed
1 carrot, halved
1 bay leaf
1 tablespoon chopped fresh marjoram
3/4 cup (180 ml) orange juice
2 teaspoons orange zest
3 teaspoons chicken stock (bouillon) powder
1/4 cup (60 ml) madeira
2 tablespoons honey
3 teaspoons cornflour (cornstarch)

- If using a pressure cooker, follow the same method as for the slow cooker, browning the duck in the pressure cooker without the lid on. Cook under low pressure for 40 minutes and allow the pressure to release naturally.
- To save some time, you can also cook this dish on high for 3–4 hours.
- In step 3, it will be easier to remove the excess fat from the sauce if you place it in the freezer for a while. The fat will congeal on top, making it easier to remove.

PREPARATION 10 minutes COOKING 6–8 hours SERVES 4

1 Season the duck all over with salt and freshly ground black pepper. Heat the oil over medium–high heat and brown the duck all over, either in your slow cooker, if it has a browning option, or in a large frying pan. Remove the duck to a plate and discard the fat.

2 Place the onion, garlic, carrot, bay leaf and marjoram in the slow cooker. Combine the orange juice, orange zest, stock powder, madeira and honey, then add to the slow cooker and mix to combine. Place the duck on top. Cover and cook on low for 6–8 hours.

3 Carefully remove the duck from the slow cooker to a warm platter. Cover loosely with foil to keep warm. Discard the carrot from the cooking juices, then remove the excess fat from the top of the sauce.

4 Mix the cornflour with enough cold water to make a smooth paste, then stir into the cooking juices. Replace the lid, increase the heat to high and cook for a further 10–15 minutes, or until the sauce has thickened slightly. Season to taste.

5 Carve the duck into quarters and arrange on warm plates. Drizzle with the sauce and serve.

PER SERVING 4363 kJ, 1042 kcal, 60 g protein, 79 g fat (23 g saturated fat), 24 g carbohydrate (17 g sugars), 1 g fibre, 806 mg sodium

In the oven

PREHEAT THE OVEN TO 180°C (350°F/Gas 4). Follow step 1 as above, browning the duck in a flameproof casserole dish on the stovetop. Follow step 2 and gently bring to a boil. Cover with the lid, transfer to the oven and bake for 2 hours. Continue as directed in steps 3 to 5.

Slow-cooker creamy rabbit with mustard

Ask your butcher to joint the rabbit for you, if you prefer. If rabbit isn't available, a tasty substitute would be chicken pieces on the bone. Serve with crusty bread to mop up the juices.

- 2 rabbits (about 750 g/1½ lb each), each cut into 6 pieces
- 1 leek, white part only, sliced
- 250 g (8 oz) small button mushrooms, trimmed
- 2 teaspoons chopped fresh thyme, plus extra sprigs to garnish
- 1 bay leaf
- 1 tablespoon dijon mustard
- ¼ cup (60 ml) dry white wine
- ¾ cup (180 ml) salt-reduced chicken stock
- 2 tablespoons reduced-fat cream
- 1 tablespoon cornflour (cornstarch)
- 1 tablespoon finely chopped fresh parsley
- ¼ teaspoon freshly ground black pepper

PREPARATION 20 minutes COOKING 6 hours SERVES 4–6

1 Cut the rabbits into six pieces each. Layer the rabbit pieces, leek and mushrooms in a 5 litre (5 quart) slow cooker. Sprinkle with the thyme and add the bay leaf.

2 Using a fork, whisk the mustard into the wine and stock, then drizzle over the rabbit. Cover and cook on low for 6 hours.

3 Stir the cream, cornflour, parsley and pepper together in a small bowl until smooth. Pour the mixture into the slow cooker, give a quick stir and replace the lid.

4 Increase the heat to high and cook for a further 15 minutes, or until the sauce has thickened slightly. Serve garnished with thyme sprigs.

PER SERVING 1564 kJ, 374 kcal, 58 g protein, 11 g fat (5 g saturated fat), 7 g carbohydrate (3 g sugars), 3 g fibre, 398 mg sodium

On the stove

Coat the rabbit pieces in the mustard, then cover and marinate in the refrigerator for 2 hours. Heat 1 tablespoon olive oil in a large, deep heavy-based frying pan and sauté the leek over medium heat for 3 minutes, or until softened. Remove to a plate.

Lightly brown the rabbit in batches. Return the leek and all the rabbit to the pan. Add the mushrooms, herbs, ½ cup (125 ml) wine and 1½ cups (375 ml) stock. Cover and bring just to a boil, then reduce the heat to low. Cover and gently simmer for 1½ hours.

Transfer the rabbit and mushrooms to a warm serving dish. Increase the heat and bring to a boil. Cook until the sauce has reduced by half, then whisk in the cream, but omit the cornflour. Pour the sauce over the rabbit and sprinkle with the parsley. Garnish with thyme sprigs and serve with crusty bread.

Rabbit in red wine sauce

Wild rabbit has a darker meat and a gamier — and many say superior — flavour than the plumper, paler-fleshed, farmed rabbits. If you can't get hold of rabbit, chicken is a fine alternative in this dish. Use 1.5 kg (3 lb) chicken pieces and reduce the cooking time by 30 minutes.

- 1.5 kg (3 lb) rabbit, cut into 6 pieces (ask your butcher to do this, if you prefer)
- 1/4 cup (35 g) plain (all-purpose) flour
- 150 g (5 oz) rindless bacon (bacon strips), diced
- 1 tablespoon olive oil, approximately
- 1 onion, finely chopped
- 2 carrots, finely chopped
- 2 cloves garlic, crushed
- 1 tablespoon tomato paste (concentrated purée)
- 2 cups (500 ml) red wine
- 1 bouquet garni
- 1–2 cups (250–500 ml) salt-reduced chicken stock

The rabbit goes well with mashed potato (see page 311) and steamed vegetables such as green beans.

PREPARATION 10 minutes COOKING 1 hour 55 minutes SERVES 6

1 Dust the rabbit pieces with the flour and season generously with salt and freshly ground black pepper.

2 Heat a large heavy-based saucepan over medium heat. Add the bacon and sauté without any oil for 3–4 minutes, or until most of the fat has been released. Remove to a plate.

3 Add the rabbit pieces in batches and brown all over for 5–7 minutes, adding the oil if necessary. Remove each batch to a plate.

4 Sauté the onion, carrots and garlic for 5 minutes, or until the onion has softened. Stir in the tomato paste until combined, then add the wine, stirring to loosen the solids from the bottom of the dish.

5 Return the bacon and rabbit to the pan. Add the bouquet garni and enough stock to just cover the rabbit. Bring to a simmer, then cover and cook over low heat for 1 hour, or until the rabbit is tender.

6 Remove the lid and simmer for a further 30 minutes, or until the sauce has reduced. Season to taste and serve.

PER SERVING 1493 kJ, 357 kcal, 43 g protein, 11 g fat (3 g saturated fat), 8 g carbohydrate (3 g sugars), 1 g fibre, 813 mg sodium

Slow cooker

If you have a slow cooker you can sauté in, or you don't mind using another pot, follow the recipe as above, up to the end of step 4. (Alternatively, omit the oil and the browning steps.) Transfer all the ingredients to the slow cooker. Gently combine, then cover and cook on low for 6 hours.

Slow-cooker Brunswick stew

Closer to a soup than a stew, this thrifty yet satisfying dish is a traditional favourite from the American South where early versions were made with rabbit and squirrel instead of chicken. It can be made a day or two ahead and reheated just before serving. Serve with cornbread.

- 2 carrots, cut into 2.5 cm (1 inch) chunks
- 2 large celery stalks, cut into 2.5 cm (1 inch) chunks
- 2 potatoes, peeled and cut into 2.5 cm (1 inch) chunks
- 1 onion, chopped
- 1 tablespoon finely chopped fresh sage
- 2 tablespoons chopped fresh flat-leaf (Italian) parsley
- 1 bay leaf
- 410 g (15 oz) can chopped tomatoes
- 1 cup (250 ml) salt-reduced chicken stock
- 1.8 kg (3¾ lb) whole chicken
- 410 g (15 oz) can butterbeans (lima beans), drained and rinsed
- 300 g (10 oz) can corn kernels, drained

The best way to extract fat from a stew is to make the dish a day ahead and refrigerate it. The fat will rise to the top and solidify, making it easier to remove.

PREPARATION 25 minutes **COOKING** 6 hours **SERVES** 4

1 Arrange the carrots, celery, potatoes and onion in a 5 litre (5 quart) slow cooker. Add the sage, parsley and bay leaf, then stir in the tomatoes and stock.

2 Wash the chicken inside and out. Pat dry with paper towels and trim off any excess fat. Place on top of the vegetables. Cover and cook on low for 5½ hours.

3 Add the beans and corn to the slow cooker. Replace the lid, increase the heat to high and cook for a further 30 minutes.

4 Take the chicken from the pot and remove the skin and bones. Pull the meat into shreds, then stir it back into the stew. Season to taste with salt and freshly ground black pepper and serve.

PER SERVING 3189 kJ, 762 kcal, 59 g protein, 41 g fat (13 g saturated fat), 35 g carbohydrate (11 g sugars), 10 g fibre, 760 mg sodium

On the stove

Place the chicken in a large heavy-based saucepan with the parsley and bay leaf. Pour in 4 cups (1 litre) salt-reduced chicken stock. Cover and bring just to a boil, then reduce the heat to low. Simmer for 1 hour, or until the chicken is tender. Transfer the chicken to a platter, then skim any fat from the stock.

Add the carrots, celery, potatoes and onion to the pan, along with the sage, tomatoes, beans and corn. Cover and simmer for 30 minutes, or until the vegetables are tender.

Pull the meat from the chicken, discarding the skin and bones. Shred the meat, stir into the stew and reheat. Season to taste and serve.

Fish and seafood

Slow-cooker seafood stew with saffron

To save time, you can cook this seafood-lover's favourite using the high setting of the slow cooker. Simply halve the cooking time in step 2 to 2 hours, and in step 3 to 1 hour. You can thicken the stew in step 5 by stirring in a little cornflour mixed with water, if you prefer.

1 tablespoon olive oil
1 onion, finely diced
2 cloves garlic, sliced
1 celery stalk, finely sliced
3 potatoes, peeled and thinly sliced
2 tomatoes, seeded and diced
1 red capsicum (bell pepper), diced
pinch of saffron threads
$^3/_4$ cup (180 ml) white wine
2 cups (500 ml) salt-reduced fish stock
2 sprigs fresh thyme
2 bay leaves
500 g (1 lb) skinless thick white fish fillets, cut into 4 cm ($1^1/_2$ inch) chunks
200 g (7 oz) calamari rings
200 g (7 oz) raw prawns (uncooked shrimp), peeled and deveined if desired
300 g (10 oz) mussels, scrubbed and beards removed
fresh basil leaves, to garnish
crusty bread, to serve

PREPARATION 20 minutes **COOKING** 6 hours 45 minutes **SERVES** 6

1 If your slow cooker has a browning option, heat the oil in it and sauté the onion, garlic and celery for 5 minutes, or until softened. (Alternatively, use a frying pan, or omit the oil and simply add the onion, garlic and celery to the slow cooker.)

2 Add the potatoes, tomatoes and capsicum to the slow cooker. Stir the saffron into the wine, then pour into the cooker with the stock. Add the thyme and bay leaves, then cover and cook on low for 4 hours.

3 Gently stir in all the seafood except the mussels. Replace the lid and cook on low for 2 hours.

4 Add the mussels, then cover and cook for a further 30 minutes, or until the shells open. Discard any mussels that do not open.

5 If the stew is too soupy or you wish to reduce the liquid, remove the seafood and keep it warm. Increase the heat to high and cook, uncovered, until the liquid has reduced slightly. Season to taste with salt and freshly ground black pepper.

6 Return the seafood to the stew. Garnish with basil leaves and serve with crusty bread.

PER SERVING 1101 kJ, 263 kcal, 35 g protein, 6 g fat (1 g saturated fat), 13 g carbohydrate (3 g sugars), 2 g fibre, 441 mg sodium

On the stove

HEAT THE OIL IN A large saucepan and sauté the onion, garlic and celery over medium heat for 5 minutes, or until softened. Add the remaining ingredients, except the seafood, basil and bread. Bring to a boil, reduce the heat, then cover and simmer for 20 minutes.

Gently stir in the seafood, and some extra stock if needed. Simmer for 10 minutes, or until the seafood is just cooked. Discard any mussels that do not open, then continue with steps 5 and 6.

Seafood paella

An ideal dish for entertaining, this eye-catching saffron-tinted rice dish is studded with white fish and seafood, and vegetables such as asparagus and artichokes. Traditionally it is cooked and presented in a paella pan, so do use one for this recipe if you happen to have one.

- 6 cups (1.5 litres) salt-reduced fish or chicken stock, or 4 cups (1 litre) stock and 2 cups (500 ml) water
- 1 small onion, halved
- large pinch of saffron threads
- 3 tablespoons olive oil
- 2 large cloves garlic, crushed
- 1 red capsicum (bell pepper), chopped
- $2\frac{1}{4}$ cups (495 g) paella or risotto rice
- 150 ml (5 fl oz) dry white wine
- 350 g (12 oz) skinless firm white fish fillets, cut into chunks
- 250 g (8 oz) peeled raw small prawns (uncooked shrimp), thawed if frozen
- 125 g (4 oz) squid, cleaned and sliced
- 150 g (5 oz) asparagus, trimmed and sliced
- 2 large tomatoes, peeled, seeded and chopped
- 12 pitted olives, sliced
- 2 tablespoons chopped fresh parsley, plus extra to garnish
- 1 tablespoon lemon juice
- 410 g (15 oz) can artichoke hearts, rinsed, drained and halved
- lemon wedges, to serve

PREPARATION 25 minutes **COOKING** 35 minutes **SERVES** 4

1 Pour the stock into a very large wide saucepan and add the onion and saffron. Bring to a boil, then reduce the heat. Cover and simmer gently for 10 minutes, then strain into a large jug.

2 Meanwhile, heat the oil in the saucepan or a paella pan and sauté the garlic and capsicum over medium heat for 2–3 minutes. Add the rice and cook, stirring often, for 5 minutes, or until the rice looks transparent.

3 Add the wine, stir, then allow it to bubble up and evaporate. Ladle about one-third of the reserved stock into the rice. When it has all been absorbed, add a further one-third of the stock, then cook gently until it has been absorbed.

4 Add the fish and seafood to the pan, along with the asparagus, tomatoes, olives, parsley, lemon juice and artichokes. Ladle in the rest of the stock. Cook gently, stirring occasionally, for 10 minutes, or until all the seafood is cooked and the rice and vegetables are tender, adding extra stock or hot water if needed.

5 Season to taste with salt and freshly ground black pepper. Tip into a serving dish, if not using a paella pan. Garnish with lemon wedges and extra parsley and serve.

PER SERVING 3379 kJ, 807 kcal, 53 g protein, 19 g fat (3 g saturated fat), 95 g carbohydrate (5 g sugars), 5 g fibre, 838 mg sodium

Basque-style fish

This one-pan-wonder bursts with sensational colours and flavours and lends itself well to most types of firm white fish. Serve with country-style bread and crunchy salad leaves.

2 tablespoons olive oil
1 onion, halved and thinly sliced
2 large red capsicums (bell peppers), thinly sliced into short strips
2 large green capsicums (bell peppers), thinly sliced into short strips
2 sprigs fresh oregano
3 cloves garlic, crushed
400 g (14 oz) large ripe tomatoes, diced
1 teaspoon sugar
good pinch of chilli powder
50 g ($1^3/_4$ oz) pitted black olives, halved
1 tablespoon white wine vinegar
400 g (14 oz) skinless thick white fish fillet, such as cod, hake, snapper, bream, flathead or barramundi
chopped fresh flat-leaf (Italian) parsley, to garnish

- Using drained roasted capsicums from a jar will save some cooking time. You could also use a 410 g (15 oz) can of chopped tomatoes instead of fresh tomatoes.
- For a different flavour and texture, add the minimum amount of salt when seasoning, and instead sprinkle slivered good-quality salted almonds over the cooked fish and vegetables before serving.

PREPARATION 25 minutes **COOKING** 15 minutes **SERVES** 4

1 Heat the oil in a large frying pan and sauté the onion, capsicums, oregano and garlic over medium heat for 5 minutes, or until the vegetables are slightly softened.

2 Add the tomatoes, sugar, chilli powder, olives and vinegar. Cook over medium–high heat, stirring frequently, for 3 minutes, or until the tomatoes are slightly softened. Season to taste with salt and freshly ground black pepper.

3 Cut the fish into four equal portions and add them to the pan, shuffling them down into the vegetables. Reduce the heat so that the vegetables bubble gently.

4 Cover with a piece of foil and cook for 5 minutes, or until the fish is just cooked. It should be firm, succulent and opaque, with flakes that just separate. Sprinkle with chopped parsley and serve.

PER SERVING 1070 kJ, 256 kcal, 24 g protein, 14 g fat (2 g saturated fat), 9 g carbohydrate (7 g sugars), 4 g fibre, 391 mg sodium

Slow cooker

If you have a slow cooker you can sauté in, or you don't mind using another pot, follow step 1 above. (Alternatively, omit the oil and the sautéing step.) Transfer all the ingredients to the slow cooker, except the fish and parsley. Gently combine, then cover and cook on low for 2 hours.

Add the fish, ensuring it is covered, then cover and cook for a further 2 hours. Sprinkle with chopped parsley and serve.

Peppered fish with lemon and basil

This fantastically healthy dish has a real peppery kick, balanced by sweet basil and capsicums. Be as adventurous as you like with the vegetables: try broccolini or beans instead of sugarsnap peas, or broad (fava) beans instead of peas. Serve with a rustic bread such as ciabatta.

- 2 tablespoons vegetable oil
- 1 onion, finely chopped
- 2 red capsicums (bell peppers), thinly sliced
- 2 yellow capsicums (bell peppers), thinly sliced
- 175 g (6 oz) sugarsnap peas
- 500 g (1 lb) skinless firm white fish fillets, cut into 4 cm ($1^1/_2$ inch) chunks
- grated zest and juice of 1 lemon
- 2 teaspoons mixed peppercorns, coarsely crushed
- $1^1/_4$ cups (195 g) frozen peas, thawed
- 1 cup (90 g) bean sprouts
- finely shredded fresh basil, to garnish

PREPARATION 15 minutes **COOKING** 15 minutes **SERVES** 4

1 Heat a wok or large frying pan over high heat and add 1 tablespoon of the oil. Stir-fry the onion for 1 minute, then add the capsicums and sugarsnap peas and stir-fry for 3–5 minutes, or until all the vegetables are tender but still crisp. Transfer to a plate using a slotted spoon and keep warm.

2 Heat the remaining oil in the wok over low heat. Add the fish and stir-fry for 4 minutes, carefully turning the chunks to keep them intact, until the fish is cooked through and flakes easily when tested with the point of a knife.

3 Add the lemon zest, lemon juice and crushed peppercorns to the wok. Return the stir-fried vegetables to the wok, along with the peas and bean sprouts. Gently stir-fry for 2–3 minutes to heat through. Scatter the basil over the top and serve.

PER SERVING 1233 kJ, 295 kcal, 32 g protein, 12 g fat (2 g saturated fat), 11 g carbohydrate (8 g sugars), 4 g fibre, 114 mg sodium

A mortar and pestle is ideal for crushing the peppercorns, but if you don't have one, put them in the corner of a strong plastic bag and press down with the end of a rolling pin or the back of a wooden spoon. Alternatively, some spice manufacturers sell mixed peppercorns in a pepper grinder, which makes the job very easy — look in the spice aisle of your local supermarket.

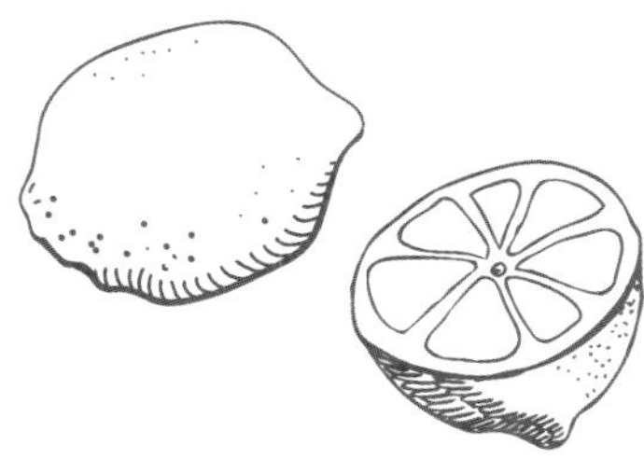

Fish and potato hotpot with spiced yogurt

This simple, chunky vegetable-laden stew comes with some added extras — a piquant yogurt topping and toasty croutons to give a tangy crunch to every lovely mouthful.

2 tablespoons olive oil
1 leek, white part only, sliced
2 celery stalks, sliced
1 carrot, diced
700 g (1 lb 7 oz) potatoes, peeled and cut into 4 cm (1½ inch) chunks
100 g (3½ oz) button mushrooms, trimmed
2 cups (500 ml) fish stock
250 g (8 oz) skinless white fish fillet, cut into bite-sized chunks
250 g (8 oz) skinless salmon fillet, cut into bite-sized chunks
1 baguette, sliced
1 tablespoon chopped fresh tarragon
2 tablespoons chopped fresh parsley

Spiced yogurt

2 tablespoons mayonnaise
2 tablespoons natural (plain) yogurt
1 garlic clove, crushed
½ teaspoon paprika
pinch of chilli powder

- Select boiling (waxy) potatoes rather than roasting (floury) potatoes for this hotpot, as the pieces will hold their shape instead of breaking apart during cooking.
- You can also use mixed fresh or frozen seafood instead of the fish.

PREPARATION 15 minutes **COOKING** 25 minutes **SERVES** 4

1 Heat the oil in a large saucepan over high heat. Add the leek, celery and carrot. Reduce the heat to medium, stir well, then cover and cook for 3 minutes.

2 Add the potatoes and mushrooms and stir in the stock. Bring to a boil, cover and simmer for 10 minutes, or until the potatoes are tender. Gently stir in all the fish and bring back to a simmer. Cover and simmer for a further 5 minutes, or until the fish is just cooked.

3 Meanwhile, preheat the grill (broiler) to its hottest setting. Place the baguette slices on a grill tray and grill (broil) for 2–3 minutes on each side, or until golden. In a small bowl, combine all the spiced yogurt ingredients.

4 Just before serving, stir the tarragon and parsley into the hotpot. Serve with the spiced yogurt and toasted baguette slices.

PER SERVING 2642 kJ, 631 kcal, 40 g protein, 22 g fat (4 g saturated fat), 68 g carbohydrate (8 g sugars), 8 g fibre, 695 mg sodium

Slow cooker

If you have a slow cooker you can sauté in, or you don't mind using another pot, follow step 1 as above. (Alternatively, omit the oil and the vegetable softening step.) Transfer all the vegetables to the slow cooker and add the stock. Gently combine, then cover and cook on low for 4 hours. Add the fish and cook for a further 2 hours, then proceed from step 3.

Spicy fish with chickpeas and spinach

Succulent chunks of fish, gently cooked in an aromatic sauce with a hearty mix of vegetables and chickpeas, make a satisfyingly healthy meal. Serve with steamed rice or crusty bread.

2 tablespoons olive oil
1 onion, finely chopped
1 green chilli, seeded and finely chopped
2 carrots, diced
2 celery stalks, diced
40 g ($1\frac{1}{2}$ oz) fresh ginger, peeled and finely chopped
2 cloves garlic, crushed
seeds from 6 green cardamom pods, crushed
1 teaspoon ground turmeric
2 cups (500 ml) salt-reduced fish, chicken or vegetable stock
420 g (15 oz) can chickpeas, drained and rinsed
500 g (1 lb) tomatoes, peeled and quartered
1 cup (155 g) frozen peas
600 g ($1\frac{1}{4}$ lb) skinless thick white fish fillets, cut into large chunks
250 g (8 oz) baby English spinach leaves

PREPARATION 20 minutes **COOKING** 25 minutes **SERVES** 4

1 Heat the oil in a large deep frying pan with a lid. Add the onion, chilli, carrots, celery, ginger, garlic and cardamom seeds. Stir well, then cover and cook over medium heat for 5 minutes, or until the onions are slightly softened.

2 Stir in the turmeric, then pour in the stock and bring to a boil. Reduce the heat, cover and simmer for 10 minutes, or until the vegetables are tender.

3 Stir in the chickpeas, tomatoes and peas. Gently mix the fish through, taking care not to break up the fish. Bring back to a simmer, then pile the spinach on top — there's no need to stir it in. Cover and cook for 5 minutes, or until the fish chunks are white and firm, and the spinach has just wilted.

4 Using a fork, gently mix the spinach through the vegetables. Ladle into shallow bowls and serve.

PER SERVING 1566 kJ, 374 kcal, 42 g protein, 14 g fat (3 g saturated fat), 20 g carbohydrate (7 g sugars), 7 g fibre, 410 mg sodium

- Salmon fillets can be used instead of white fish; use cannellini beans in place of the chickpeas.
- This recipe can be transformed into a hearty vegetarian meal. Use vegetable stock and replace the fish with either a 420 g (15 oz) can each of red kidney beans and borlotti (cranberry) beans (added with the chickpeas), or 8 halved, hard-boiled eggs, added at the end of cooking to gently heat through.

Slow cooker

If you have a slow cooker you can sauté in, or you don't mind using another pot, follow step 1 as above. (Alternatively, omit the oil and the vegetable softening step.) Transfer all the ingredients to the slow cooker, except the frozen peas, fish and spinach. Gently combine, then cover and cook on low for 2 hours.

Add the fish, replace the lid and cook for a further $1\frac{1}{2}$ hours. Add the fully thawed peas and cook for 20 minutes, then add the spinach and cook for a final 5 minutes, until wilted.

Slow-cooker octopus in tomato and red wine

This simple method for cooking octopus ensures a tender result. Red wine, tomato and a hint of chilli complement the octopus beautifully and impart a fabulously rich hue.

1 tablespoon olive oil
4 cloves garlic, sliced
4 French shallots (eschalots), sliced
¼–½ teaspoon dried red chilli flakes, or taste
1 kg (2 lb) cleaned octopus, cut into 3–4 cm (1¼–1½ inch) chunks
200 ml (7 fl oz) red wine
410 g (15 oz) can chopped tomatoes
1 tablespoon tomato paste (concentrated purée)
1 teaspoon sugar
1 bay leaf
⅔ cup (100 g) fresh or frozen peas
flat-leaf (Italian) parsley sprigs, to garnish
rustic farmhouse bread rolls, to serve

PREPARATION 10 minutes **COOKING** 6–8 hours 15 minutes **SERVES** 4–6

1 Preheat the slow cooker to high. Add the oil, garlic, shallots and chilli flakes, then cover and cook for 10–15 minutes, or until the onion has softened slightly, stirring now and then. (If your slow cooker has a browning option, use this instead and sauté for 5 minutes.)

2 Reduce the setting to low. Add the octopus, wine, tomatoes, tomato paste, sugar and bay leaf and gently combine. Cover and cook on low for 6–8 hours, adding the peas for the last 30 minutes.

3 If you wish to reduce the liquid, increase the heat to high and leave the lid off. Season with salt and freshly ground black pepper. Garnish with parsley and serve with rustic farmhouse rolls.

PER SERVING 1366 kJ, 326 kcal, 40 g protein, 8 g fat (1 g saturated fat), 14 g carbohydrate (6 g sugars), 3 g fibre, 687 mg sodium

You can also make this dish in a pressure cooker. Sauté the garlic mixture in the oil over medium heat without the lid on, until the shallots have softened. Add the remaining ingredients except the peas, parsley and bread. Cook under low pressure for 45 minutes and allow the pressure to release naturally. Add the peas and simmer without the lid on for 5 minutes, or until the peas are cooked. Finish the recipe as directed in step 3.

On the stove

Heat the oil in a large heavy-based saucepan and sauté the garlic, shallots and chilli flakes over medium heat until the shallots have softened. Add the ingredients as directed in step 2, then bring to a boil. Reduce the heat to low, cover and simmer for 1½–2 hours, or until the octopus is tender.

Add the peas (if using frozen, ensure they are fully thawed first) and simmer for 5 minutes, or until the peas are cooked. Finish the recipe as directed in step 3.

Slow-cooker creamy salmon stew

Poaching salmon in a slow cooker ensures it stays beautifully moist and tender. Fennel, dill and vermouth complement salmon superbly, with a few spring greens adding crunch and colour.

- 1 tablespoon butter
- 1 leek, white part only, thinly sliced
- 1 small fennel bulb, thinly sliced
- 4 potatoes, peeled and thinly sliced
- 2 sprigs fresh dill, chopped, plus extra chopped dill to garnish
- 2–3 cups (500–750 ml) salt-reduced chicken or fish stock
- 2 tablespoons cornflour (cornstarch)
- 1/4 cup (60 ml) vermouth
- 4 x 180 g (6 oz) skinless salmon fillets, small bones removed
- 150 g (5 oz) sugarsnap peas, or halved asparagus spears
- 2 tablespoons lemon juice
- 1/3 cup (90 g) sour cream

PREPARATION 15 minutes **COOKING** 3 hours 45 minutes **SERVES** 4

1 Preheat the slow cooker to low. Add the butter and leek and stir to combine. (If your slow cooker has a browning option, sauté the leek for 5 minutes, or until softened.)

2 Add the fennel, potatoes and dill, then pour in enough stock to just cover the vegetables. Mix the cornflour and vermouth to a smooth paste, then stir it through the mixture. Cover and cook on low for 2 hours.

3 Place the salmon on top of the vegetables, then add more stock if necessary to cover the fish. Replace the lid and cook for 1 hour. Add the peas or asparagus and cook for a further 30 minutes.

4 Remove the fish and vegetables from the slow cooker and keep warm. Stir the lemon juice and sour cream through the cooking juices.

5 If you wish to reduce the liquid, increase the heat to high and leave the lid off. Season well with salt and freshly ground black pepper. Serve the sauce with the fish and vegetables, garnished with extra dill.

PER SERVING 2253 kJ, 538 kcal, 42 g protein, 26 g fat (11 g saturated fat), 28 g carbohydrate (7 g sugars), 5 g fibre, 470 mg sodium

On the stove

Melt the butter in a large saucepan and sauté the leek over medium heat for 5 minutes, or until softened. Add the ingredients as instructed in step 2, then cover and cook over low heat for 15 minutes.

Add the salmon, replace the lid and cook for 10 minutes. Add the peas or asparagus and cook for a further 10 minutes. Finish the recipe as directed in steps 4 and 5.

Slow-cooker stuffed calamari

Chorizo adds a spicy, smoky note to the robust stuffing. Lightly browning the calamari tubes before simmering them in the sauce will enhance the final taste and give them a golden lustre.

8 calamari, each measuring about 18 cm (7 inches)
crusty bread, to serve

Stuffing

1 chorizo sausage, skinned
1/2 cup (30 g) panko breadcrumbs
1 egg
2 1/2 tablespoons grated parmesan
1 tablespoon lemon juice
2 tablespoons chopped fresh flat-leaf (Italian) parsley

Sauce

2 cups (500 ml) tomato passata (puréed tomatoes)
3/4 cup (180 ml) white wine
2 cloves garlic, crushed
2 tablespoons balsamic vinegar
1 tablespoon chopped fresh flat-leaf (Italian) parsley

- Panko breadcrumbs are available from most supermarkets. Larger and flakier than regular breadcrumbs, they are used in Japanese tempura dishes for their lovely crisp and crunchy texture.
- You can also make this dish in a pressure cooker. Follow the slow cooker instructions, then cook under low pressure for 10–15 minutes and allow the pressure to release naturally. Finish the recipe as directed in step 4.

PREPARATION 30 minutes **COOKING** 3–4 hours **SERVES** 4

1 Clean and skin the calamari, reserving the tentacles. Roughly chop the tentacles and place in a food processor. Add the stuffing ingredients and blend until they form a paste.

2 Spoon the stuffing into the calamari tubes, but don't fill them more than three-quarters full or they will burst during cooking. Use a toothpick to close the end of each calamari tube.

3 Place the calamari tubes in the slow cooker. Combine the passata, wine and garlic and pour over the calamari. Cover and cook on low for 3–4 hours.

4 Remove the calamari from the slow cooker and place on warm plates. Stir the vinegar and parsley through the sauce. Drizzle the sauce over the calamari and serve with crusty bread.

PER SERVING 1362 kJ, 325 kcal, 44 g protein, 6 g fat (3 g saturated fat), 14 g carbohydrate (9 g sugars), 3 g fibre, 1283 mg sodium

In the oven

Preheat the oven to 180°C (350°F/Gas 4). Prepare and stuff the calamari as directed in steps 1 and 2, then arrange the stuffed calamari in a shallow baking dish. Combine all the sauce ingredients, except the parsley, and drizzle over the calamari. Cover with foil, transfer to the oven and bake for 35 minutes, or until the calamari is cooked through. Stir the parsley through the sauce and serve with crusty bread.

Slow-cooker seafood curry

Deeply yellow turmeric imparts an appealing tint and distinctive aroma to this creamy seafood hotpot, spiced with paprika and garam masala. All you need with it is some steamed white rice.

- 1 tablespoon vegetable oil
- 1 onion, finely chopped
- 2 red chillies, seeded and chopped
- 10 curry leaves
- 1 tablespoon tamarind concentrate
- 1 teaspoon garam masala
- 1/2 teaspoon ground turmeric
- 1/2 teaspoon hot paprika
- 1/2 teaspoon salt
- 1/2 teaspoon freshly ground black pepper
- 420 ml (15 fl oz) coconut milk
- 410 g (15 oz) can chopped tomatoes
- 4 small new potatoes, scrubbed and quartered
- 100 g (3 1/2 oz) green beans, trimmed and halved
- 400 g (14 oz) firm white fish fillet
- 350 g (12 oz) mixed raw seafood, such as prawns (shrimp), scallops and calamari rings
- coriander (cilantro) leaves, to garnish

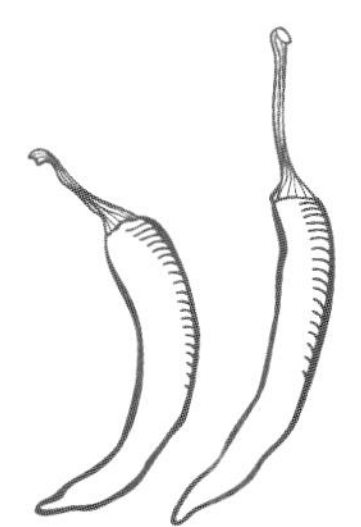

PREPARATION 10 minutes **COOKING** 3 hours 10 minutes **SERVES** 4

1 Preheat the slow cooker to high. Add the oil, onion, chillies and curry leaves, then cover and cook for 10 minutes, or until the onion has softened slightly, stirring now and then. (If your slow cooker has a browning option, use this instead and sauté for 5 minutes.)

2 Stir in the tamarind and spices until well combined, then the coconut milk and tomatoes. Add the potatoes and beans. Cover and cook on low for 2 1/4 hours.

3 Add the seafood and cook for a further 45 minutes. Break the fish fillet into chunks. Ladle the curry into warm shallow serving bowls, garnish with coriander and serve.

PER SERVING 2218 kJ, 530 kcal, 54 g protein, 30 g fat (21 g saturated fat), 24 g carbohydrate (10 g sugars), 6 g fibre, 913 mg sodium

On the stove

Heat the oil in a large saucepan and sauté the onion, chillies and curry leaves over medium heat for 5 minutes, or until the onion has softened. Add the remaining ingredients, except the fish, seafood and bread. Bring to a boil, reduce the heat, then cover and simmer for 10 minutes, or until the potato is cooked.

Cut the fish into large chunks and add with the seafood. Cover and simmer for 5–8 minutes, or until the seafood is cooked. Garnish with coriander and serve.

Slow-cooker Vietnamese seafood broth

This fragrant seafood bowl will have you slurping with satisfaction. Serve with an array of South-East Asian herbs and vegetables, such as bean sprouts, spring onion (scallion) slices, diced tomato, chopped chilli, and mint and coriander leaves, so people can add their own.

1/4 cup (60 ml) tamarind concentrate
1/4 cup (60 ml) fish sauce
3 tablespoons soft brown sugar, or to taste
2 lemongrass stems, bruised
1/4 small pineapple, peeled and cut into 3 cm (1 1/4 inch) chunks
2 tomatoes, diced
100 g (3 1/2 oz) snake beans, trimmed and cut into 4 cm (1 1/2 inch) lengths
750 g (1 1/2 lb) firm white fish fillets, cut into chunks

Stock

1 kg (2 lb) fish bones
1 leek, white part only, roughly chopped
3 cm (1 1/4 inch) piece of fresh ginger, peeled and roughly chopped
2 cloves garlic
2 kaffir lime (makrut) leaves
1/2 bunch (45 g) coriander (cilantro), roots scrubbed, stems and leaves roughly chopped

Wok-ready noodles can be added for the final 10–15 minutes of cooking.

PREPARATION 20 minutes **COOKING** 5 hours 30 minutes **SERVES** 4

1 Place the stock ingredients in the slow cooker with 6 cups (1.5 litres) water. Cover and cook on low for 3–4 hours. Strain the stock and discard the solids.

2 Return 4 cups (1 litre) of the stock to the slow cooker. Stir in the tamarind, fish sauce and sugar until combined. Add the lemongrass, pineapple, tomatoes and snake beans and gently combine. Add the fish, then cover and cook on low for 1 1/2 hours.

3 Discard the lemongrass. Ladle the fish, pineapple and vegetables into warm bowls. Ladle the broth over the top and serve with your choice of fresh herbs, spices and chopped vegetables.

PER SERVING 208 kJ, 50 kcal, 12 g protein, <1 g fat (<1 g saturated fat), 4 g carbohydrate (3 g sugars), <1 g fibre, 333 mg sodium

On the stove

Place the stock ingredients in a large saucepan with 6 cups (1.5 litres) water. Bring to a gentle boil, then reduce the heat, cover and simmer for 25 minutes. Strain the stock and discard the solids.

Return 4 cups (1 litre) of the stock to the pan and add the other ingredients as directed in step 2. Cover and simmer for 15–20 minutes, or until the fish is tender, adding more stock if necessary.

- If raw prawns aren't available, you can use cooked peeled prawns. Add them at the very end of cooking just to warm them through, before you leave the dish to stand before serving.
- Jambalaya is a versatile dish. As well as seafood, it often contains chicken and ham or chopped smoked spicy sausages, such as andouille or chorizo.

Seafood jambalaya

A close cousin of Spanish paella, jambalaya is a Creole dish from the US state of Louisiana, and a melting pot of French, Spanish, African and American cuisines. In the old days just about any edible creature was fair game for this dish. Glam up this seafood version by adding crab or even lobster.

- 3 tablespoons olive oil
- 1 large red onion, finely chopped
- 2 garlic cloves, finely chopped
- 1/2 head of celery, finely diced, leaves reserved for garnishing
- 1 red capsicum (bell pepper), chopped
- 1/2 teaspoon chilli powder, or to taste
- 1 teaspoon ground cumin
- 1 1/4 cups (250 g) long-grain white rice
- 2 x 410 g (15 oz) cans chopped tomatoes
- 1 tablespoon chopped fresh thyme or 1 teaspoon dried thyme
- 300 g (10 oz) skinned firm white fish fillet, cut into four pieces
- 8 large raw prawns (uncooked shrimp), peeled and deveined
- 2 tablespoons chopped fresh flat-leaf (Italian) parsley
- 1 lemon, cut into wedges

PREPARATION 30 minutes **COOKING** 35–40 minutes **SERVES** 4

1 Heat the oil in a large deep frying pan with a lid. Sauté the onion, garlic, celery, capsicum, chilli and cumin over medium–low heat for 10–12 minutes, or until softened. Add the rice and cook, stirring often, for 2 minutes.

2 Meanwhile, drain the tomatoes in a sieve set over a heatproof measuring jug or bowl to catch the juices. Bring a kettle of water to a boil.

3 Add the drained tomatoes to the rice mixture. Sprinkle the thyme over the top, stir well and reduce the heat a little.

4 Make up the tomato juice to 4 cups (1 litre) with boiling water. Pour over the rice, stir well and bring to a boil. Reduce the heat, cover the pan with the lid slightly ajar, and gently simmer for 10 minutes.

5 Season the rice to taste with salt and freshly ground black pepper. Place the fish pieces on top, partly cover the pan and cook for 5 minutes. Carefully stir the rice and turn the fish over, then add the prawns. Partly cover and cook for a further 5 minutes, or until the prawns have turned pink, the fish pieces are cooked, and the rice is tender. The dish should be moist, not dry.

6 Remove from the heat, cover tightly and leave to stand for 5 minutes. Scatter the celery leaves and parsley over the top and serve with lemon wedges to squeeze over.

PER SERVING 2184 kJ, 523 kcal, 31 g protein, 17 g fat (3 g saturated fat), 62 g carbohydrate (10 g sugars), 6 g fibre, 391 mg sodium

Vegetables, grains and pasta

Slow-cooker black bean stew

This dish is similar to feijoada, a traditional Brazilian black bean stew. You can use canned beans, adding them to the slow cooker during the last 2 hours of cooking. Serve with steamed rice.

- 400 g (14 oz) dried black beans
- 410 g (15 oz) can chopped tomatoes
- 3 tablespoons tomato paste (concentrated purée)
- 1 onion, finely diced
- 5 cloves garlic, crushed
- 2 bay leaves
- 600 g ($1^{1}/_{4}$ lb) pork belly or pork shoulder, cut into large chunks
- 1 chorizo sausage, cut into 6 chunks
- 1 ham hock
- coriander (cilantro) leaves, to garnish
- chopped orange segments, to serve (optional)

If using a pressure cooker, follow the same method as for the slow cooker, browning the pork and chorizo and softening the onions in the pressure cooker in 2 tablespoons olive oil, without the lid on. Add the remaining ingredients and stir together. Cook under low pressure for 40 minutes and allow the pressure to release naturally.

PREPARATION 20 minutes, plus overnight soaking **COOKING** 8 hours **SERVES** 6

1 Put the beans in a bowl, cover with plenty of cold water and leave to soak overnight. Drain well.

2 Add the tomatoes and tomato paste to the slow cooker and mix to combine. Pour in 4 cups (1 litre) water, then stir in the onion, garlic and bay leaves. Add the pork, chorizo and ham hock. (If your slow cooker has a browning option, first brown the pork and chorizo in 2 tablespoons olive oil, then the onion and garlic, then add the other ingredients; browning will improve the final flavour.)

3 Cover and cook on low for 8 hours. Season to taste if needed with salt and freshly ground black pepper. Garnish with coriander and serve with chopped orange segments if desired.

PER SERVING 3314 kJ, 792 kcal, 27 g protein, 56 g fat (20 g saturated fat), 47 g carbohydrate (5 g sugars), 12 g fibre, 262 mg sodium

On the stove/In the oven

Heat 2 tablespoons olive oil in a flameproof casserole dish. Brown the pork and chorizo, then remove to a plate. Sauté the onion and garlic over medium heat for 5 minutes, or until softened.

Mix in the tomatoes and tomato paste, then pour in 6 cups (1.5 litres) water. Add the remaining ingredients, except the orange segments, and bring to a simmer.

Cover and cook over low heat on the stovetop or in a preheated 160°C (320°F/Gas 2–3) oven for 3 hours, or until beans are tender, checking the liquid from time to time and adding more as needed. Garnish with coriander and serve with chopped orange segments if desired.

Creamy vegetable fricassee

An elegant array of vegetables is lightly cooked in a tarragon-flavoured stock, finished with crème fraîche or sour cream to make a wonderful, creamy coating sauce. Served with wholegrain or seeded bread, this dish contains balanced plant proteins and easily stands as a meal on its own.

1 tablespoon olive oil
250 g (8 oz) carrots, cut into batons
250 g (8 oz) small new potatoes, scrubbed and either halved or quartered, depending on their size
150 g (5 oz) button mushrooms, trimmed and halved
400 ml (14 fl oz) salt-reduced vegetable stock
2 tablespoons dry white wine
2 teaspoons fresh tarragon leaves, or ½ teaspoon dried tarragon, plus extra fresh leaves to garnish
1 cup (155 g) frozen broad (fava) beans, thawed
150 g (5 oz) asparagus spears, trimmed
3 tablespoons light sour cream or crème fraîche
⅓ cup (50 g) unsalted cashew nuts
wholegrain or seeded bread, to serve

You can partly prepare this dish up to 6 hours ahead. Cook the vegetables up to the end of step 2 and allow them to cool. When ready to serve, gently reheat, then continue from step 3.

PREPARATION 10 minutes **COOKING** 25 minutes **SERVES** 4

1 Heat the oil in a large flameproof casserole dish over medium heat. Add the carrots, potatoes and mushrooms and sauté for 4 minutes, or until lightly browned.

2 Pour in the stock and wine, then stir in the tarragon. Bring to a boil, then reduce the heat, cover and gently simmer for 10 minutes, or until the vegetables are almost cooked.

3 Stir in the broad beans and lay the asparagus on top. Cover and simmer for a further 5 minutes, or until the vegetables are tender. Lift out the vegetables onto a plate, using a slotted spoon.

4 Stir the sour cream into the liquid in the casserole dish. Gently heat through, then season to taste with salt and freshly ground black pepper. Return the vegetables to the dish, coating them with the sauce.

5 Scatter the cashews over the top and garnish with extra tarragon leaves. Serve with wholegrain or seeded bread.

PER SERVING 1179 kJ, 282 kcal, 10 g protein, 18 g fat (6 g saturated fat), 18 g carbohydrate (7 g sugars), 8 g fibre, 455 mg sodium

Slow cooker

If you have a slow cooker you can sauté in, or you don't mind using another pot, follow step 1 as above. (Alternatively, omit the oil and the sautéing step.) Transfer the carrots, potatoes and mushrooms to the slow cooker, along with the stock, wine and tarragon. Gently combine, then cover and cook on low for 7 hours.

Stir in the fully thawed broad beans and lay the asparagus on top. Cover and cook for a further 1 hour. Lift out the vegetables onto a plate, using a slotted spoon, then continue from step 4.

Slow-cooker spicy vegetable and pumpkin hotpot

Middle Eastern spices add an aromatic warmth to this wholesome vegetarian casserole. It is a great recipe for a cook-ahead meal — all the flavours will mature and improve if the dish is chilled overnight, then thoroughly reheated for serving.

- 1 leek, white part only, halved lengthwise and sliced
- 2 parsnips, halved lengthwise and thickly sliced
- 2 zucchini (courgettes), thickly sliced
- 1 red capsicum (bell pepper), chopped
- $^1/_2$ teaspoon ground turmeric
- $^1/_2$ teaspoon ground coriander
- $^1/_2$ teaspoon ground cumin
- pinch of dried red chilli flakes, or to taste (optional)
- $^1/_2$ cup (90 g) dried apricots, roughly chopped
- 420 g (15 oz) can butterbeans (lima beans), drained and rinsed
- 600 g ($1^1/_4$ lb) pumpkin (winter squash), peeled, seeded and cut into 4 cm ($1^1/_2$ inch) chunks
- 1 cup (250 ml) salt-reduced vegetable stock
- $^1/_4$ cup (40 g) toasted pine nuts
- chopped fresh parsley or coriander (cilantro), to garnish

To toast your own pine nuts, simply spread them in a frying pan and fry over medium heat without any oil for 1–2 minutes, or until they start to brown. Keep an eye on them and stir them often. As soon as they have browned, tip them onto a plate to cool, so they don't burn.

PREPARATION 25 minutes **COOKING** 6 hours **SERVES** 4

1 Combine the leek, parsnips, zucchini and capsicum in a 4–5 litre (4–5 quart) slow cooker. Sprinkle with the spices, then add the apricots and butterbeans. Arrange the pumpkin on top.

2 Pour the stock over. Cover and cook on low for 6 hours. Season to taste with salt and freshly ground black pepper.

3 Serve sprinkled with the pine nuts and garnished with chopped parsley or coriander.

PER SERVING 1199 kJ, 287 kcal, 13 g protein, 9 g fat (<1 g saturated fat), 37 g carbohydrate (22 g sugars), 11 g fibre, 441 mg sodium

On the stove

Heat 1 tablespoon olive oil in a large saucepan and sauté the leek and capsicum over medium heat for 5 minutes, or until softened. Add the remaining ingredients, the pine nuts and chopped herbs, increasing the stock to 2 cups (500 ml).

Cover and bring to a boil, then reduce the heat and simmer for 20–25 minutes, or until the vegetables are tender.

- Use any combination of canned beans available, such as red kidney, cannellini or mixed beans, to suit your preference.
- It's easy to make your own breadcrumbs. For fresh crumbs, cut the crusts off bread that isn't too stale. Cut the slices in half and briefly pulse in a food processor until crumbs form. To make dry breadcrumbs, process some stale bread in a food processor; there's no need to remove the crusts.

Mixed bean cassoulet

This vegetarian version of the hearty French country classic uses canned beans for a quick and easy one-pot. The enticing breadcrumb and herb crust contains nuts for extra crunch and protein.

- 1 tablespoon olive oil
- 1 onion, chopped
- 2 cloves garlic, crushed
- 1 butternut pumpkin (squash), peeled, seeded and diced
- 300 ml (10 fl oz) salt-reduced vegetable stock
- 410 g (15 oz) can chopped tomatoes
- 1 tablespoon tomato paste (concentrated purée)
- 2 bay leaves
- 2 sprigs fresh thyme
- 420 g (15 oz) can butterbeans, drained and rinsed
- 420 g (15 oz) can borlotti (cranberry) beans, drained and rinsed

Herb crust

- 1 cup (60 g) dry wholemeal (whole-wheat) breadcrumbs
- ⅓ cup (50 g) mixed nuts, coarsely chopped
- 2 tablespoons chopped fresh flat-leaf (Italian) parsley

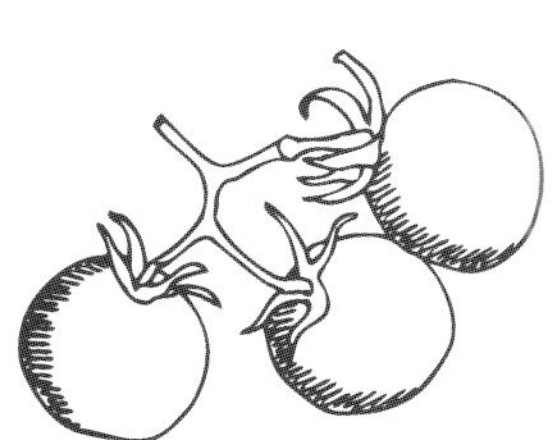

PREPARATION 20 minutes **COOKING** 55 minutes **SERVES** 4

1 Preheat the oven to 200°C (400°C/Gas 6). Heat the oil in a flameproof casserole dish and sauté the onion over medium heat for 5 minutes, or until softened. Add the garlic and pumpkin and cook for a further minute, stirring all the time.

2 Add the stock, tomatoes, tomato paste, bay leaves, thyme and beans and combine well. (The mixture may look slightly dry at this stage, but the pumpkin will produce extra juices as it cooks.) Slowly bring to a boil, then cover the dish, transfer to the oven and cook for 25 minutes.

3 Combine the herb crust ingredients. Remove the casserole from the oven and season to taste with salt and freshly ground black pepper. Scatter the breadcrumb mixture over the top.

4 Return the casserole to the oven, without the lid. Bake for a further 20 minutes, or until the crust is lightly browned. Serve hot.

PER SERVING 1872 kJ, 447 kcal, 18 g protein, 16 g fat (2 g saturated fat), 58 g carbohydrate (14 g sugars), 15 g fibre, 914 mg sodium

Slow cooker

If you have a slow cooker you can sauté in, or you don't mind using another pot, follow step 1 above. (Alternatively, omit the oil and the sautéing step.) Reduce the stock to 150 ml (5 fl oz) and transfer to the slow cooker with all the other ingredients, except those for the herb crust. Gently combine, then cover and cook on low for 6 hours. Omit the herb crust and instead serve with grainy bread.

Provençal bean hotpot

Bursting with antioxidants, this enticing dish stars healthy high-fibre legumes, simmered with loads of fresh Mediterranean vegetables and herbs. Soak your own beans if you have time, or just use canned beans for the ultimate in one-pot cooking convenience.

2 cups (440 g) dried mixed beans, such as chickpeas, red kidney beans, cannellini beans and butterbeans (lima beans), or 2 x 420 g (15 oz) cans mixed beans, drained and rinsed
1 tablespoon olive oil
1 onion, chopped
2 cloves garlic, crushed
1 red capsicum (bell pepper), diced
1 yellow capsicum (bell pepper), diced
750 g (1½ lb) ripe tomatoes, peeled and diced
finely grated zest of 1 lemon
2 tablespoons lemon juice
¼ cup (30 g) pitted black olives
½ cup (15 g) roughly chopped fresh flat-leaf (Italian) parsley
3 tablespoons roughly chopped fresh oregano
3 tablespoons roughly chopped fresh basil
lemon wedges, to serve
4 thick toasted sourdough slices, to serve

PREPARATION 20 minutes, plus overnight soaking if using dried beans
COOKING 25 minutes, or 45 minutes if using dried beans **SERVES** 4

1 If using dried beans, place them in a large bowl, cover with plenty of cold water and leave to soak overnight.

2 Drain the soaked dried beans and place in a large saucepan over high heat with plenty of fresh water. Bring to a boil, then boil for 30 minutes, or until the beans are tender. Drain well.

3 Meanwhile, heat the oil in a large non-stick frying pan and sauté the onion, garlic and capsicums over medium heat for 8 minutes, or until softened.

4 Stir in the tomatoes, lemon zest, lemon juice and ½ cup (125 ml) water and bring to a boil. Add the cooked or canned beans, along with the olives, half the parsley and half the oregano. Season with freshly ground black pepper and simmer for 10 minutes, or until the beans are soft and the mixture has thickened.

5 Sprinkle with the basil and remaining parsley and oregano. Serve with lemon wedges and toasted sourdough slices.

PER SERVING 1623 kJ, 388 kcal, 25 g protein, 9 g fat (1 g saturated fat), 47 g carbohydrate (10 g sugars), 23 g fibre, 110 mg sodium

---

- Dried beans are easy to cook, but acidic ingredients, such as tomatoes, can slow the cooking time and cause the beans to harden. For best results always make sure dried beans and lentils are cooked to your liking before combining them in a dish with your other ingredients.
- A speedy way to cook dried beans is in a pressure cooker. Soak them, drain and place in the cooker with fresh water. Cook under high pressure for about 10 minutes.

Sweet potato curry with paneer

So simple and quick to prepare, this mild, sweet, gingery vegetable curry is an all-round winner, whatever the season. Some red lentils would also go well in this dish. All you'll need alongside the curry are some naan bread, chapattis or steamed rice.

1 tablespoon vegetable oil
1 onion, chopped
2 cloves garlic, crushed
500 g (1 lb) orange sweet potatoes (kumara), peeled and cut into chunks
1 tablespoon mild curry powder
1 tablespoon finely chopped fresh ginger
410 g (15 oz) can chopped tomatoes
100 ml (3½ fl oz) salt-reduced vegetable stock
1 cup (155 g) frozen peas or shelled fresh peas
250 g (8 oz) paneer or firm tofu, cut into chunks
fresh mint leaves, to garnish

- Paneer is a soft, lightly pressed Indian cheese that is available in Indian grocery stores.
- For extra texture, scatter a handful of toasted almonds or walnuts over the curry just before serving.

PREPARATION 10 minutes **COOKING** 30 minutes **SERVES** 4

1 Heat the oil in a large frying pan sauté the onion and garlic over medium heat for 5 minutes, or until softened.

2 Add the sweet potatoes and cook, stirring, for 2 minutes. Stir in the curry powder and ginger and cook for 30 seconds.

3 Stir in the tomatoes and stock. Bring to a boil, then reduce the heat, cover and simmer for 12–15 minutes, or until the sweet potato is tender when pierced with a knife.

4 Stir in the peas and simmer for 3 minutes, then add the paneer and cook for a further 2 minutes, or until heated through.

5 Season to taste with salt and freshly ground black pepper. Garnish with the mint and serve.

PER SERVING 1419 kJ, 339 kcal, 15 g protein, 10 g fat (3 g saturated fat), 28 g carbohydrate (13 g sugars), 7 g fibre, 199 mg sodium

Red lentil and vegetable dal

A dal is a dish of simmered lentils, flavoured with aromatic spices and usually served as a sauce. Adding extra vegetables transforms it into a light and easy low-fat vegetarian meal. Serve with a selection of Indian-style breads and natural yogurt or raita.

1 onion, chopped
2 large garlic cloves, crushed
1 green chilli, seeded and chopped
1 carrot, grated
1 eggplant (aubergine), chopped
1 tablespoon vegetable oil
1 teaspoon ground cumin
1 teaspoon mild curry powder
2 teaspoons black mustard seeds
150 g (5 oz) split red lentils
800 ml (28 fl oz) salt-reduced vegetable stock
1 zucchini (courgette), halved and sliced
1 large tomato, chopped
2 tablespoons chopped fresh coriander (cilantro)

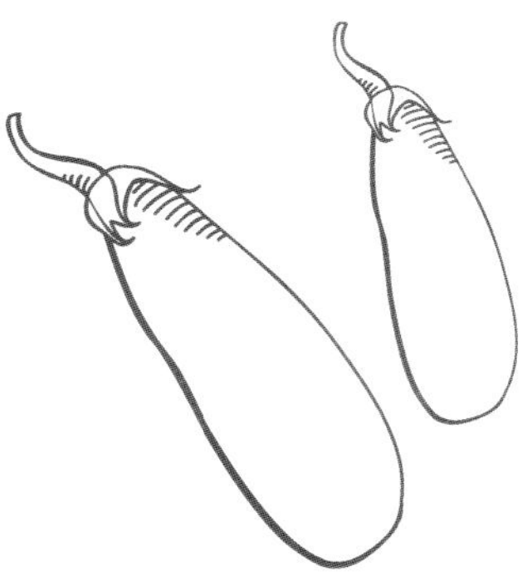

PREPARATION 15 minutes **COOKING** 30 minutes **SERVES** 4

1 Place the onion, garlic, chilli, carrot and eggplant in a flameproof casserole dish or large saucepan. Stir in the oil and 2 tablespoons water. Heat until the mixture starts to sizzle, then cover and cook gently for 5 minutes, or until the eggplant has softened.

2 Stir in the spices and cook for 1 minute, then stir in the lentils and stock. Bring to a boil, then add the zucchini and tomato.

3 Cover and simmer gently for 15 minutes. Remove the lid and cook for a further 5 minutes, or until the lentils burst open and thicken the dal. Season to taste with salt and freshly ground black pepper, sprinkle with the coriander and serve.

PER SERVING 856 kJ, 205 kcal, 12 g protein, 7 g fat (<1 g saturated fat), 25 g carbohydrate (9 g sugars), 9 g fibre, 839 mg sodium

Slow cooker

If you have a slow cooker you can sauté in, or you don't mind using another pot, follow step 1 as above. (Alternatively, omit the vegetable softening step.) Transfer all the ingredients to the slow cooker, except the coriander, and gently combine.

Cover and cook on low for 8 hours, or on high for 4 hours. Season to taste, sprinkle with the coriander and serve.

- The dal can be made a day in advance, then reheated; you may need to add a little more water if it has thickened too much. It is also suitable for freezing.
- For a more authentic dal, use yellow split peas instead of the lentils. These will need to be soaked in cold water for about 2 hours first.
- Instead of zucchini, stir in 250 g (8 oz) baby English spinach leaves at the end of the cooking time and leave to wilt for about 2 minutes before seasoning.

Thai pumpkin and eggplant curry

Other vegetables also work well in this curry — try chopped onion, potatoes, carrots and green beans, or whole peas. For extra protein, add chickpeas, lentils or diced tofu for a vegetarian meal, or even beef, chicken or firm fish fillets. Serve with steamed rice or cooked rice noodles.

1 tablespoon peanut or corn oil
4 tablespoons red curry paste, or to taste
270 ml (9½ fl oz) can light coconut cream
500 g (1 lb) pumpkin (winter squash), peeled, seeded and cut into 2.5 cm (1 inch) cubes
300 g (10 oz) Lebanese or Thai eggplants (aubergines), sliced
4 tablespoons chopped coriander (cilantro) leaves

- The long, thin Lebanese eggplant and small, round Thai eggplant are available in season from good greengrocers and Asian grocery stores.
- There is no need to salt Lebanese or Thai eggplant.
- Instead of red curry paste, try a green or massaman curry paste and add 2–3 teaspoons sugar to reduce the curry 'heat'.
- Instead of coriander, use Thai basil leaves and/or thinly sliced kaffir lime (makrut) leaves. If using lime leaves, first remove the stems by folding the leaf in half and pulling the spine downwards.

PREPARATION 10 minutes **COOKING** 15 minutes **SERVES** 4

1 Heat the oil in a large saucepan over medium heat. Add the curry paste and fry gently for 2 minutes, or until the paste begins to release its fragrant aromas, stirring occasionally.

2 Stir in the coconut cream and ½ cup (125 ml) water and bring to a boil. Add the pumpkin and eggplants, reduce the heat and simmer for 10–12 minutes, or until the pumpkin is tender.

3 Serve in small bowls, sprinkled with the coriander.

PER SERVING 916 kJ, 219 kcal, 5 g protein, 16 g fat (10 g saturated fat), 14 g carbohydrate (9 g sugars), 3 g fibre, 39 mg sodium

Speedy spinach and lentil curry

There are many Indian-style curry sauces sold in supermarkets these days, so pick your favourite for this amazingly simple recipe. For a milder and creamier sauce, add yogurt or coconut milk.

1 cup (250 ml) ready-made Indian-style curry sauce, such as korma or rogan josh
1 large onion, cut into wedges
420 g (15 oz) can lentils, drained and rinsed
250 g (8 oz) baby English spinach leaves
2 tablespoons chopped fresh coriander (cilantro) leaves
lemon wedges, to serve (optional)

- Serve with steamed basmati or jasmine rice (Thai fragrant rice) — see page 310.
- Replace the lentils with canned chickpeas or mixed beans.
- Use dried lentils rather than canned lentils if using a slow cooker.

PREPARATION 5 minutes **COOKING** 10 minutes **SERVES** 4

1 Pour the curry sauce and ¾ cup (180 ml) water into a large saucepan, combine well and bring to a boil. Add the onion and simmer over medium–low heat for 5 minutes.

2 Stir the lentils and spinach into the curry. Simmer for 2–3 minutes, or until the spinach has wilted and the lentils have heated through.

3 Season to taste with salt and freshly ground black pepper, garnish with the coriander and serve with lemon wedges if desired.

PER SERVING 663 kJ, 158 kcal, 7 g protein, 8 g fat (2 g saturated fat), 15 g carbohydrate (7 g sugars), 6 g fibre, 966 mg sodium

Slow cooker

In a slow cooker, combine 1 cup (185 g) brown or green dried lentils, the curry sauce, onion and 2 cups (500 ml) water. Gently combine, then cover and cook on low for 8 hours.

Stir the spinach leaves into the curry, then cover and cook for a further 5 minutes, or until the leaves have just wilted. Finish as directed in step 3.

Add the rice and stir until coated with the oil.

Stir in the hot stock, one ladleful at a time.

When the rice is tender, stir in the mozzarella.

Pumpkin and corn risotto

A vibrant, golden yellow vegetarian risotto that looks good, tastes wonderful — and is good for you too. The mozzarella added right at the end melts into creamy goodness. This risotto is perfect for lunch or a light dinner and is good served with a crisp green leaf salad.

2 tablespoons olive oil
1 onion, finely chopped
1 clove garlic, crushed
1 cup (220 g) risotto rice
500 g (1 lb) pumpkin (winter squash), or 1 small butternut pumpkin (squash), peeled, seeded and cut into small chunks
2 large fresh sage leaves, finely chopped
pinch of saffron threads
850 ml (29 fl oz) salt-reduced vegetable stock, hot
1 cup (150 g) frozen corn kernels
125 g (4 oz) mozzarella, diced
⅓ cup (50 g) pepitas (pumpkin seeds)

- The secret of a good risotto lies in using the right rice — arborio, carnaroli or vialone nano — and a well-flavoured stock that should be added to the risotto gradually.
- In summer you can replace the pumpkin with zucchini (courgettes). Cut into small pieces and add to the risotto with the corn in step 4, as it does not need a long cooking time.
- For a 'green' risotto, omit the saffron, sage and pumpkin. Instead add 150 g (5 oz) chopped baby English spinach leaves and 2 tablespoons chopped fresh basil with the corn in step 4.

PREPARATION 15 minutes **COOKING** 30 minutes **SERVES** 4

1 Heat the oil in a large heavy-based saucepan or large deep frying pan with a lid. Sauté the onion and garlic over medium heat for 5 minutes, or until softened.

2 Add the rice and stir until coated with the oil. Stir in the pumpkin and sage and cook for a further 2 minutes. Stir the saffron into the hot stock, then pour about one-quarter of the stock into the pan. Stir frequently until it has almost all been absorbed.

3 Continue adding the stock, only a ladleful at a time, making sure each one is almost completely absorbed before adding the next, and stirring frequently to produce a creamy texture.

4 With the last addition of stock, add the corn and stir well. Once all the stock has been absorbed and the rice is tender, which will take about 20 minutes, stir in the mozzarella.

5 Season to taste with salt and freshly ground black pepper. Cover and leave to stand for 5 minutes. Sprinkle with the pepitas and serve.

PER SERVING 2279 kJ, 545 kcal, 20 g protein, 24 g fat (8 g saturated fat), 62 g carbohydrate (12 g sugars), 5 g fibre, 995 mg sodium

Slow cooker

Preheat the slow cooker to high. Combine the oil, onion and garlic in the cooker, then cover and cook for 15 minutes. Stir in the rice and pumpkin, coating them with the oil. Stir in the stock and cook on high for 1 hour. Stir in the corn, then cover and cook for a further 30 minutes.

Stir in the mozzarella and season to taste. Cover and leave to stand for 5 minutes. Sprinkle with the pepitas and serve.

Quick bean and chorizo hotpot

Just about anything goes in this heart-warming hotpot. Use bacon instead of chorizo, or add chopped black olives, and herbs such as fresh basil, oregano or thyme. Use canned herbed tomatoes instead of paprika and Tabasco, or serve sprinkled with crunchy breadcrumbs.

- 2 chorizo sausages, about 300 g (10 oz), diced
- ½ teaspoon smoked paprika
- 1 green or red capsicum (bell pepper), diced
- 2 x 420 g (15 oz) cans mixed beans, drained and rinsed
- 800 g (28 oz) can chopped tomatoes
- 1–2 teaspoons Tabasco sauce, or to taste
- ⅓ cup (35 g) grated pecorino or parmesan

PREPARATION 5 minutes **COOKING** 15 minutes **SERVES** 4

1. Heat a flameproof shallow casserole dish (or a frying pan with a heatproof handle) over medium–high heat. Sauté the chorizo for 2–3 minutes. Stir in the paprika and capsicum and cook for 1 minute.

2. Stir in the beans, tomatoes and Tabasco sauce. Bring to a gentle boil, then reduce the heat and simmer for 6–8 minutes.

3. Meanwhile, preheat the grill (broiler) to high. Sprinkle the cheese over the hotpot, then place under the hot grill and cook for 2–3 minutes, or until the cheese starts to melt. Serve hot.

PER SERVING 1510 kJ, 361 kcal, 22 g protein, 17 g fat (8 g saturated fat), 30 g carbohydrate (11 g sugars), 11 g fibre, 1454 mg sodium

---

To make mini bean casseroles, place a large saucepan over medium–high heat. Add the diced chorizo and cook for 2 minutes, stirring occasionally. Reduce the heat to medium, stir in the tomatoes, capsicum and beans and simmer for 6–8 minutes. Divide the mixture among four 1 cup (250 ml) heatproof ramekins and sprinkle with the cheese. Grill (broil) for 2 minutes, or until the cheese has melted. Serve hot.

Bean and vegetable surprise

Even kids love vegetables when they're packaged up like this — teamed with baked beans, spiced with barbecue sauce and topped with melting cheese and sliced potatoes. You can also use peeled sweet potatoes; blanch them for 3 minutes in boiling water with some lemon juice to stop them browning.

- 600 g (1¼ lb) thin-skinned potatoes, scrubbed and very thinly sliced
- 25 g (1 oz) butter, or 1½ tablespoons olive oil
- 1 teaspoon sun-dried tomato paste
- 420 g (15 oz) can baked beans
- 125 g (4 oz) frozen peas
- 1 cup (125 g) frozen green beans
- 200 g (7 oz) can corn, drained
- 2 tablespoons barbecue sauce
- 100 g (3½ oz) smoked cheese, roughly chopped

- There are many varieties of potato, and some are better suited than others to different cooking methods. Look for those labelled 'all purpose' or 'general purpose' to simplify your shopping and food preparation.
- Any combination of prepared frozen, blanched fresh, or left-over cooked vegetables can be used in this dish.
- To add extra protein, use frozen soybeans instead of the peas or green beans.

PREPARATION 15 minutes **COOKING** 40 minutes **SERVES** 4

1 Preheat the oven to 200°C (400°F/Gas 6). Half-fill a flameproof casserole dish with lightly salted boiling water. Add the potato slices and return to a boil. Half-cover with the lid and simmer for 4 minutes, or until the potatoes are just tender, but not breaking up.

2 Drain the potatoes well, reserving 4 tablespoons of the cooking water. Tip the potato slices into a bowl, add the butter or oil and gently toss using two wooden spoons to lightly coat all over. Set aside.

3 Blend the sun-dried tomato paste and the reserved hot water in the casserole dish. Stir in the baked beans, peas, green beans, corn and barbecue sauce. Gently heat until the mixture is barely warm, and the peas and green beans have thawed.

4 Spread the mixture out in the dish, in an even layer. Scatter with the cheese. Arrange the potato slices over the top, overlapping them slightly so they completely cover the bean and cheese mixture.

5 Transfer to the oven and bake, uncovered, for 30 minutes, or until the potatoes are tender and the top is golden brown.

PER SERVING 1559 kJ, 372 kcal, 17 g protein, 13 g fat (8 g saturated fat), 45 g carbohydrate (12 g sugars), 10 g fibre, 965 mg sodium

White beans with silverbeet

This simple, versatile and health-giving dish could be a vegetarian main course, or served as part of a buffet or banquet. It is also wonderful as a side dish to meat or chicken.

- 2 tablespoons olive oil
- 1 small onion, finely chopped
- 1 carrot, finely chopped
- 1 teaspoon dried oregano
- 1 bay leaf
- 2 cloves garlic, crushed
- 250 g (8 oz) silverbeet (Swiss chard), tough stems removed, leaves coarsely chopped
- 1 cup (250 ml) salt-reduced chicken stock
- 3 x 420 g (15 oz) cans cannellini or butterbeans (lima beans), drained and rinsed
- ½ cup (50 g) grated parmesan

Instead of cannellini beans, you can use another type of white bean — or for a nutty flavour, try making this dish with chickpeas. Vary the herbs, too. Fresh thyme, parsley or chervil all work well.

PREPARATION 10 minutes **COOKING** 25 minutes **SERVES** 8

1 Heat the oil in a large non-stick frying pan over medium heat. Sauté the onion, carrot, oregano and bay leaf for 8 minutes, or until the onion and carrot are very soft. Add the garlic and sauté for 30 seconds.

2 Add the silverbeet and stock and cook for 2 minutes, or until the silverbeet begins to wilt, stirring occasionally. Stir in the beans, then cover and simmer for 10 minutes.

3 Remove the lid and cook for a further 5 minutes, or until the silverbeet is tender. Season to taste with salt and freshly ground black pepper. Remove the bay leaf, sprinkle with the parmesan and serve.

PER SERVING 603 kJ, 144 kcal, 9 g protein, 7 g fat (2 g saturated fat), 12 g carbohydrate (3 g sugars), 7 g fibre, 467 mg sodium

Ratatouille

In an old-style ratatouille, the vegetables are cooked separately and the dish is assembled at the end. This quick, one-pan method is just as good — and far more convenient.

- 2 tablespoons olive oil
- 1 onion, chopped
- 2 cloves garlic, crushed
- 1 red capsicum (bell pepper), cut into small chunks
- 2 zucchini (courgettes), cut in half lengthwise, then into bite-sized chunks
- 1 eggplant (aubergine), cut into bite-sized chunks
- 5 ripe tomatoes, cored and chopped
- 2 tablespoons shredded fresh basil, plus extra leaves to garnish

---

- If your tomatoes aren't super-ripe, you can enrich the dish by adding 1 tablespoon tomato paste (concentrated purée), or use an 800 g (28 oz) can of chopped Italian tomatoes.
- When seasoning tomato-based dishes, a good pinch of sugar often rounds out the flavour.
- To make a delicious vegetarian meal, add a drained 420 g (15 oz) can of chickpeas towards the end of cooking and heat through. Serve with crusty bread.

PREPARATION 20 minutes **COOKING** 35 minutes **SERVES** 6

1 Heat the oil in a large heavy-based saucepan and sauté the onion over medium–low heat for 7 minutes, or until soft and golden. Add the garlic and sauté for a further 1 minute.

2 Add the capsicum and cook for 2 minutes, stirring occasionally. Add the zucchini and eggplant and stir until well combined.

3 Stir in the tomatoes and bring to a boil. Reduce the heat to low and partially cover with a lid. Simmer, stirring occasionally, for 20 minutes, or until the vegetables are tender.

4 Stir in the basil and season with salt and freshly ground black pepper. Serve hot or warm, scattered with extra basil leaves.

PER SERVING 392 kJ, 94 kcal, 3 g protein, 7 g fat (<1 g saturated fat), 6 g carbohydrate (5 g sugars), 4 g fibre, 13 mg sodium

Slow cooker

If you have a slow cooker you can sauté in, or you don't mind using another pot, follow step 1 as above. (Alternatively, omit the oil and the sautéing step.) Transfer all the ingredients to the slow cooker, except the basil. Gently combine, then cover and cook on low for 4 hours. Stir in the basil and season to taste. Serve garnished with extra basil.

Vegetarian chilli beans

Served with steamed rice or crusty bread, this dish makes a complete one-pot meal. You can also use the beans as a filling for warmed tortillas, with shredded lettuce, sour cream and avocado.

- 1 tablespoon olive oil
- 1 onion, chopped
- 2 cloves garlic, crushed
- 1 teaspoon paprika
- 1 teaspoon ground cumin
- 1/2 teaspoon dried red chilli flakes
- 800 g (28 oz) can chopped tomatoes
- 150 g (5 oz) chopped roasted capsicum (bell pepper)
- 2 x 420 g (15 oz) cans red kidney beans, drained and rinsed
- 300 g (10 oz) jar tomato salsa
- 3 spring onions (scallions), sliced on the diagonal
- 3 tablespoons chopped fresh parsley

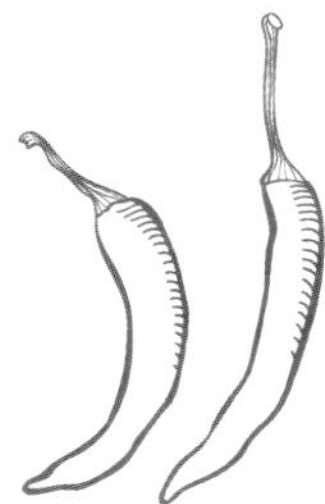

PREPARATION 10 minutes **COOKING** 20 minutes **SERVES** 4

1 Heat the oil in a saucepan over medium heat and sauté the onion for 5 minutes, or until softened. Stir in the garlic, paprika, cumin and chilli flakes and cook for a further 1 minute.

2 Stir in the tomatoes, capsicum, beans and salsa and bring to a boil. Reduce the heat and simmer for 10 minutes, or until the mixture has thickened, stirring occasionally.

3 Stir in the spring onions and parsley and serve.

PER SERVING 1051 kJ, 251 kcal, 12 g protein, 7 g fat (<1 g saturated fat), 33 g carbohydrate (16 g sugars), 13 g fibre, 894 mg sodium

---

- Roasted capsicum can be bought in jars and at the delicatessen counter in supermarkets. Drain off the oil before using.
- For a chilli beef version, cook 250 g (8 oz) lean minced (ground) beef with the onion, then continue with the recipe.
- Freeze any leftover chilli in an airtight container. Thaw it in the fridge for 24 hours before reheating.

- Some companies produce packaged biryani spice mixes, which you can use instead of the spices in this recipe.
- A good accompaniment to the biryani is a simple cucumber or tomato salad. Combine 1 chopped cucumber and a few mint leaves or 2 chopped tomatoes and a few sprigs of fresh coriander (cilantro).
- Make sure the casserole dish you use is flameproof and suitable for stovetop use as well as for the oven.

Mixed vegetable biryani

Here is a vegetarian one-pot feast of golden saffron-scented basmati rice combined with spiced vegetables. Serve with a cooling banana mint raita or a simple cucumber and mint salad.

1½ cups (300 g) basmati rice, rinsed
pinch of saffron threads
3 tablespoons vegetable oil
1 onion, thinly sliced
⅓ cup (40 g) raisins
1 cinnamon stick, broken in half
8 black peppercorns
6 cloves
seeds from 6 green cardamom pods, crushed
1 tablespoon coriander seeds, lightly crushed
2 teaspoons ground cumin
½ teaspoon cayenne pepper
4 cloves garlic, crushed
200 g (7 oz) new potatoes, scrubbed and cubed
1 carrot, thinly sliced
150 g (5 oz) thin green beans, trimmed and chopped
1 zucchini (courgette), thinly sliced
1 cup (155 g) frozen peas, thawed
¾ cup (200 g) thick (Greek-style) yogurt
3 hard-boiled eggs, shelled and quartered
1 tablespoon flaked almonds, lightly toasted
fresh coriander (cilantro) leaves, to garnish

PREPARATION 20 minutes **COOKING** 1 hour **SERVES** 6

1 Put the rice in a large flameproof casserole dish with the saffron, 2¼ cups (560 ml) water and a pinch of salt. Stir together and bring to a boil. Reduce the heat to low, then cover the pan tightly with a lid. Leave to simmer for 10 minutes, or until the liquid has been absorbed and the rice is just starting to become tender. Remove the rice from the dish and set aside.

2 Heat 1 tablespoon of the oil in the casserole dish. Add the onion and sauté over medium–low heat for 10 minutes, or until golden. Remove the onion to a plate. Add the raisins to the dish and stir for 30 seconds to coat with the oil, then remove and set aside with the onion.

3 Heat the remaining oil in the dish. Add the cinnamon, peppercorns, cloves, cardamom and coriander seeds and stir for 1 minute. Reduce the heat to low. Add the cumin, cayenne pepper and garlic and stir for a further 30–60 seconds, or until the spices smell aromatic.

4 Stir in all the vegetables, then gradually add the yogurt, still over low heat. Stir in ⅓ cup (80 ml) water, cover the pan tightly and leave the vegetables to gently simmer for 12 minutes.

5 Spoon the cooked rice on top of the vegetables. Cover tightly and gently cook for a further 10–15 minutes, or until both the rice and vegetables are tender. (Alternatively you can layer the vegetable curry and rice in the dish, cover tightly and bake in a preheated 180°C/350°F/ Gas 4 oven for 20–30 minutes.)

6 Scatter the reserved onion and raisins over the top of the biryani. Garnish with the egg quarters, sprinkle with the almonds and coriander and serve.

PER SERVING 1844 kJ, 441 kcal, 13 g protein, 17 g fat (4 g saturated fat), 60 g carbohydrate (11 g sugars), 5 g fibre, 91 mg sodium

Spicy vegetable tagine

Although a one-pot dish on its own, this tagine is superb with the quick and easy couscous recipe given below. If you can't find dried cherries, use dried or frozen cranberries instead.

- 2 tablespoons olive oil
- 1 large red onion, chopped
- 4 cloves garlic, sliced
- 1 tablespoon shredded fresh ginger
- 500 g (1 lb) butternut pumpkin (squash), peeled, seeded and cut into bite-sized chunks
- 1 teaspoon ground cinnamon
- 1 teaspoon ground cumin
- 1 teaspoon ground coriander
- seeds from 6 green cardamom pods, lightly crushed
- 3 bay leaves
- 800 g (28 oz) can chopped tomatoes
- 250 g (8 oz) large carrots, thickly sliced
- 300 ml (10 fl oz) vegetable stock
- 1/3 cup (40 g) raisins
- 1/3 cup (30 g) dried cherries
- 125 g (4 oz) okra, sliced lengthwise into thirds
- 1 large red capsicum (bell pepper), chopped
- 420 g (15 oz) can chickpeas or red kidney beans, drained and rinsed
- 1/3 cup (30 g) toasted flaked almonds
- chopped flat-leaf (Italian) parsley leaves, to garnish

For a quick spicy couscous, put 350 g (12 oz) instant couscous in a large heatproof bowl. Stir in 2 cups (500 ml) boiling vegetable stock, 1 tablespoon olive oil, 1 teaspoon chilli sauce or harissa, 1/2 teaspoon ground coriander and 1/2 teaspoon ground cumin. Cover and leave for 5 minutes for the liquid to absorb. Just before serving, separate the grains with a fork.

PREPARATION 25 minutes **COOKING** 30 minutes **SERVES** 4

1 Heat the oil in a large saucepan and sauté the onion over high heat for 2–3 minutes, or until beginning to soften and colour. Toss in the garlic and ginger and cook for a few more seconds. Tip in the pumpkin and sauté for 1 minute.

2 Reduce the heat and add all the spices, along with the bay leaves, tomatoes and carrots. Pour in the stock, then stir in the raisins and cherries. Bring back to a boil, reduce the heat, then cover and simmer for 10 minutes.

3 Stir the okra and capsicum into the stew. Cover and leave to simmer for 5 minutes.

4 Stir in the chickpeas and simmer for a further 5–10 minutes, or until all the vegetables are tender but still retain their shape and texture. Sprinkle with the toasted almonds and parsley and serve.

PER SERVING 1498 kJ, 358 kcal, 11 g protein, 15 g fat (2 g saturated fat), 49 g carbohydrate (25 g sugars), 14 g fibre, 589 mg sodium

Slow cooker

Browning the onion adds depth of flavour to the dish, so if you have a slow cooker you can sauté in, or you don't mind using another pot, follow step 1 as above. (Alternatively, reduce the oil to 1 tablespoon and omit the sautéing step.)

Reduce the stock to 150 ml (5 fl oz) and add to the slow cooker with all the remaining ingredients, except the almonds and parsley. Gently combine, then cover and cook on low for 6 hours. Sprinkle with the toasted almonds and parsley and serve.

Slow-cooker layered potato bake

This classic side dish works well in the slow cooker. Choose boiling (waxy) potatoes, and if the skin is clean just give them a rinse and leave it on, saving lots of time. For a light meal, simply serve the potato bake with a simple green salad topped with tomato wedges and a light oil dressing.

- vegetable oil, for brushing
- 1.25 kg ($2\frac{1}{2}$ lb) desiree potatoes, very finely sliced
- 1 onion, halved and finely sliced
- 3 cloves garlic, finely sliced
- 1 tablespoon finely chopped fresh rosemary leaves
- 1 cup (250 ml) milk
- 1 cup (250 ml) cream
- $\frac{2}{3}$ cup (85 g) grated cheddar

PREPARATION 20 minutes **COOKING** 6 hours **SERVES** 6–8

1 Brush the inside of a 5 litre (5 quart) slow cooker with oil. Arrange one-quarter of the potato slices in a layer over the base. Scatter with one-third of the onion, garlic and rosemary, then lightly season with salt and freshly ground black pepper.

2 Continue layering the ingredients, finishing with a layer of potato. Pour the milk and cream over, then sprinkle with the cheese. Cover and cook on low for 6 hours.

PER SERVING 1661 kJ, 397 kcal, 11 g protein, 25 g fat (16 g saturated fat), 33 g carbohydrate (5 g sugars), 5 g fibre, 227 mg sodium

- You can replace the rosemary with thyme, or use a mixture of each.
- The cream gives this dish its characteristic richness, but if you would like a lighter version, omit the cream and increase the milk to 2 cups (500 ml).

In the oven

Preheat the oven to 180°C (350°F/Gas 4). Brush an 8 cup (2 litre) shallow baking dish with vegetable oil. Layer the ingredients in the dish as directed in steps 1 and 2, leaving off the cheese. Cover with foil and bake for 1 hour.

Sprinkle with the cheese, replace the foil and bake for a further 1 hour, or until the potato is tender.

Slow-cooker tortellini with chicken

This recipe uses fresh tortellini, sold in the refrigerated section of the supermarket. The pasta pieces sometimes clump together in the packet, so gently pull them apart before adding them to the dish. To keep the cooker at a constant heat, replace the lid as quickly as possible after adding the pasta.

500 g (1 lb) boneless, skinless chicken thighs
150 g (5 oz) button mushrooms, thickly sliced
1½ cups (375 ml) chicken stock
1½ cups (375 g) tomato passata (puréed tomatoes)
500 g (1 lb) spinach and ricotta tortellini
1 cup (45 g) baby English spinach leaves
grated parmesan, to serve

- Use any filled pasta, such as ravioli or agnolotti. A cheese or vegetable-filled pasta works best, given there is already meat in the dish.
- If you aren't a fan of mushrooms, replace them with diced pumpkin (winter squash) or sweet potato, or add some thawed frozen peas or chopped green beans when you add the pasta.

PREPARATION 15 minutes **COOKING** 6 hours **SERVES** 4

1 Trim the excess fat from the chicken and cut the meat into 4 cm (1½ inch) chunks. Place in a 5 litre (5 quart) slow cooker with the mushrooms, stock and passata. Stir to combine, then cover and cook on low for 5½ hours.

2 Add the pasta and give a quick stir. Replace the lid and cook for a further 30 minutes.

3 Fold the spinach through; it will quickly wilt in the hot mixture. Season to taste with salt and freshly ground black pepper, sprinkle with parmesan and serve.

PER SERVING 1501 kJ, 359 kcal, 34 g protein, 13 g fat (4 g saturated fat), 26 g carbohydrate (10 g sugars), 4 g fibre, 911 mg sodium

In the oven

You can cook this dish in the oven, though you will need to boil the tortellini according to the packet directions first, and brown the chicken in a little olive oil. Layer the cooked pasta and chicken in a baking dish with the pasta and spinach, omitting the stock. Sprinkle with grated cheddar or mozzarella.

Bake in a preheated 180°C (350°F/Gas 4) oven for 20 minutes, or until the cheese is golden brown.

Slow-cooker mushroom risotto

Everyone loves a good risotto, but sometimes all the stirring involved seems a bit of a chore. Well, relax. This simply delicious risotto virtually cooks itself for a fuss-free meal or side dish.

10 g (1/4 oz) dried porcini mushrooms
3 tablespoons butter
1 small onion, finely chopped
1 clove garlic, crushed
1 1/2 cups (330 g) arborio or risotto rice
1/4 cup (60 ml) white wine
4 cups (1 litre) salt-reduced chicken stock, heated
200 g (7 oz) mixed fresh mushrooms, such as button, Swiss brown and oyster, halved or sliced
1 tablespoon chopped fresh parsley
1/2 cup (50 g) grated parmesan, plus extra shaved parmesan to serve

---

Porcini mushrooms have a beautifully earthy, slightly nutty flavour. They are not so easy to come by fresh, but the dried variety are readily available from gourmet food stores and some larger supermarkets. The dried mushrooms need to be rehydrated in water before using in dishes. Be sure to reserve the soaking liquid to use as stock.

PREPARATION 15 minutes **COOKING** 1 hour 25 minutes **SERVES** 4

1 Put the porcini mushrooms in a small heatproof bowl. Pour 1/2 cup (125 ml) boiling water over and leave to soak for 20 minutes.

2 Meanwhile, heat the slow cooker to high. Add about 1 tablespoon of the butter, and all the onion and garlic. Cover and cook for 10–15 minutes, or until the onion has softened slightly, stirring now and then. (If your slow cooker has a browning option, use this instead and sauté for 5 minutes.)

3 Add the rice and stir to combine, ensuring the grains are coated in the butter. Add the soaked porcini mushrooms and their liquid, along with the wine, hot stock and fresh mushrooms. Stir to combine.

4 Cover and cook for 1 hour 10 minutes, or until most of the liquid has been absorbed and the rice is tender.

5 Stir the parsley and grated parmesan through, along with the remaining butter. Season to taste with salt and freshly ground black pepper, top with shaved parmesan and serve.

PER SERVING 2140 kJ, 511 kcal, 17 g protein, 17 g fat (11 g saturated fat), 70 g carbohydrate (4 g sugars), 2 g fibre, 932 mg sodium

In the oven

Preheat the oven to 180°C (350°F/Gas 4). Follow steps 1 to 3 as above, using a flameproof casserole dish on the stovetop. Briefly bring to a boil, then cover and transfer to the oven. Bake for 30 minutes, or until the rice is just tender. Continue as directed in step 5.

Slow-cooker quinoa pilaf

A healthy South American grain, quinoa makes a nice change from rice or couscous as a side dish, or as a light vegetarian meal. This dish serves two people as a main, or four people as a side.

1 cup (200 g) quinoa
2 cups (500 ml) vegetable stock
1⅓ cups (60 g) baby English spinach leaves, shredded
1 tablespoon extra virgin olive oil
1 tablespoon lemon juice
2 teaspoons finely grated lemon zest
100 g (3½ oz) fetta, crumbled
2 tablespoons toasted slivered almonds

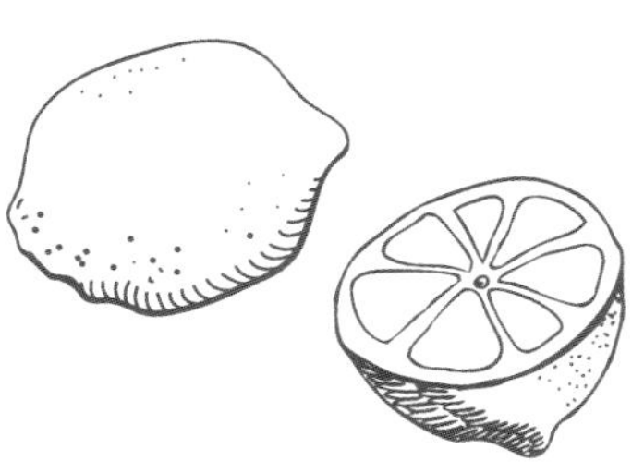

PREPARATION 15 minutes **COOKING** 2 hours **SERVES** 2–4

1 Place the quinoa in a fine sieve and rinse under running water. Leave for about 10 minutes to drain well.

2 Tip the quinoa into a 4 litre (4 quart) slow cooker and stir in the stock. Cover and cook on low for 1½ hours. Stir in the spinach, replace the lid and cook for a further 30 minutes.

3 Drizzle the quinoa with the oil and lemon juice. Add the lemon zest and fluff up the grains with a fork or large metal spoon. Mix the fetta through, sprinkle with the almonds and serve.

PER SERVING 2892 kJ, 691 kcal, 26 g protein, 32 g fat (10 g saturated fat), 77 g carbohydrate (5 g sugars), 8 g fibre, 1572 mg sodium

On the stove

Rinse and drain the quinoa as directed in step 1. Place in a large saucepan and stir in the stock. Cover and bring to a boil, then reduce the heat to low and cook for 12 minutes, or until the quinoa has absorbed all the stock. Stir in the spinach, replace the lid and leave to stand for 5 minutes for the spinach to wilt. Finish the recipe as directed in step 3.

Kedgeree

A popular breakfast dish from the days of the British Raj, kedgeree is equally as good for lunch or an easy light dinner. Add a contemporary twist by using canned salmon instead of smoked cod.

- 400 g (14 oz) smoked cod, or any other smoked fish
- 2 cups (500 ml) milk, approximately
- 2 tablespoons butter
- 1 small onion, finely chopped
- 1 teaspoon curry powder
- 3 cups (555 g) cold, cooked long-grain rice
- 4 hard-boiled eggs, shelled and quartered
- 2 tablespoons finely chopped fresh parsley
- lemon wedges, to serve

This is an ideal recipe for using up leftover rice, and any type of leftover cooked fish.

PREPARATION 10 minutes **COOKING** 25 minutes **SERVES** 4

1 Place the fish in a large deep frying pan with a lid. Pour in enough milk to just cover the fish. Bring to a simmer over medium heat, then reduce the heat to low. Cover and gently simmer for 15 minutes, or until the fish is just cooked — the flesh will be opaque and will flake easily when tested with a fork. Drain, then break into large flakes.

2 Wipe out the frying pan, then melt the butter in the pan over medium heat. Sauté the onion and curry powder for 5 minutes, or until the onion has softened.

3 Add the rice and stir well to coat in the butter. Add the fish and stir gently for 3 minutes, or until heated through.

4 Top with the egg quarters, sprinkle with the parsley and serve hot, with lemon wedges on the side.

PER SERVING 2047 kJ, 489 kcal, 33 g protein, 20 g fat (10 g saturated fat), 45 g carbohydrate (7 g sugars), 1 g fibre, 847 mg sodium

Risoni hotpot

Besides the salami, this versatile recipe can be whipped up from a handful of tasty ingredients from your pantry cupboards. Serve with good crusty bread to soak up those lovely juices.

1 tablespoon olive oil
1 onion, sliced
2 cloves garlic, crushed
180 g (6 oz) sliced salami, roughly chopped
800 g (28 oz) can chopped tomatoes
4 cups (1 litre) salt-reduced chicken stock
1 cup (220 g) risoni pasta
250 g (8 oz) marinated artichoke quarters
1/3 cup (50 g) sliced black olives
2 tablespoons chopped fresh parsley

- You can buy marinated artichokes by weight from the delicatessen section of supermarkets.
- For a hotter dish, add some chopped fresh chilli with the salami.
- For a heartier meal, add some chopped roasted capsicum (bell pepper), eggplant (aubergine) and sun-dried tomatoes.

PREPARATION 10 minutes **COOKING** 20 minutes **SERVES** 4

1 Heat the oil in a small saucepan and sauté the onion over medium heat for 5 minutes, or until softened. Add the garlic and salami and cook for a further 1 minute.

2 Pour in the tomatoes and stock and bring to a boil. Add the risoni and simmer for 8 minutes, stirring occasionally to stop the pasta sticking to the base of the pan.

3 Stir in the artichoke and olives and simmer for 2 minutes to heat through. Sprinkle with the parsley and serve.

PER SERVING 2260 kJ, 540 kcal, 21 g protein, 31 g fat (7 g saturated fat), 44 g carbohydrate (11 g sugars), 6 g fibre, 1842 mg sodium

Ravioli with beef and tomatoes

Dried oregano and rosemary add a Mediterranean flavour to this easy-cook beef and tomato sauce, in which fresh ravioli is then simply simmered. A vegetable-filled ravioli is ideal for this dish.

4 tablespoons olive oil
200 g (7 oz) minced (ground) beef
200 g (7 oz) minced (ground) pork
1 onion, diced
2 cloves garlic, finely chopped
1 teaspoon dried oregano
½ teaspoon dried rosemary
2 cups (500 ml) chicken stock
250 g (8 oz) zucchini (courgettes), cut into small cubes
800 g (28 oz) can chopped tomatoes
400 g (14 oz) ravioli
¼ cup (40 g) toasted pine nuts
small fresh basil leaves, to garnish
grated parmesan, to serve

For a quicker preparation time, omit the pine nuts and basil leaves, and simply stir 4 tablespoons basil pesto into the stew once it has been cooked.

PREPARATION 15 minutes **COOKING** 25 minutes **SERVES** 4

1 Heat half the oil in a heavy-based saucepan. Add the beef and pork and fry over high heat for 2 minutes, or until the meat has changed colour, breaking up the lumps with a wooden spoon.

2 Add the onion and garlic and sauté for 1 minute. Sprinkle with the oregano and rosemary and season with salt and freshly ground black pepper. Stir in the stock, bring to a boil, then reduce the heat to low. Cover and simmer for about 8 minutes.

3 Stir in the zucchini and cook for 5 minutes. Mix the tomatoes through and bring to a boil. Carefully stir in the ravioli and allow to gently heat in the sauce for about 5 minutes (check the packet for specific directions as the pasta cooking times can vary).

4 Sprinkle with the pine nuts, garnish with basil leaves and drizzle with the remaining 2 tablespoons oil. Serve with grated parmesan for sprinkling over.

PER SERVING 2407 kJ, 575 kcal, 34 g protein, 37 g fat (8 g saturated fat), 27 g carbohydrate (13 g sugars), 6 g fibre, 935 mg sodium

Slow cooker

You can cook this dish in a slow cooker, although the beef, pork, onion and garlic need to be sautéed first. (If your slow cooker doesn't have a browning option, use a frying pan and follow steps 1 and 2, then transfer the mixture to the slow cooker.)

Transfer all the ingredients to the slow cooker, except the zucchini, ravioli, pine nuts, basil and parmesan. Gently combine, then cover and cook on low for 7 hours.

Stir in the zucchini and ravioli. Cover and cook for a further 30 minutes, then continue from step 4.

Penne with tuna

This easy pasta dish with its no-cook topping is a great choice when time is short. Paired with a simple salad and perhaps some garlic bread, it makes a quick and satisfying midweek meal.

- 375 g (13 oz) penne or other short pasta
- 150 g (5 oz) green beans, trimmed and halved
- 1 tablespoon extra virgin olive oil
- 1 small red onion, finely sliced
- 200 g (7 oz) cherry tomatoes, halved
- 185 g (6 oz) can tuna in oil, drained and flaked

- This is a very versatile dish. Replace the tuna with canned or smoked salmon, and use peas instead of green beans.
- Instead of fresh tomatoes, use sun-dried tomatoes packed in oil, and toss some of the oil through the pasta.

PREPARATION 10 minutes **COOKING** 15 minutes **SERVES** 4

1 Bring a large saucepan of lightly salted water to a boil. Stir in the pasta and return to a boil. Cook, uncovered, for 8 minutes.

2 Add the beans, then return to a boil. Cook for a further 2 minutes, or until the pasta is al dente and the beans are cooked.

3 Drain the pasta and beans, then return them to the saucepan. Drizzle with the oil and add the onion, tomatoes and tuna. Season with freshly ground black pepper, gently toss together and serve.

PER SERVING 1962 kJ, 469 kcal, 19 g protein, 14 g fat (2 g saturated fat), 66 g carbohydrate (2 g sugars), 5 g fibre, 157 mg sodium

- To quickly trim and halve the beans, simply line them up on a chopping board, slice the ends off in one go, then cut the beans in half.
- For a vegetarian version, replace the tuna with crumbled ricotta or fetta, adding some canned chickpeas and finely grated lemon zest.

One-pot steak and fusilli casserole

Slim pasta spirals called fusilli help make a substantial casserole with beef and vegetables. Add the dried, uncooked pasta towards the end of the cooking time so that it retains its al dente texture while still absorbing the flavours of the other ingredients.

- 1 tablespoon olive oil
- 350 g (12 oz) lean braising steak, cut into 1 cm (1/2 inch) cubes
- 1 onion, chopped
- 410 g (15 oz) can chopped tomatoes
- 2 tablespoons tomato purée or tomato paste (concentrated purée)
- 2 cloves garlic, crushed
- 4 cups (1 litre) salt-reduced beef or vegetable stock
- 3 large carrots, sliced
- 4 celery stalks, sliced
- 1 small swede (rutabaga), about 400 g (14 oz), chopped
- 250 g (8 oz) fusilli or other pasta spirals
- 1 tablespoon chopped fresh oregano, or 1 teaspoon dried oregano

---

- For a more Mediterranean flavour, replace the carrots and swede with 2 chopped capsicums (bell peppers), adding them with the onion. Also add 175 g (6 oz) button mushrooms with the pasta.
- Try venison steak instead of the beef, and use whole baby carrots and baby turnips instead of the sliced carrots and chopped swede.

PREPARATION 15 minutes **COOKING** 1 hour 45 minutes **SERVES** 4

1 Heat the oil in a large flameproof casserole dish and brown the beef over medium–high heat, turning to brown all over. Remove to a plate using a slotted spoon.

2 Sauté the onion in the dish for 5 minutes, or until softened. Add the tomatoes, tomato purée or paste, garlic and half the stock. Stir well and bring to a boil.

3 Return the beef to the casserole. Add the carrots, celery and swede and season with salt and freshly ground black pepper. Bring to a gentle boil, then reduce the heat, cover and gently simmer for 1 hour, or until the meat is tender.

4 Stir in the pasta, oregano and the remaining stock. Bring back to a simmer, then reduce the heat and cover. Cook for 20–25 minutes, or until the pasta is al dente. Serve hot.

PER SERVING 2018 kJ, 482 kcal, 34 g protein, 10 g fat (3 g saturated fat), 63 g carbohydrate (15 g sugars), 9 g fibre, 1381 mg sodium

Slow cooker

Browning the beef and onion adds depth of flavour to this dish, so if you have a slow cooker you can sauté in, or you don't mind using another pot, follow steps 1 and 2 as above. (Alternatively, omit the oil and the browning and sautéing steps.)

Transfer all the ingredients to the slow cooker, except the pasta. Gently combine, then cover and cook on low for 7 hours. Stir in the pasta, then cover and cook for a further 45 minutes.

Slow-cooker pasta with meatballs

Such an easy way to make a favourite pasta dish — a true one-pot meal. Use a different short pasta shape if you like, such as spirals. If you don't have fresh basil handy, use parsley instead.

500 g (1 lb) minced (ground) beef
250 g (8 oz) minced (ground) pork
2 cloves garlic, crushed
1/2 cup (40 g) fresh breadcrumbs
1/4 cup (25 g) finely grated parmesan, plus extra to serve
1 carrot, finely chopped
2 celery stalks, finely chopped
750 g (1 1/2 lb) tomato passata (puréed tomatoes)
1 cup (250 ml) salt-reduced vegetable or chicken stock
300 g (10 oz) penne
pinch of sugar, or to taste
basil leaves, to garnish

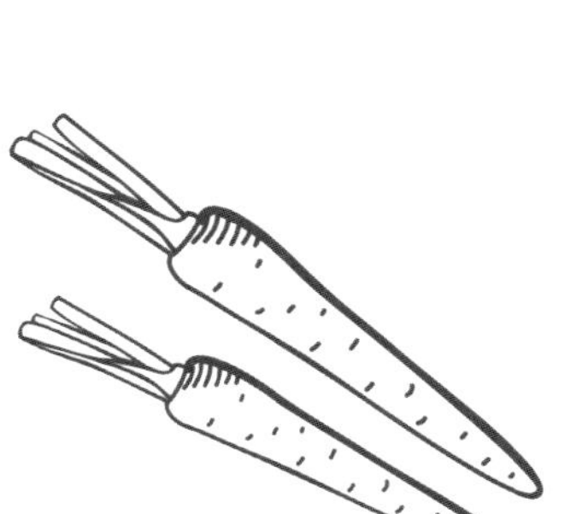

PREPARATION 25 minutes **COOKING** 6 hours 45 minutes **SERVES** 6

1 Place the beef, pork, garlic, breadcrumbs and parmesan in a bowl. Season with salt and freshly ground black pepper and mix well using your hands. Roll level tablespoons of the mixture into balls.

2 Combine the carrot and celery in a 5 litre (5 quart) slow cooker. Pour in the passata, stock and 4 cups (1 litre) water. Add the meatballs, then cover and cook on low for 6 hours.

3 Stir in the pasta, replace the lid and cook for a further 45 minutes, or until the pasta is tender and the sauce is thick.

4 Season with salt, pepper and a pinch of sugar to taste. Serve topped with extra parmesan and some basil leaves.

PER SERVING 1864 kJ, 445 kcal, 34 g protein, 13 g fat (5 g saturated fat), 47 g carbohydrate (8 g sugars), 5 g fibre, 834 mg sodium

On the stove

Make the meatballs as directed in step 1. Heat 1 tablespoon olive oil in a large, deep heavy-based frying pan and cook the meatballs in batches over medium–high heat until browned. Remove to a plate. Sauté the carrot and celery in the pan over medium heat for 5 minutes, or until softened slightly.

Add the passata and stock and bring to a boil. Return the meatballs to the pan, partially cover, then cook over low heat for 15 minutes, or until the meatballs are cooked through.

Meanwhile, cook the pasta in a large pan of boiling salted water until al dente. Serve the meatballs and sauce over the drained pasta.

Assorted
Cadbury's
Chocolate

Desserts

Slow-cooker self-saucing chocolate pudding

This fabulous old family favourite works a treat in the slow cooker, and is so easy to throw together. Scoop it straight from the cooker into serving bowls and watch it be devoured.

- vegetable oil, for brushing
- 1 cup (150 g) self-raising flour
- 2 tablespoons unsweetened cocoa powder
- 1/2 cup (115 g) caster (superfine) sugar
- 1 egg
- 1/2 cup (125 ml) milk
- 1 teaspoon vanilla extract
- 60 g (2 oz) butter, melted and cooled
- sifted icing (confectioners') sugar, for dusting
- vanilla ice-cream, to serve

Chocolate sauce

- 3/4 cup (140 g) soft brown sugar
- 2 tablespoons unsweetened cocoa powder

PREPARATION 15 minutes **COOKING** 2 hours 30 minutes **SERVES** 6

1 Lightly brush the inside of a 4 litre (4 quart) slow cooker with oil. Preheat the cooker to high.

2 Sift the flour and cocoa powder into a bowl, then stir in the sugar and make a well in the centre. Whisk together the egg, milk, vanilla and butter, add to the dry ingredients and fold together until smooth. Spoon the mixture into the slow cooker.

3 To make the chocolate sauce, put the sugar and cocoa powder in a jug. Stir in 1 3/4 cups (435 ml) boiling water and mix well to dissolve the sugar. Slowly pour the chocolate sauce over the batter, pouring it over the back of a spoon to help disperse the liquid evenly.

4 Cover and cook on low for 2 1/2 hours. Lightly dust with icing sugar and serve with ice-cream.

PER SERVING 1560 kJ, 373 kcal, 5 g protein, 12 g fat (7 g saturated fat), 62 g carbohydrate (44 g sugars), 1 g fibre, 283 mg sodium

In the oven

PREHEAT THE OVEN TO 180°C (350°F/Gas 4). Lightly brush an 8 cup (2 litre) baking dish with vegetable oil. Prepare the batter as directed in step 2 and spoon it into the dish, then continue with step 3. Transfer the dish to the oven and bake for 40 minutes. Serve as directed in step 4.

Rice pudding

Creamy rice pudding is delicious on its own, but for a special touch, top each bowl with berries, or fresh or poached fruit. If your favourite fruit is out of season, canned fruit will do instead.

1 cup (250 ml) cream
$2\frac{1}{2}$ cups (625 ml) milk
$\frac{1}{3}$ cup (75 g) sugar
1 teaspoon vanilla extract
1 cup (220 g) medium-grain white rice
2 mangoes, peeled and diced
fresh mint leaves, to garnish

You can also add some sliced banana to the rice a few minutes before the end of cooking, and serve with a sprinkling of ground cinnamon.

PREPARATION 5 minutes **COOKING** 30 minutes **SERVES** 4

1 Pour the cream into a large saucepan. Add 2 cups (500 ml) of the milk and stir in the sugar.

2 Add the vanilla and bring to a rolling boil over medium heat. Stir in the rice and gently simmer for 25 minutes, stirring regularly.

3 When the rice is getting dry, stir in the remaining $\frac{1}{2}$ cup (125 ml) milk. Serve topped with the mango and garnished with mint.

PER SERVING 2851 kJ, 681 kcal, 11 g protein, 34 g fat (22 g saturated fat), 85 g carbohydrate (41 g sugars), 2 g fibre, 83 mg sodium

Slow cooker

GREASE THE INSIDE OF THE slow cooker with softened butter. Add the cream, all the milk, the sugar, vanilla and rice. Stir until well combined, then cover and cook on low for 3 hours.

Bread and butter pudding

This simplest of puddings uses honey instead of sugar, enriching the flavour. Serve warm, straight from the oven, with a drizzle of cream or some good-quality ice-cream.

1½ tablespoons butter, plus some extra melted butter, for brushing
8 thick bread slices
½ cup (175 g) honey, plus extra for drizzling
4 eggs
1 cup (250 ml) cream
2 cups (500 ml) milk
¼ teaspoon ground cinnamon

Instead of honey, use ¼ cup (55 g) caster (superfine) sugar and whisk it with the eggs in step 3. Replace the plain bread with fruit bread, or sprinkle ½ cup (95 g) mixed dried fruit or ½ cup (60 g) sultanas (golden raisins) over the bread before adding the eggs.

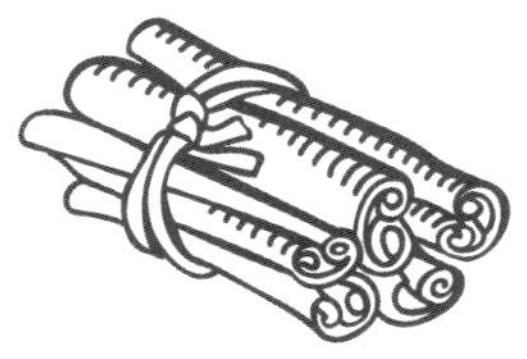

PREPARATION 10 minutes, plus 10 minutes standing
COOKING 45 minutes **SERVES** 6

1 Preheat the oven to 160°C (320°F/Gas 2–3). Brush a shallow rectangular baking dish with a little melted butter.

2 Spread each slice of bread with the butter and honey. (To make the honey easy to spread, warm it for 30 seconds in the microwave.) Cut each slice into four triangles, then arrange them in the baking dish, overlapping the slices as needed.

3 In a bowl, lightly whisk together the eggs, cream, milk and cinnamon. Pour the egg mixture over the bread and place a saucer on top. (Weighing the bread down with a saucer allows the egg mixture to soak into the bread, giving a rich, dense pudding.) Leave to stand for 10 minutes, then remove the saucer.

4 Place the dish in a larger baking dish and transfer to the oven. Carefully pour enough hot water into the larger baking dish to come halfway up the side of the smaller dish.

5 Bake for 45 minutes, or until the pudding is just set and golden. Serve warm, with a drizzle of extra honey.

PER SERVING 211 kJ, 504 kcal, 11 g protein, 31 g fat (19 g saturated fat), 47 g carbohydrate (30 g sugars), 1 g fibre, 342 mg sodium

Slow cooker

Butter a 6 cup (1.5 litre) heatproof tin or dish that will fit in your slow cooker. Follow steps 2 and 3 as above, layering the bread triangles in the slow cooker and then pouring the milky egg mixture over. Cover with a sheet of oiled foil and tie with kitchen string to seal.

Place in the slow cooker, on top of a trivet or upturned saucer. Pour 4 cups (1 litre) of hot water into the slow cooker bowl. Cover and cook on low for 4–5 hours, or until the pudding has set; the shallower the dish, the shorter the cooking time will be.

Golden syrup dumplings

Economical and filling, these divine dumplings have sustained many generations of families through chilly winter nights. Be gentle when handling the dough, or the dumplings will be tough. If you don't have a lid for your frying pan, cover it with a large baking tray.

1 cup (150 g) self-raising flour
50 g (1¾ oz) butter, chopped
½ cup (125 ml) milk
1 cup (350 g) golden syrup
cream or vanilla ice-cream, to serve

Sometimes called 'light treacle', golden syrup is a honey-coloured treacle with a distinctive taste. If you don't happen to have any, try using equal quantities of regular treacle, light molasses and corn syrup instead.

PREPARATION 15 minutes **COOKING** 15 minutes **SERVES** 4

1 Sift the flour into a bowl. Using your fingertips, rub in 1 tablespoon of the butter until evenly combined. Make a well in the centre, add the milk and mix with a non-serrated knife until the mixture starts to clump together. Gather the dough into a ball. Pinch off level tablespoons and lightly roll into 12 small balls.

2 Put the remaining butter in a large deep frying pan with the golden syrup and 1 cup (250 ml) water. Stir over medium heat until melted and combined, then bring to a boil.

3 Carefully add the dumplings, then cover and cook for 5 minutes. Using a spoon, gently turn the dumplings over. Increase the heat to medium–high and cook, uncovered, for a further 5 minutes.

4 Drizzle the dumplings with the syrup from the pan. Serve warm, with cream or vanilla ice-cream.

PER SERVING 2048 kJ, 489 kcal, 5 g protein, 12 g fat (8 g saturated fat), 94 g carbohydrate (67 g sugars), 1 g fibre, 477 mg sodium

Slow cooker

Combine the golden syrup, 30 g (1 oz) butter and 1 cup (250 ml) boiling water in the slow cooker. Mix until well combined, then cover and cook on high for 1 hour. Meanwhile, prepare the dumplings as directed in step 1. Drop them into the syrup mixture and turn the slow cooker setting to high. Cover and cook for a further 25 minutes, or until the dumplings are cooked. Gently turn to coat the dumplings in the syrup and serve as directed in step 4.

Plum cobbler

In this old-fashioned pudding, plump, juicy plums gently stew beneath a light, scone-like topping. Peaches, nectarines or apricots are equally good. If fresh plums are not in season, use canned ones instead. You won't need to add sugar to canned fruit, but do drain it well before using.

1 kg (2 lb) plums, halved and stoned
1 tablespoon caster (superfine) sugar
1½ cups (225 g) self-raising flour
100 g (3½ oz) butter, chopped
⅓ cup (60 g) soft brown sugar
⅓ cup (80 ml) milk
1 egg
1 teaspoon vanilla extract
ice-cream, cream or custard, to serve
sifted icing (confectioners') sugar, for dusting (optional)

Try a quick crumble topping instead. Rub 100 g (3½ oz) chilled chopped butter into 1 cup (150 g) plain (all-purpose) flour. Mix in ½ cup (50 g) rolled (porridge) oats, ½ cup (95 g) soft brown sugar, and ½ teaspoon ground cinnamon or mixed spice if desired. Sprinkle over the fruit and bake for 30 minutes, or until golden brown.

PREPARATION 20 minutes **COOKING** 35 minutes **SERVES** 6

1 Preheat the oven to 180°C (350°F/Gas 4). Arrange the plums in a 6 cup (1.5 litre) baking dish. Sprinkle the caster sugar over the plums and gently toss to coat.

2 Sift the flour into a large bowl. Using your fingertips, rub in the butter until combined. Stir in the brown sugar and make a well in the centre.

3 Whisk together the milk, egg and vanilla. Add to the dry ingredients and fold together until just combined — do not overbeat.

4 Place large spoonfuls of the batter next to each other, covering the fruit; this will give a 'cobbled' effect. Bake for 25–35 minutes, or until the topping has risen and is golden brown.

5 Serve hot, with your choice of ice-cream, cream or custard, and lightly dusted with icing sugar if desired.

PER SERVING 1577 kJ, 377 kcal, 6 g protein, 16 g fat (10 g saturated fat), 52 g carbohydrate (24 g sugars), 5 g fibre, 402 mg sodium

Slow cooker

Grease the inside of a 4 litre (4 quart) slow cooker with softened butter and preheat on high. Arrange the plums in the slow cooker, sprinkle with the caster sugar and gently toss to coat the plums.

Prepare the topping as directed in steps 3 and 4, then spoon over the plums. Cover and cook on high for 2 hours. Serve as directed in step 5.

Slow-cooker berry cobbler

Here's a simple way to transform summer berries into a sumptuous dessert — without the oven heating up your kitchen. You can use any combination of berries, up to the total weight.

vegetable oil, for brushing
1 cup (150 g) self-raising flour
1/4 teaspoon ground cinnamon
3/4 cup (140 g) brown sugar
60 g (2 oz) butter, chopped
1 egg, lightly beaten
1/4 cup (60 ml) milk
250 g (8 oz) raspberries
250 g (8 oz) blueberries
2 tablespoons plain (all-purpose) flour
2 tablespoons caster (superfine) sugar
cream or vanilla ice-cream, to serve

PREPARATION 20 minutes **COOKING** 2 hours **SERVES** 6

1 Lightly brush the inside of a 4 litre (4 quart) slow cooker with oil. Preheat the cooker to high.

2 Sift the self-raising flour and cinnamon into a large bowl, then stir in the brown sugar. Rub in the butter using your fingertips until evenly incorporated. Make a well in the centre.

3 Whisk the egg and milk together and stir into the dry ingredients to make a thick batter.

4 Toss the berries with the plain flour and caster sugar. Spread in an even layer over the base of the slow cooker.

5 Dollop the batter evenly over the berries. Cover and cook on high for 2 hours. Serve warm, with cream or ice-cream.

PER SERVING 1422 kJ, 340 kcal, 5 g protein, 11 g fat (6 g saturated fat), 56 g carbohydrate (35 g sugars), 4 g fibre, 266 mg sodium

In the oven

Preheat the oven to 180°C (350°F/Gas 4). Lightly grease a 6 cup (1.5 litre) baking dish. Follow steps 2 to 4 as above, spreading the coated berries in the baking dish. Dollop the batter over the top, then bake for 35 minutes. Serve warm, with cream or ice-cream.

Slow-cooker crustless lime cheesecake

Lusciously creamy with a lovely tang of lime, this cheesecake is almost hands-free in terms of effort required. We've topped it with fresh berries, but you can use your choice of fresh or poached fruit.

250 g (8 oz) cream cheese, softened
200 g (7 oz) fresh ricotta
300 g (10 oz) sour cream
1 cup (230 g) caster (superfine) sugar
grated zest of 3 limes
150 g (5 oz) raspberries
125 g (4 oz) blueberries
fresh mint leaves, to garnish
sifted icing (confectioners') sugar, for dusting (optional)

The cheesecake can also be cooked in a pressure cooker. Prepare a cake tin or heatproof container as directed in step 1. Follow steps 2 and 3, placing the cheesecake on a trivet in the pressure cooker and adding some water to the cooker. Cook under low pressure for 20 minutes, then allow the pressure to release naturally. Chill and decorate the cheesecake as directed in steps 4 and 5.

PREPARATION 15 minutes, plus at least 4 hours cooling
COOKING 2 hours 30 minutes **SERVES** 6–8

1 Grease and line an 18 cm (7 inch) springform cake tin that fits inside your slow cooker; you can also use a loaf (bar) tin or baking dish with a 5 cup (1.25 litre) capacity. Wrap a sheet of foil around the base and sides of the cake tin or dish.

2 Combine the cream cheese, ricotta, sour cream, sugar and lime zest in a food processor. Blend until smooth.

3 Spoon the mixture into the prepared tin or dish, then place in the slow cooker. Pour enough water into the cooker to come halfway up the outside of the tin.

4 Cover and cook on low for 2½ hours. Remove the tin or dish from slow cooker. Allow to cool slightly, then refrigerate for 4 hours or overnight, until the cheesecake has set.

5 Remove the cheesecake from the tin. Decorate with the berries and garnish with mint leaves. Serve dusted with icing sugar if desired.

PER SERVING 2306 kJ, 551 kcal, 8 g protein, 38 g fat (24 g saturated fat), 45 g carbohydrate (45 g sugars), 2 g fibre, 256 mg sodium

In the oven

Preheat the oven to 160°C (320°F/Gas 2–3). Use a 20 cm (8 inch) springform cake tin and follow steps 1 and 2 as above. Spoon the cheesecake mixture into the cake tin. Transfer the cake tin to the oven and bake for 50–60 minutes, or until the cheesecake is just set. Chill and decorate the cheesecake as directed in steps 4 and 5.

- To remove the furry skin from fresh apricots, cut a small shallow cross into the bottom of each one. Place them in a bowl of boiling water for 60 seconds, then remove with a slotted spoon and cool them in a cold water bath. Gently rub the skins; they should slip off quite easily.
- Canned apricots may be substituted for fresh ones in most recipes; those packed in water or juice (rather than sugary syrup) are generally the best choice.

Fresh apricots poached in syrup

Make the most of plump juicy apricots when they're in season and dish up this super-quick treat. Vanilla and ginger are the perfect partners for their exquisite sweetness.

$^1/_2$ cup (110 g) sugar
$^1/_2$ teaspoon ground ginger
1 vanilla bean, halved
8 fresh apricots, peeled

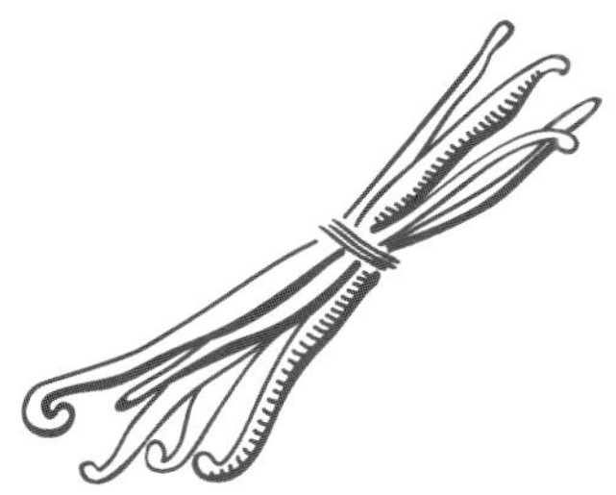

PREPARATION 5 minutes, plus chilling **COOKING** 15 minutes **SERVES** 4

1 Place the sugar, ginger and vanilla bean in a saucepan. Pour in 1 cup (250 ml) water and stir over low heat, without boiling, until the sugar has dissolved. Bring to a boil, reduce the heat and simmer without stirring for 3 minutes.

2 Add the apricots. Reduce the heat to a simmer, then cover and cook gently for 10 minutes, or until the apricots are tender.

3 Remove from the heat and allow the apricots to cool in the syrup. Transfer to a container and chill before serving.

PER SERVING 633 kJ, 151 kcal, 1 g protein, <1 g fat (<1 g saturated fat), 36 g carbohydrate (35 g sugars), 2 g fibre, 2 mg sodium

Slow cooker

Prepare the syrup as directed in step 1. Place the apricots in a 4 litre (4 quart) slow cooker and pour the syrup over. Cover and cook on low for 5 hours. Cool the apricots in the syrup and chill before serving.

Baked apples

Choose a cooking apple for this marvellous dish, as they hold their shape well during baking. Brown sugar adds a lovely caramel flavour to the syrup, but you can use maple syrup or honey instead. Also experiment by adding your favourite chopped nuts to the filling.

6 granny smith apples
50 g (1¾ oz) butter, melted
⅓ cup (60 g) soft brown sugar
¼ cup (30 g) sultanas (golden raisins)
¼ cup (35 g) currants
¼ cup (40 g) chopped raisins
1 teaspoon mixed spice (pumpkin pie spice)
custard, cream or vanilla ice-cream, to serve

- With these golden baked apples you can use any combination of dried fruit, up to about ¾ cup (140 g). If using large fruits such as dried apricots or dates, finely chop them first.
- For a quick, luxurious filling, try using a good-quality fruit mince (mincemeat).

PREPARATION 15 minutes **COOKING** 45 minutes **SERVES** 6

1 Preheat the oven to 170°C (340°F/Gas 3). Remove the cores from the apples using an apple corer. Use a small sharp knife to score a line through the skin, around the middle of each apple.

2 In a large bowl, mix the butter, sugar, dried fruit and mixed spice until well combined. Press the mixture into the cavities in the apples, then arrange the apples in a large baking dish. Bake for 45 minutes, or until the apples are tender.

3 Drizzle the apples with the juices left in the baking dish. Serve warm, with custard, cream or vanilla ice-cream.

PER SERVING 929 kJ, 222 kcal, 1 g protein, 7 g fat (5 g saturated fat), 40 g carbohydrate (39 g sugars), 4 g fibre, 72 mg sodium

Slow cooker

Core and fill the apples as directed in steps 1 and 2. Pour water into the slow cooker to a depth of about 2 cm (¾ inch), then arrange the apples in the cooker. Cover and cook on high for 2½ hours, or until tender. Serve as directed in step 3.

Cherry brandy clafoutis

Clafoutis is a classic French dessert in which fruit is baked in a sweetened batter. It is simply sensational made with plump fresh cherries; remove the stems and stones before adding them to the batter. Canned cherries also work well when time is short, or cherries are not in season.

2 x 420 g (15 oz) cans pitted cherries in syrup
2 tablespoons brandy
½ cup (75 g) plain (all-purpose) flour
⅓ cup (60 g) soft brown sugar or light muscovado sugar
1 cup (250 ml) low-fat milk
3 eggs
1 teaspoon vanilla extract
sifted icing (confectioners') sugar, for dusting (optional)

- When fresh peaches are in season, replace the canned cherries with 4 ripe but firm peaches, peeled and sliced, and use peach schnapps instead of the brandy. Flavour the batter with 1 teaspoon mixed spice (pumpkin pie spice) instead of vanilla, adding it to the flour.
- Bake the clafoutis in individual dishes, if you prefer. Divide the cherries equally among four 300 ml (10 fl oz) individual flan dishes, or other ovenproof dishes, spreading them in an even layer. Bake for 20 minutes.

PREPARATION 10 minutes **COOKING** 25 minutes **SERVES** 4

1 Preheat the oven to 200°C (400°F/Gas 6). Drain the cherries, then tip them onto paper towels and pat dry.

2 Evenly spread the cherries in a 25 cm (10 inch) round china, ceramic or porcelain flan dish (tart pan), or other ovenproof dish. Drizzle the brandy over the cherries and set aside.

3 Sift the flour into a bowl and add the sugar. In a pouring jug, beat together the milk, eggs and vanilla, then whisk into the flour mixture to make a smooth batter.

4 Pour the batter slowly over the fruit. Bake for 20–25 minutes, or until the batter is lightly set and pale golden. Serve warm, lightly dusted with icing sugar if desired.

PER SERVING 1258 kJ, 301 kcal, 11 g protein, 4 g fat (1 g saturated fat), 52 g carbohydrate (35 g sugars), 2 g fibre, 91 mg sodium

Saffron-scented pears

Firm pears are ideal for gentle poaching as they hold their shape. The longer the pears sit in the syrup after poaching at the end of step 2, the better they'll taste, so this dessert is well suited to preparing ahead. A slow cooker is also ideal for poaching; see the directions below the recipe.

1 cup (250 ml) white wine
1 cup (220 g) sugar
1 vanilla bean, halved
$\frac{1}{2}$ cinnamon stick
$\frac{1}{2}$ teaspoon saffron threads
2 teaspoons grated orange zest
6 firm pears, such as beurre bosc

- Choose firm, just-ripe pears; softer varieties such as williams or bartlett will fall apart during poaching.
- For a gourmet touch, serve crisp sweet biscuits (cookies) on the side.

PREPARATION 5 minutes **COOKING** 1 hour 55 minutes **SERVES** 6

1 Combine all the ingredients, except the pears, in a saucepan in which the pears will fit snugly upright. Pour in 1 cup (250 ml) water and stir over low heat, without boiling, until the sugar has dissolved. Bring to a boil, reduce the heat and simmer without stirring for 3 minutes.

2 Meanwhile, peel the pears, leaving the stems intact. Add them to the saucepan, standing them upright. Cover and simmer over very low heat for $1\frac{1}{2}$ hours, or until they begin to take on a glazed appearance.

3 Close to serving time, remove the pears and gently simmer the syrup for 20 minutes, or until it has reduced and is almost toffee-like. Pour the syrup over the pears and serve.

PER SERVING 1068 kJ, 255 kcal, <1 g protein, <1 g fat (<1 g saturated fat), 58 g carbohydrate (53 g sugars), 3 g fibre, 13 mg sodium

Slow cooker

PREPARE THE SYRUP AS DIRECTED in step 1. Peel the pears, leaving the stems intact, and place in a 4 litre (4 quart) slow cooker. Pour the syrup over, then lay the pears on their sides to make sure they are submerged. Cover and cook on high for 4 hours.

Near serving time, remove the pears. Transfer the syrup to a saucepan and gently simmer for 20 minutes, or until it has reduced and is almost toffee-like. Serve the syrup drizzled over the pears.

Slow-cooker lemon delicious

This is a very aptly named pudding in which the batter magically separates into a creamy curd, topped by a fluffy sponge layer. You can vary the recipe by using limes or oranges instead of lemons — or why not experiment by using a combination of different citrus fruits?

60 g (2 oz) butter, at room temperature, chopped, plus extra for greasing
3/4 cup (170 g) caster (superfine) sugar
1 tablespoon finely grated lemon zest
3 eggs, separated
1 1/4 cups (310 ml) milk
1/3 cup (80 ml) lemon juice
1/3 cup (50 g) self-raising flour, sifted

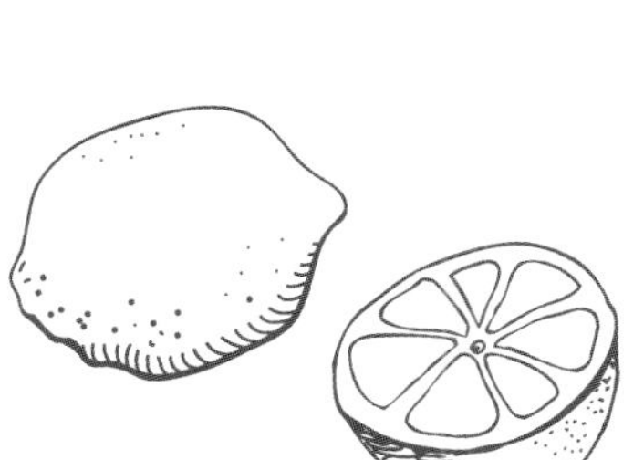

PREPARATION 20 minutes **COOKING** 2 hours **SERVES** 6

1 Lightly grease the inside of a 4 litre (4 quart) slow cooker with butter. Preheat the cooker to high.

2 In a large mixing bowl, cream the butter, sugar, lemon zest and egg yolks using electric beaters until light and fluffy. Stir in the milk and lemon juice, then fold the flour through — don't worry if the mixture looks a little curdled.

3 Using clean beaters, beat the eggwhites to soft peaks. Fold the eggwhites through the batter, then gently pour into the slow cooker.

4 Cover the cooker and reduce the heat to low. Cook for 2 hours, or until the sponge is springy to a gentle touch in the centre.

PER SERVING 1239 kJ, 296 kcal, 6 g protein, 14 g fat (8 g saturated fat), 37 g carbohydrate (31 g sugars), <1 g fibre, 191 mg sodium

In the oven

Preheat the oven to 180°C (350°F/Gas 4). Lightly grease a 6 cup (1.5 litre) baking dish. Follow steps 2 and 3 as directed, pouring the mixture into the baking dish. Transfer to the oven and bake for 40 minutes.

Slow-cooker coconut and mango pudding

This moist pudding is great eaten hot or cold — and perfect to prepare when your favourite fruit is out of season. It is delicious on its own, or serve drizzled with a little cream.

125 g (4 oz) butter, at room temperature, chopped, plus extra for greasing
1/2 cup (115 g) caster (superfine) sugar
2 eggs
1 teaspoon ground ginger
420 g (15 oz) can mangoes (in natural juice), drained, reserving the juice
1 1/2 cups (225 g) self-raising flour, sifted
150 ml (5 fl oz) coconut milk
shredded coconut, to garnish

PREPARATION 20 minutes **COOKING** 2 hours **SERVES** 8

1 Grease a 4 cup (1 litre) pudding basin (mould) with butter. Line the bottom with baking (parchment) paper.

2 In a large mixing bowl, cream the butter and sugar using electric beaters until light and fluffy. Add the eggs one at a time, beating well after each addition. Stir in the ginger and reserved mango juice. Fold the flour through, then the coconut milk.

3 Pour the batter into the pudding basin and seal the lid. Place the pudding in a 5 litre (5 quart) slow cooker, then pour enough boiling water into the cooker to come halfway up the side of the pudding basin.

4 Cover and cook on high for 2 hours, replenishing the liquid in the cooker with boiling water as needed to maintain the original level.

5 Remove the pudding basin from the slow cooker. Stand the pudding in the basin for 5 minutes, before turning out onto a serving plate.

6 Chop the mangoes and pile them on top of the pudding. Sprinkle with shredded coconut and serve.

PER SERVING 1489 kJ, 356 kcal, 5 g protein, 19 g fat (13 g saturated fat), 41 g carbohydrate (21 g sugars), 2 g fibre, 333 mg sodium

On the stove

COMPLETE STEPS 1 AND 2 as above. Pour the batter into the pudding basin and seal the lid. Place the pudding in a large saucepan, then pour enough boiling water into the saucepan to come halfway up the side of the pudding basin.

Bring to a boil, reduce the heat, then cover and simmer for 1 3/4 hours, or until a skewer inserted into the middle of the pudding comes out clean. Finish as directed in steps 5 and 6.

Slow-cooker butterscotch pudding

This warming treat is a welcome no-fuss dessert on a cold winter's night. For a nutty surprise, fold some chopped pecans or walnuts through the batter before cooking the pudding.

vegetable oil, for brushing
1$\frac{1}{3}$ cups (200 g) self-raising flour
$\frac{1}{3}$ cup (60 g) soft brown sugar
100 g (3$\frac{1}{2}$ oz) butter, melted and cooled
1 egg
$\frac{1}{2}$ cup (125 ml) milk
1 teaspoon vanilla extract
cream or vanilla ice-cream, to serve

Butterscotch sauce

$\frac{1}{2}$ cup (95 g) soft brown sugar
2 tablespoons butter, chopped

In the oven

Preheat the oven to 180°C (350°F/Gas 4). Lightly brush a 6 cup (1.5 litre) baking dish with vegetable oil. Prepare the batter as directed in step 2 and spoon it into the dish, then continue with step 3. Transfer the dish to the oven and bake for 35 minutes. Serve warm, with cream or ice-cream.

PREPARATION 20 minutes **COOKING** 2 hours 30 minutes **SERVES** 6

1 Lightly brush the inside of a 4 litre (4 quart) slow cooker with oil. Preheat the cooker to high.

2 Sift the flour and sugar into a bowl and make a well in the centre. Whisk the butter, egg, milk and vanilla together with a fork, add to the dry ingredients and fold together until evenly combined. Spoon the mixture into the slow cooker.

3 To make the butterscotch sauce, put the sugar and butter into a jug. Stir in 1$\frac{1}{2}$ cups (375 ml) boiling water and mix well to dissolve the sugar and melt the butter. Slowly pour the sauce over the batter, pouring it over the back of a spoon to help disperse the liquid evenly.

4 Cover and cook on low for 2$\frac{1}{2}$ hours. Serve warm, with cream or vanilla ice-cream.

PER SERVING 1719 kJ, 411 kcal, 5 g protein, 22 g fat (13 g saturated fat), 50 g carbohydrate (26 g sugars), 1 g fibre, 422 mg sodium

Cooking basics

While the recipes in this book are not difficult in terms of technique, some simple principles will help guarantee cooking success. Here we explain how Asian hotpots work, cover some basic stewing essentials, and offer some easy side dishes to complete the meal.

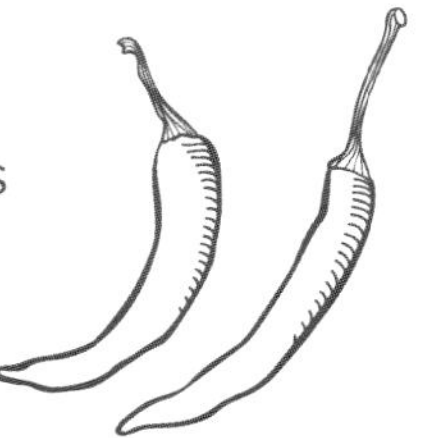

Cooking an Asian-style hotpot

The term 'hotpot' covers myriad variations, and while we generally think of the Asian-style hotpots discussed here, it is very possible that this style of cooking developed simultaneously in different locations.

Legend has it that the original Mongolian hotpot was developed by nomadic Mongols, who used their iron helmets as cooking vessels over campfires when travelling through isolated places.

The popularity of the dish spread throughout China, where it is called a 'steamboat', and appears in slightly different guises in many Asian countries.

The appeal of the hotpot lies in the sociable manner of sharing a meal, with each diner being able to choose their preferred ingredients, cooked to their liking. What probably started as a style of cooking born of necessity has become popular in restaurants, both high-end and local family-style establishments.

Taiwan, Vietnam, Korea, Singapore and Malaysia all have their own hotpots, featuring local seafood, spicy condiments and herbs.

HOTPOTS IN JAPAN

In Japan, hotpot is known as nabenomo. Sukiyaki is a popular type of hotpot, as is shabu shabu. Styles vary between regions, but generally sukiyaki and shabu shabu use thinly sliced beef, firm tofu, leafy green vegetables, mushrooms and noodles. The major differences lie in the broth: sukiyaki is a little sweeter and shabu shabu more savoury. The style of cooking varies slightly, too: where sukiyaki has all the ingredients cooked together, for shabu shabu the diner dips each piece separately. Interestingly, shabu shabu takes its name from the sound made by the food when swished around in the broth.

How does it work?

These days, a hotpot is basically a pot of simmering broth on the table, kept hot over flame, coals or another heat source. Platters of thinly sliced meats (often lamb or mutton), tofu, and green vegetables such as cabbage and broccoli are offered, and diners use a long fork to dip a piece of food into the broth, letting it cook briefly. Sauces are available for seasoning the cooked food.

Depending on the local cuisine, a starch such as rice, noodles or possibly bread is part of the meal.

The pot can be a large communal one, or there may be smaller individual pots for each diner.

What do you need?

If making an Asian-style hotpot, you'll need a few specific cooking and serving utensils.

HOTPOT This keeps the broth at a simmer on the table, for cooking the food. For best results, bring the broth to the boil on the stove first, then transfer to the hotpot.

A traditional hotpot vessel is an unusual shape, as it has the broth in a ring-shaped bowl, kept hot by coals set over a grill in a central chimney section. You can use a fondue pot, if you have one, or even an electric frying pan or wok.

If your vessel isn't very large, you can top it up with hot stock from the stove. Proper hotpots are available from Asian shops, or can be purchased online. The simpler models are not very expensive.

SMALL SERVING BOWLS AND CHOPSTICKS Set the table with a bowl and a set of chopsticks for each diner.

LONG FONDUE-STYLE FORKS Supply one fork for each diner to dip their chosen ingredients into the hot broth and cook to their individual preference.

LADLE AND TONGS You will need a ladle for the broth and tongs for retrieving any recalcitrant pieces of food.

Simple Mongolian hotpot

This basic hotpot recipe can be varied according to your taste. Serve with dipping sauces such as soy sauce, hoisin sauce, chilli sauce, sesame oil or sesame paste.

PREPARATION 15 minutes **COOKING** 10 minutes **SERVES** 4

500 g (1 lb) good-quality lamb fillet
1/4 Chinese cabbage (wombok)
200 g (7 oz) firm tofu
150 g (5 oz) mushrooms, halved, or quartered if large
dipping sauces, to serve
6 cups (1.5 litres) diluted lamb, beef or chicken stock
2 cloves garlic, crushed
1 teaspoon finely grated fresh ginger
100 g (3 1/2 oz) mung bean vermicelli (cellophane noodles)

- Cut the lamb into very thin slices across the grain. (To make this easier, first wrap the meat well with plastic wrap and place it in the freezer until firm, though not frozen solid.)
- Cut the cabbage leaves into smaller pieces, and the tofu into cubes. Arrange on separate serving plates, with the mushrooms. Place the dipping sauces in bowls.
- Combine the stock, garlic and ginger in a saucepan, then bring to a boil on the stove. Transfer to a hotpot. Keep the stock at a simmer on the table.
- Ask diners to select pieces of food to dip into the broth. They then transfer to their own small bowl and add condiments to taste.
- At the end of the meal, the stock will have taken on flavour from the various foods, and can be served as a soup to finish. Soak the noodles in boiling water for 5 minutes, then drain well and add to the stock.

Variations

MEAT You can replace the lamb with beef, pork or chicken, or use a combination.

SEAFOOD Seafood is perfect for hotpots as it cooks quickly. Add prawns (shrimp), scallops, mussels, sliced squid or abalone, or cubes of firm white fish.

VEGETABLES Use Asian leafy greens such as bok choy or gai larn instead of, or as well as, the cabbage; use mushrooms such as shiitake, enoki or oyster.

NOODLES Try different types of noodles, such as rice noodles or hokkien (egg) noodles. Dumplings and won tons can also be cooked in the hotpot.

Chicken hotpot

Ideal for entertaining, this fun dish begs to be cooked in a large pot on a portable burner in the middle of the table. Alternatively, everything can be cooked at once on the stove and served in individual bowls. See the Mongolian hotpot recipe for versatile ingredient variations.

PREPARATION 15 minutes **COOKING** 10 minutes **SERVES** 4

100 g (3 1/2 oz) rice vermicelli noodles
6 Chinese cabbage (wombok) leaves, chopped
1 small carrot, finely sliced
12 small shiitake or oyster mushrooms, halved
4 spring onions (scallions), cut into short lengths
250 g (8 oz) baby bok choy, chopped
6 cups (1.5 litres) dashi, chicken or vegetable stock
400 g (14 oz) skinless, boneless chicken breasts, thinly sliced
300 g (10 oz) firm tofu, cut into cubes
ponzu sauce, for dipping (see page 31)

- Soak the noodles according to the packet instructions. Drain well and arrange on a platter with the cabbage, carrot, mushrooms, spring onions and bok choy.
- Bring the stock to a boil in a wok or large saucepan. Reduce the heat to low, add the chicken and simmer for 2–3 minutes, or until nearly cooked through. Add the tofu and cook for 2–3 minutes, or until hot.
- Add a selection of the vegetables with some noodles and cook for 1–2 minutes, or until tender.
- Remove all the ingredients from the wok a few at a time, then dip into the ponzu dipping sauce. Once all of the ingredients are eaten, drink any remaining stock as a soup, or with any remaining noodles.

Choosing cuts of meat

Not all 'one-pot' cooking is slow cooking, although it often is, as this method lends itself so beautifully to stews, soups and casseroles. One-pot cooking is time saving, as usually the preparation time is short, and even if the cooking time is long it is mostly unattended. It is economical, too, as cheaper cuts of meat are those that are most suited.

Slow one-pot cooking is, in essence, peasant-style cuisine, developed over the years by necessity and thrift. Tough, cheap cuts of meat, old chickens, offal, readily available game, dried beans and grains and long-lasting root vegetables were used to make meals that could simmer away unattended while the work was done. The long, slow cooking rendered the meat tender.

Cheap cuts of meat are not only acceptable in slow cooked dishes, but in fact result in a better dish than if expensive cuts were to be used. The fat and connective tissue they contain break down over a long time at reasonably low temperatures. Just as you wouldn't use these cuts seared quickly in a frying pan, neither should you use a lean fillet of beef or lamb in a stew — in both cases, the meat will be tough and unappealing. Meat cooked on the bone, such as a slow-roasted lamb leg, is especially successful.

BEST CUTS TO USE	
Beef and veal	Chuck steak, skirt steak, round steak, boneless shin (gravy beef), osso buco (bone-in shin), brisket, topside roast, blade roast, silverside, ribs, oxtail.
Lamb	Neck chops, forequarter chops, shanks, shoulder, leg.
Pork	Shoulder, forequarter chops, neck.
Poultry	Any cut, but those on the bone are best, such as thighs on the bone or drumsticks. Duck and turkey are suitable, and even whole chickens work well.

Preparing meat for slow cooking

Cheap meat cuts are inherently fatty, so it is a good idea to cut off large visible areas of fat. There will be plenty of fat, even if it is not totally obvious, marbled throughout the meat.

It can be cheaper to buy the meat in a piece, and cut it up yourself — it depends if you prefer to save the time or the money. Cutting it yourself allows you to make pieces of uniform size, as packaged diced meat can sometimes be quite irregularly cut. Generally, you would cut the meat into pieces about 3 cm ($1\frac{1}{4}$ inches) in size.

Browning the meat

Browning the meat — whether in a slow cooker insert, in the oven or on the stove — before starting the long, slow stewing process contributes colour and flavour to the finished dish.

To sear effectively, cook the meat in small batches, so you don't overcrowd the pan. Adding too much meat at once will cause the temperature to drop, and instead of caramelising, the meat will turn grey and start to stew. Set each batch aside on a plate while you cook the remaining batches. Add a little more oil to the pan if necessary and then sauté the onion (and garlic, if using) until soft and lightly golden. Individual recipes vary, but this is a good rule of thumb for a fabulous stew, soup or casserole.

If you are browning the meat in a different pan to the one you will be slow cooking the stew in, it is worth deglazing the pan. This is a simple way of making the most of all the lovely brown residue left behind in the pan. Once all the meat and any vegetables have been browned and set aside, add a little of the cooking liquid to the hot pan and heat it, scraping the bottom of the pan to loosen and dissolve the cooked-on residue.

Thickening the stew

The sauce or liquid in stews and other slow-cooked dishes can be thickened in a number of ways, and the method used will depend on the ingredients in the dish.

Sometimes vegetables such as potatoes are included, which help thicken the sauce as they release starch. The meat may be tossed in flour before browning, which also contributes to thickening the sauce. Other times, flour is sprinkled onto the pan juices after browning the meat, and cooked for few minutes to remove the raw taste. Stock or other liquid is then gradually added, in the manner of deglazing the pan, to create a thicker sauce.

In our spiced braised beef (see page 75), a little cornflour is mixed with water to make a smooth paste, then stirred into the stew for the final 15 minutes to help thicken it.

A very simple way (which is not suitable for slow cookers) is to remove the lid of the pan for the last part of cooking, so any excess liquid evaporates and the sauce reduces, concentrating the flavour.

A common way to thicken slow-cooker dishes is with cornflour (cornstarch), stirred into a small amount of liquid to make a paste, and added close to finishing time.

When to add the vegetables

Recipes vary, but generally when cooking a stew or casserole by conventional methods, you add harder vegetables, such as turnips and carrots, earlier in the cooking time. Potatoes, sweet potatoes and pumpkin (winter squash) tend to fall apart if cooked too long, so these will be added slightly later in the cooking process.

Vegetables such as peas, green beans and broccoli are better added near the end of cooking time, to preserve some colour and texture, whereas leafy greens such as English spinach will wilt quickly in the heat, so can be added right at the last minute.

With a slow cooker it is fine to add most vegetables right at the start — because it cooks food so gently, there is little danger of overcooking the vegetables. More tender vegetables, such as greens, can be added later in the cooking time; check your recipe for specific instructions.

COOKING DRIED BEANS

The slow cooker may seem ideal for cooking dried beans, but it is essential to boil dried beans before adding them to a slow cooker dish. Dried beans, particularly red kidney beans, contain a toxin that needs to first be eliminated by boiling.

For best results, soak dried beans overnight, drain them, then boil in fresh water until tender; this will take anywhere between 45 minutes and 1½ hours, depending on the size of the bean.

Beans can be cooked successfully in a pressure cooker, preferably after soaking overnight.

You can also use canned beans in our recipes, as they are convenient, safe, and won't turn to mush in a slow cooker.

Side dishes

While many recipes in this book are complete meals in themselves, others may need an extra element to round out the nutrition, or to soak up a lovely broth or sauce. Here's a selection of classic accompaniments that are big on effect but require very little effort.

A simple side salad turns our chicken-stuffed capsicums (see page 148) into a satisfying main meal.

One-pot dishes usually contain everything you need for a complete meal. Occasionally something 'on the side' is called for, particularly when there is a luscious sauce or gravy to be mopped up. The easiest accompaniment to soups and stews is crusty bread, but here we give you our 'best ever' side dishes, which are quick and easy to prepare while your other pot simmers away.

While each of these accompaniments ideally suits specific dishes, they are virtually interchangeable, so use whatever you have on hand, or mix it up occasionally for mealtime variety. Adding the bulk of one of these economical components will make your meal go further.

Mashed potato

A popular side dish in many cuisines, mashed potato is wonderful as an accompaniment to meat stews and casseroles. Mashed potato is versatile, easy to make, filling and comforting.

'Mash' isn't limited to potatoes, however. You can mash any firm or starchy vegetable, such as sweet potato, pumpkin (winter squash), celeriac, parsnips or carrots. A combination of potato with a less starchy vegetable, such as cauliflower, also works well.

TO PREPARE Peel 600 g (1 lb 5 oz) baking (floury) potatoes, such as russet (idaho), king edward, coliban, dutch cream or sebago. Cut into evenly sized pieces. Place in a saucepan, cover with cold water and bring to a boil. Cook until tender when pierced with a small sharp knife; the actual cooking time will depend on how large you've cut them. They should be very soft all the way through.

Drain well, then return to the pan and place over low heat for a minute to evaporate any residual water. Remove from the heat and use a potato masher to break the potatoes up, then beat with a wooden spoon until smooth. Add a knob of butter and/or a dash of milk, to your liking. Season to taste. Serves 4.

Couscous

Instant couscous is a terrific time-saving product to keep in your pantry. It goes well with spicy Moroccan-style dishes that have plenty of thin sauce which will absorb into the couscous.

TO PREPARE Pour 1¼ cups (310 ml) water or stock into a saucepan, cover and bring to a boil. As soon as it boils, turn off the heat. Uncover briefly to add 1 cup (185 g) couscous, then put the lid back on straight away. Swirl the pan to combine the couscous and hot liquid. Leave to stand for 5 minutes, then uncover and drizzle with 1 tablespoon olive oil. Use a fork to mix through and fluff up the grains. Serves 4.

Rice

Rice is *the* staple food for so many people on the planet. There are many different types of rice, some with particular properties and best served in specific ways.

As an accompaniment, a fairly fluffy, dry cooked rice is ideal, as it will soak up all the lovely flavours in your dish. Long-grain basmati is perfect with Indian curries, whereas jasmine rice (Thai fragrant rice) suits spicy stir-fries and other South-East Asian dishes.

TO PREPARE Check the packaging because instructions vary according to type, but if you have had trouble in the past with gluggy rice, the simple boiling method is often the easiest.

Bring a large saucepan of water to a boil, then add 1 cup (200 g) rice. Return to the boil, then cook for 10 minutes. Remove from the heat and test a few grains — they should be tender but slightly firm. If they still have a starchy centre, cook for a few minutes more. The main thing is to keep an eye on the pan, as rice can turn to mush quickly. Pour cooked rice into a large colander and drain well. Serves 4.

Salads

Salads are so quick and versatile: toss some mixed salad leaves with herbs, sliced salad vegetables or some lightly blanched harder vegetables such as broccoli.

Roasted vegetables (leftovers, or from a jar) are great in a salad; so are olives, cheeses such as fetta, and croutons or nuts for crunch.

TO PREPARE Wash mixed green leaves and baby spinach. Using a peeler, peel off long strips of carrot. Toss gently to combine. Just before serving, dress with olive oil or a nut oil, and a tangy component such as vinegar or citrus juice.

Pasta

While not always obvious as a side dish to stews and casseroles, pasta is ideal for making a meal go further. It particularly suits a generously sauced, meat-based dish such as stroganoff. Use any type of pasta you have on hand — wide long noodles such as tagliatelle or fettuccine, or short pasta such as fusilli or penne.

Fresh pasta takes only a couple of minutes to cook, but dried pasta is convenient for its longer shelf life.

TO PREPARE Whichever type of pasta you use, the method is always the same — the only aspect that will differ will be the actual cooking time.

Bring a large pot of water to a boil. Add some salt and your required quantity of pasta. Stir to separate the pasta, then allow to boil vigorously for the time recommended on the pasta packet. Always begin checking just before the suggested time. Pasta should be 'al dente' — tender, but still firm and slightly resistant. Drain well and serve.

Noodles

There are many different types of South-East Asian noodles. Some are made from rice, some from wheat flour, and some contain eggs. Noodles can be purchased fresh or dried; some varieties are pre-cooked, so all you need to do is soak them in boiling water before serving.

Rice noodles make a lovely alternative to rice for dishes such as fragrant stir-fries or Thai-style curries.

TO PREPARE Always check the packet instructions, as the preparation required for different types of noodles varies greatly.

Polenta

Polenta is most commonly made from cornmeal. It is cooked with water or stock to a thick, soft, porridge-like consistency, and makes an excellent side dish served with meat or vegetarian stews. Polenta can also be spread into a tin and left to set, after which it can be sliced and then baked or fried. Look for instant polenta, which takes only a few minutes to cook.

TO PREPARE Heat 3 cups (750 ml) water or stock in a medium saucepan; for a creamier polenta, replace 1 cup (250 ml) of the water with 1 cup (250 ml) milk. Add 1 cup (180 g) instant polenta in a slow stream, stirring constantly. Keep stirring over medium heat for 2–3 minutes, or until the polenta is thick and soft. Add a knob of butter, or a little grated parmesan. Serves 4.

Index

Q

R

S

T

V

W

Y

Z

Note to readers

Weights and measures

Sometimes conversions within a recipe are not exact but are the closest conversion that is a suitable measurement for each system.

Use either the metric or the imperial measurements; do not mix the two systems.

Can sizes

Can sizes vary between countries and manufacturers; if the stated size is unavailable, use the nearest equivalent.

Here are the metric and imperial measurements for can sizes used in this book: 225 g = 8 oz; 300 g = 10 oz; 350 g = 12 oz; 400/410 g = 14 oz = 398 ml/410 ml; 425 g = 15 oz = 540 ml; 800 g = 28 oz = 796 ml.

Nutritional analysis

Each recipe is accompanied by a nutrient profile showing kilojoules (kJ), calories (kcal), protein, fat (including saturated fat), carbohydrate (including sugars), fibre and sodium. Serving suggestions, garnishes and optional ingredients are not included in the nutritional analysis. For the recipe analysis we used FoodWorks ® based on Australian and New Zealand food composition data.

Oven temperatures

These recipes have been written for a regular oven. If you have a fan-forced (convection) oven, reduce the temperature by 20°C (70°F).

If you have a broiler (grill) where the temperature cannot be adjusted by a temperature dial or knob, lower the rack from the element as follows:

Medium heat: about half or two-thirds of the way down.
Medium–high heat: about a third of the way down.

Alternative terms and substitutes

beef bolar blade – blade
capsicum – bell pepper, sweet pepper
cream – where type of cream is not specified, use pure, light, single or pouring cream
eggplant – aubergine, brinjal
English spinach – baby spinach; not the heavily veined, thick-leafed vegetable sold as spinach or silverbeet (Swiss chard)
fish substitutes – for blue-eye, bream, ling, snapper, flathead, use any firm white-fleshed fish such as cod, coley, hake or kabeljou
hokkien noodles – 2-minute noodles or other fast-cooking noodle
low-fat milk – 1% milk
milk – use full-cream (whole) milk unless the recipe specifies otherwise
oregano – oreganum
pepitas (pumpkin seeds) – use sunflower seeds
rice noodles – rice vermicelli
salt-reduced – low-sodium
self-raising flour – self-rising flour
silverbeet – Swiss chard, often sold as spinach in South Africa
slotted spoon – draining spoon
sugar – use white (granulated) sugar unless otherwise stated
Swiss brown mushrooms – brown mushrooms
vanilla extract – vanilla essence
vegetable oil – use canola oil
wholegrain mustard – seeded mustard
wholemeal – whole-wheat
zucchini – baby marrow, courgette

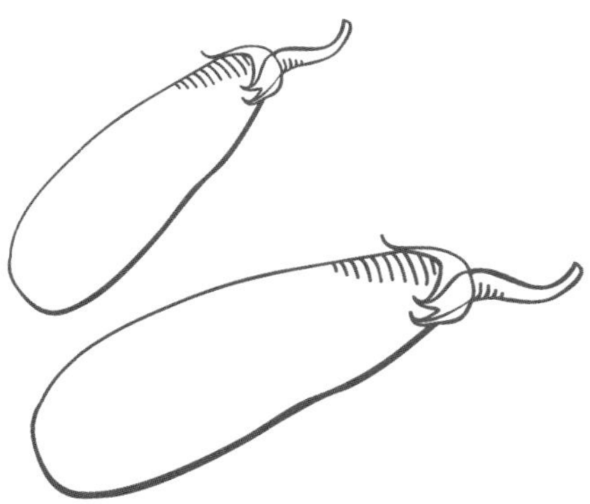

Hotpot, Crockpot, One Pot

Additional Text Tracy Rutherford
Copy Editor Katri Hilden
Designers Susanne Geppert, Clare O'Loughlin
Senior Designer Donna Heldon
Nutritional Analysis Alex Newman
Proofreader Susan McCreery
Indexer Diane Harriman
Senior Production Controller Monique Tesoriero
Editorial Project Manager General Books Deborah Nixon

READER'S DIGEST GENERAL BOOKS

Editorial Director Lynn Lewis
Managing Editor Rosemary McDonald
Art Director Carole Orbell

CREDITS

Cover, chapter openers, pages 32, 40, 44, 54, 64, 75, 83, 108, 111, 115, 119, 131, 132, 136, 140, 148, 172, 176, 184, 187, 188, 192, 196, 208, 211, 215, 216, 222, 226, 257, 258, 261, 262, 274, 278, 289, 290, 301, 302, 305

Photographer Steve Brown
Stylist Trish Heagerty
Food preparation Nick Eade
Recipes Grace Campbell, Tracy Rutherford

page 61: Natasha Milne (photographer), Yael Grinham (stylist), Peta Dent (food preparation)

With thanks to Mud Australia and Tiles by Kate.

Hotpot, Crockpot, One Pot contains some material first published in the following Reader's Digest books: *The Anti-Ageing Diet Cookbook, The Complete Book of Herbs, Cooking for One or Two, Cooking Smart for a Healthy Heart, Eat Well Live Well: Fruit and Desserts, Eat Well Live Well: Perfect Pasta, Eat Well Live Well: Soups and Casseroles, Eat Well Stay Well, 5 Ingredient Cookbook, 5-10-15 Cookbook, The GI Cookbook, Grandma's Quick & Thrifty Cookbook, The Great Chicken Cookbook, The Great Potato Cookbook, 30-Minuten-Küche: Leckere Suppen und Eintöpfe, Healthy One-Dish Cooking, Midweek Meals Made Easy, Quick & Easy Cooking, Super Foods Super Easy, Vegetables for Vitality*

Hotpot, Crockpot, One Pot is published by
Reader's Digest (Australia) Pty Limited,
80 Bay Street, Ultimo NSW 2007, Australia
www.readersdigest.com.au, www.readersdigest.co.nz,
www.readersdigest.co.za, www.rdasia.com

First published 2013

National Library of Australia Cataloguing-in-Publication entry

Title: Hotpot, Crockpot, One Pot
ISBN: 978-1-922083-31-9 (hbk.)
ISBN: 978-1-922083-32-6 (pbk.)
Notes: Includes index.
Subjects: One-dish recipes. Casserole cooking.
Dewey Number: 641.82

Prepress by Sinnott Bros, Sydney
Printed and bound by Leo Paper Products, China

We are interested in receiving your comments on the contents of this book. Write to: The Editor, General Books Editorial, Reader's Digest (Australia) Pty Limited, GPO Box 4353, Sydney, NSW 2001, or email us at bookeditors.au@readersdigest.com

To order additional copies of this book, please contact us as follows:
www.readersdigest.com.au, 1300 300 030 (Australia);
www.readersdigest.co.nz, 0800 400 060 (New Zealand);
www.readersdigest.co.za, 0800 980 572 (South Africa);
www.rdasia.com; or email us at
customerservice@readersdigest.com.au

Concept code:
AU 0904/IC

Product codes:
041 4900 (hbk), 041 4901 (pbk)